CW01072512

A PRIESTHOOD IN TUNE

Prayer is the world in tune
— *Henry Vaughan*, The Morning-Watch

Thomas Lane CM

A Priesthood
in Tune

THEOLOGICAL REFLECTIONS
ON MINISTRY

THE COLUMBA PRESS
DUBLIN 1993

First edition, 1993, published by
THE COLUMBA PRESS
93 The Rise, Mount Merrion, Blackrock, Co. Dublin, Ireland

Cover by Bill Bolger
Origination by The Columba Press
Printed by
Loader Jackson, Arlesey

ISBN: 1 85607 068 9

Nihil Obstat:
Jerome McCarthy DD
Censor Deputatus

Imprimi Potest:
✠ Desmond,
Archbishop of Dublin,
30th July 1993

The *Nihil Obstat* and the *Imprimi Potest* are a declaration that a book or publication is considered to be free from doctrinal or moral error. This declaration does not imply approval of, or agreement with the contents, opinions or statements expressed.

Copyright © 1993, Thomas Lane CM

Contents

Introduction

The preaching of Jesus was an invitation to be in tune with the good news of the kingdom of God. Some who heard it opened their ears and their hearts to receive it. Others were like the children who refused to dance to the sound of the flute or to mourn at the sound of a dirge (Mt 11:17). The tune of the kingdom of God provides a whole programme for Christian living, inviting us to sing and make melody to the Lord in our hearts (Eph 5:19). Over the centuries, the image of being in tune has helped many Christian writers and preachers to describe the continual call to discipleship.

For the past three decades, I have engaged in much teaching and preaching on the topic of priesthood. In the pages that follow, I have attempted to give some unity to what I have been saying about the priesthood of Jesus Christ, the priesthood of all the baptised, and the ministerial priesthood. The image that has helped me most is the image of being in tune. The poet Henry Vaughan described prayer as 'the world in tune'. One could say that good priestly ministry is the Church in tune. All those participating in the priesthood of Jesus Christ are called to be in tune with the mind and heart of the great High Priest who was continually in tune with the will of his Father and the action of the Holy Spirit.

It is my hope that this book will be of interest and use to all who are enchanted by the music of the kingdom of God. In particular, I hope that it will be of use to all men and women who are called to public ministry in the Church. I am particularly concerned to show the relationship between ordained ministry and other forms of Church ministry. Some of the chapters make no explicit mention of the topic of priesthood. Some concentrate on the priesthood of Jesus Christ, source of all priesthood. Some highlight the priestly call of all the baptised. Some dwell more on ordained ministry. I see the subject of each of the chapters as part of the necessary setting for our understanding of all ministry in the name of Jesus Christ. In the arranging of the topics, I have tried to be faithful to what has been handed on to us and to be alert to the searching questions that keep surfacing in the Church today. The scope of the book is, naturally, limited. Though I have dealt with some aspects of religious life, I have presented ordained ministry mostly in the setting of diocesan priesthood. My emphasis is on the Western, Catholic tradition. Though I have drawn a good deal on recent agreed statements on ministry, I have not dealt directly with contemporary ecumenical issues. My reading which has brought me in contact with the Eastern tradition has given me a continued appreciation of the place of the Holy Spirit in any understanding of Church and of priesthood.

In recent years we have seen the publication of many fine works on the topic of Christian priesthood. Many of these have dwelt especially on the historical development of the theology and practice of ministry. I have made no attempt to add to such studies. Instead I have tried to distil the basic message of the centuries and to interpret it in ways I consider helpful for today. At the end of the book, I have listed some of the works which I have found particularly helpful. At the end of each chapter, I list a few of the sources on which I have especially leaned.

I wish to thank my colleagues in All Hallows, Dublin, and Damascus House, London, who have encouraged and helped me in the writing of this book. In particular I want to thank Fr Kevin Rafferty, Fr Brian Nolan, Fr Eugene Duffy, Fr Eamonn Conway, Sr Dorothy Balfe, who carefully read the text and made valuable suggestions. The continual help and care of Margaret Doyle and Fr Eugene Sweeney kept reminding me of the qualities of the God of the covenant.

I pray that the book will make some little contribution to the tuning of the Church and to the making of a world in tune.

Thomas Lane, C.M., All Hallows, Dublin
Birthday of the Blessed Virgin Mary, September 8th, 1993

PART I

The Call of Christians

CHAPTER 1

The good news of the kingdom

Every Christian is called to be a bearer of good news. The reason is that Jesus Christ came with good news. He proclaimed 'the good news of the kingdom' (Mt 4:23). The coming of the kingdom of God had for long been the hope of the people of Israel. They knew that God was the king of the universe and the Lord of all history, especially of their own history, but they also knew that all was not well. They were keenly aware that they were somehow caught in the grip of Satan who personified the many forces of evil. In the presence of these they felt powerless. Jesus brought the 'good news of God' by saying that 'the time is fulfilled, and the kingdom of God has come near' (Mk 1:14-15). The God of the covenant was beginning to rule with power.

The God of the covenant
The covenant had always expressed God's loving-kindness and his faithfulness. In the person and ministry of Jesus, these two covenant qualities were about to burst their banks. Up to now, Satan had been like the man who is strong, fully armed, guarding his castle, and sure of the safety of his property. But Jesus was stronger than he. In his ministry, he attacked Satan, overpowered him, took away his armour and divided his plunder (Lk 11:21-22). Jesus had been given ultimate control over sickness, over sin, over death. The reason was that God's own power was at work in him. Now was the moment of the coming of God's rule, God's reign, God's kingdom. As his reign unfolded, it became clear that there was no limit to his goodness (cf Mt 5:48). This was the good news.

In the preaching of Jesus, the God of the covenant was revealed as showing qualities of loving-kindness and fidelity that were hitherto undreamt of. The compassion and love of the Father was unconditional. They went out to all those who hitherto would have been regarded as outside the pale of divine, or certainly of human, toleration. There was a complete reversal of values. Those who did not seem to count were now shown to be at the very centre of

God's plan. Those who had been, in a variety of ways, poor, were declared to be blessed by God. They were a shining expression of God's regarding as precious those who in human eyes were despicable. In their helplessness and dependency, they touched the heart-strings of the God of compassion and loving-kindness. In their lowliness, many of them actually expressed the kind of human, gentle qualities which Jesus regarded as essential for responding to the action of God's rule. What was true of the poor was true too of the various categories of sinners. From being on the very outer circles of human respectability, they were now brought into the inner circle of God's mercy. Jesus offered them the forgiveness that only God can give, and he even called them to intimate discipleship. The same applied to all those experiencing any form of human oppression. The ministry of Jesus, healing the sick, exorcising those in the grip of Satan, raising from the dead, forgiving sinners, re-assuring the poor, was a daily sign that God was already reigning, with loving power, now. Each of his miracles was an opening of human eyes and hearts to the kind of loving world that God wanted to bring into existence. In each of his parables, drawn as they were from the whole range of daily experiences, Jesus alerted his hearers to at least one aspect of the reign of God.

Like children

The reign of God as Father calls for an attitude by which we become children again. The attitude is not an optional extra for the disciple of Jesus; it is a requirement. This is, in varying ways, a recurring theme in the gospels. It has many implications. In essence, it is a call to that attitude towards God that keeps us continually in tune with the mind and heart of our loving Father; it is a continual call to a recognition of creatureliness, to trust, to a daily acknowledgment of and response to a personal and loving power, greater than ourselves, at work in our lives.

It is in the context of this call to become as little children that we must see the urgent call of Jesus to faith, to repentance, to a change that comes right from the heart, to complete conversion. The offer of the kingdom is a gift from the loving Father. It must be received with love, with trust, with joy, with abandonment. But the Father wishes that the child will grow fully in the Father's likeness. This call to growth is part of the call into the kingdom. Precisely because the Father is infinitely prodigal in his compassion and forgiveness, he is infinitely demanding on the possibilities for growth in those who accept his reign. There must be no limits to the disciples' goodness because there are no limits to the heavenly Father's goodness. At every moment, the fact that the reign of God has come is a call for a decision, a decision for greater goodness. Jesus had come as the one blessed by his Father and he named many kinds of people who through him are blessed by his Father. This is the key to the great programme of blessedness, the charter of the kingdom which has come to be called the 'beatitudes'. Those who live the beatitudes in a practical way, and those who enable others to live them, will be declared blessed at the final coming of the Son of Man (Mt 25:34). In the preaching and ministry of Jesus, this offer of blessedness and salvation goes out to all. But, as has always been the mysterious way of God, Jesus leaves his hearers free to accept it or reject it. In this free accepting or rejecting is played out the drama of human salvation.

No boundaries
Everything that Jesus said and did had multiple implications for the present and for the future. The kingdom of God was present in every stage of his work. In his casting out of Satan by the Spirit of God, the kingdom of God had come (Mt 12:28). The eyes that saw Jesus in action and the ears that heard him were already blessed with the blessedness that only the coming of the kingdom could bring (Mt 13:16). But the kingdom was not yet fully manifested; what was happening contained the seeds of the future. Similarly, any decision made for accepting or rejecting the kingdom had multiple implications for the present and for the future. No wonder that sowing time and harvest time were key words in the proclamation of Jesus. Every act of peace, justice, forgiveness and of the other qualities that characterise the coming of the kingdom had implications that reached far beyond the persons and events that they directly affected. The breadth of the claims, invitations and demands of Jesus were the foundations for the universalism that would later characterise the self-understanding of Christ's Church on every level. There must be no limit to our forgiveness; nobody is outside the ambit of being called neighbour; enemies

are to be not only tolerated but loved. All accepted conventions about moral behaviour are turned inside out. What G.K. Chesterton called the paradoxes, the apparent contradictions, of Christianity arise out of the fact that God is at the same time absurdly prodigal in his compassion and stern in his urgent call to complete conversion. Boundless grace is a call for a response that knows no boundaries. This call of God for a boundless response is motivated by the fact that he is continually, in the words of one of the parables, seeing us, being moved to compassion for us, running towards us, putting his arms round us, kissing us, clothing us, declaring us found after our loss, inviting us to celebrate (Lk 15:20-24). Every time we return again to the Father is salvation for ourselves and the making of salvation for many others. The celebration to which he invites us is foreshadowed in the table-fellowship of Jesus with tax-collectors, sinners, and the bearers of various forms of society's stigmas. All the celebrations of table-fellowship, and the eucharist itself, are stages in the preparation of that final banquet in which Jesus the Messiah will fasten his belt, invite his guests to sit down to eat and come round in person to serve them (Lk 12:37). This will be the perfect celebration of agapé, the distinctively Christian way of loving.

Jesus is the good news
The qualities of the God of the covenant were shown most of all in the dying and rising of Jesus. The Father who was at the centre of the preaching and teaching of Jesus allowed his Son to endure all the testings and all the agony that are part of the human condition. It was not a question of a vindictive God demanding vicarious punishment of an innocent victim. Once again it was the paradox of an infinitely compassionate God drawing limitless good out of the network of human malice. The resurrection of Jesus was the fidelity of the God of the covenant turning the enemy, death, into the makings of life without limit. Those who had experienced Jesus preaching the kingdom came to see that very kingdom embodied in a unique way in his own death and resurrection and in the sending of the Spirit who had been close to him from conception to resurrection. No wonder that his disciples came to speak, not directly about the kingdom of God, but about the total mystery of the life, death, and resurrection of Jesus. No wonder they

kept searching for names and words which would describe the subject of that mystery. Some of the names and words they remembered as having been used by Jesus himself. Some they found by searching the scriptures and elsewhere for the most apt way of describing God's fulfilment of his promises in Jesus Christ. Sometimes they combined the two processes. Each of the four gospels has its own focus.

Each of the evangelists knew that the name of Jesus was synonymous with the saving activity of God. Each had his own emphasis in presenting that saving activity. For Mark, Jesus is the Son of God, and the teacher of the kind of discipleship that derives from Jesus' living of that title. Matthew sees Jesus as the new Moses, giving a new law, from the perspective of a new mountain, to a new people. Luke links the whole ministry of Jesus with Jerusalem which had been so much a symbol of God's way of dealing with his people. For John, Jesus is the taking flesh of the Word of God who existed before creation and since creation had been coming into the world – the Word who embodies God's own light and glory and can identify with God's own 'I am' (8:58).

Each of the other New Testament writers provides his own characteristic portrait of Jesus. To complete their portraits, they draw in various ways on the great personages, the great events, and the great books of the Hebrew bible. Jesus is the new Adam, the new Moses, the new David, the new High Priest, the new Servant. His story is the new Exodus of a new people. He is the expression of all the Wisdom of God. Each of these titles, these events, these books, threw light on the limitless riches of the kingdom of God and the infinite riches hidden in the person of Jesus who proclaimed it. In the course of Christian history the redemptive work of Jesus came to be further articulated by believers. They were able to find a variety of starting points for understanding that redemptive work. Some started with the suffering servant who gave his life as a ransom for many (Mt 20:28). Some understood redemption in terms of the light which Jesus brought into every area of human darkness, enabling his disciples, in turn, to be the light of the world (Mt 5:14). Others, again, put the emphasis on the conquest of Satan by the only one who was strong enough and armed enough to overpower him (Lk 11:22).

Every Christian generation has provided its own insights into and synthesis of the work of Jesus in bringing about the reign of God and the Church which is the sign and instrument of its presence. For some generations, the stress was on doing full justice to both the divine and the human reality of Jesus. Sometimes an historical crisis or event was the occasion for searching for a new insight into and understanding of the saving mystery of Christ and of new ways of imaging the one who promised to be actively with his Church 'always, to the end of the age' (Mt 28:20). The reign of God has always, under a variety of names, been the Church's good news. It is always a present reality because the risen Jesus who first proclaimed it is, in every sense, a present reality.

Prophet, priest, king
In his proclamation of the good news of the kingdom, it seems clear that Jesus saw himself as a prophetic person. He started his ministry in the 'school' of John the Baptist who had come in the prophetic tradition. At the beginning of his public ministry, he identified with the prophetic figure, anointed by the Spirit, of whom Isaiah had spoken (Lk 4:18). He compared the way he himself was treated to the way the prophets had been treated (Mk 6:4). As his mission unfolded, he must have become more and more identified with the Moses-like figure whom God promised to raise up at the end of time (Deut. 18:15), calling people to conversion and repentance.

From the way he related to the official priesthood, from his re-evaluation of the kind of sacrifices that really pleased God (Mt 9:15), from his strong claims about the place and purpose of the temple, from the way in which he freely gave his own life as a ransom for many (Mt 20:28), the title of priest came to be a fitting word to describe his mission and work.

Though he was reluctant to be identified with any form of kingship that would tally with worldly expectations (Jn 18:36), he was so much taken up with the message of the reign of God, that he came to be recognised as Messiah-king and seen as the shepherd-king, the servant-king.

The promotion of the good news of the reign of God has always been and must always be the first concern of all disciples of Jesus

Christ, prophet, priest and king. His desire is that they 'strive first for the kingdom of God and his righteousness' (Mt 6:33). The final manifestation of the kingdom will be a harvest-time in which all the seeds that have been sown in the name of Jesus will be seen to produce their proper fruits (Mt 13:24-43). In the sowing of good seeds and in their cultivation, the Lord of the harvest wishes to involve many labourers (Mt 9:37-38). Over the centuries, the fellow-labourers with the Lord have come to be called by a variety of names. All the names could be said to be variations on the names that came to sum up the ministry of Jesus himself: prophet, priest, and shepherd-king. All ministry in Christ's Church is a continuation of and reflection of his own prophetic, priestly, and kingly mission. The test of its effectiveness is the extent to which it is carried out in his name and by the power of his Spirit.

The New Jerome Biblical Commentary, (Geoffrey Chapman, 1989).
Articles on: Jesus, pp 1316 - 1328 (John P. Meier);
Covenant, pp 1297 - 1301, (John L. McKenzie).

CHAPTER 2

Disciples and apostles

The Church is 'the whole community of the disciples' (Acts 6:2). A disciple is one who learns. A Christian disciple is one who keeps learning from the 'one teacher, the Christ' (Mt 23:10). Jesus himself was a learner as well being as a teacher. The gospels indicate that he learned much of his style of teaching and preaching from observing the daily happenings in the society of which he was part. There are good indications that, in learning his own mission, he was influenced by the various religious movements of his time, notably the one in which his cousin, John the Baptist, played such a part. As he learned the religious traditions of his people, the example of his family was strengthened by his regular experiences in synagogue and temple. As his mission unfolded, he learned by continually listening to the voice of his Father and learning from him. Indeed there were some topics on which he had received no communication of knowledge from his Father (Mk 13:32). Before that Father he was in the position of the son who can do nothing on his own, but only what he sees the father doing (Jn 5:19). He was ready to be taught aspects of his mission by encounters with such people as the Canaanite woman (Mt 15:21-28). As he pondered on the fate of prophets before him, he saw more clearly the implications of his own growing rejection by the religious leaders (Mt 23:37). It was out of the many sufferings that he had to endure as he followed in the same tradition that he 'learned obedience' and was 'made perfect' (Heb 5:8-9).

The maker of disciples
It is to this disciple-teacher that many disciples were drawn during his public ministry. There is no way of counting the number of these disciples. But it is clear that there was a special group who came to be called 'the disciples'. The initiative in calling the disciples came from Jesus himself. Following on this initial call, the chosen disciples developed a continuous fascination with the person of Jesus. Jesus, in turn, initiated them into the secrets of the

17

workings of the kingdom which he preached (Mk 4:11). Each, in different ways, was introduced to a personal relationship with Jesus. This relationship involved a sharing in every aspect of his own life and saving mission. To each, the call was urgent and radical. It could involve the breaking up of normal family ties (Mt 10:35) and it might leave no space for even the burying of the dead (Mt 8:21-22). The standards of discipleship were high and uncompromising; putting a stumbling block in the way of a disciple would have dire consequences (Mk 9:42). To 'follow' Jesus involved such an attachment to his person that no human being, no thing, no event should be allowed to be an obstruction. The result was that the radical life-style of the disciple should mirror accurately the life-style of the teacher. This included gentleness and humility in heart (Mt 11:28), poverty (Lk 9:3), continual readiness to 'change and become like children' (Mt 18:3). As the mission of Jesus unfolded, he made it clear that somehow his disciples would have to face a destiny like his own; following him must involve denying themselves, taking up their cross, accepting failure (Mk 8:34-35); any sharing in his glory must involve drinking the cup of suffering that he drank and being plunged into the whole of his paschal mystery (Mk 10:38).

Discipleship was not all suffering. The renewal of all things was coming and the disciples would share intimately in the glory of the Son of Man (Mt 19:28). The little flock would, through the Father's good pleasure, receive the kingdom (Lk 12:32). Nothing, not even the cup of cold water, would go unrewarded (Mt 10:42). Discipleship is an introduction into the whole intimate life of God himself who is the ultimate teacher (Jn 6:45). It is out of all these aspects of following Jesus that disciples must be recognisable as living witnesses of all that he stands for. Though he is the only 'true light which enlightens everyone' (Jn 1:9), the disciples, because they share in every aspect of his life so intimately, are the 'light of the world' and the 'salt of the earth' (Mt 5:13-14).

In one sense, there is only one form of Christian discipleship. Negatively, it is described in stark terms in the list of renunciations which Jesus one day announced to 'large crowds who were travelling with him' (Lk 14:25). Positively it is portrayed in terms of the easy yoke and the light burden that is assured to all the weary people who come to Jesus carrying heavy burdens (Mt 11:28-29). In another sense, there is a great variety of forms of discipleship. There were the special 'twelve' who travelled with Jesus, sharing intimately in his messianic ministry. There were the seventy-two whom Jesus, according to St Luke's account, appointed and sent 'ahead of him in pairs to every town and place where he himself intended to go' (Lk 10:1-20); they were to bring a message of peace and they had authority over all the manifestations of the power of the enemy; on their return, they were assured that they could rejoice because their names were written in heaven. There were the various people who, presumably in their own family settings, lived the kind of lives that were pleasing to the Lord. These included such people as the woman who performed the good service which would continue to be told 'in remembrance of her' (Mk 14:9), and the sisters who welcomed him into their home (Lk 10:38). Significantly, it was to one of these that he spoke one of his most radical words about discipleship: 'there is need of only one thing' (v 42). In the fourth gospel, the mysterious figure of the 'beloved disciple', while being represented as a historical personage, is a symbol too of the kind of person who is continually in tune with the mind and heart of the Lord, and who is always quick to recognise him. The end of the gospel according to St Matthew is a command to 'make disciples of all nations' (28:19). In Acts, it would appear that all believers are seen as disciples (Acts 6:1-2); they were following the One whom they saw as the only way (Acts 9:2; 22:4; cf Jn 14:6).

Tensions for disciples

In the early Christian centuries, the followers of Jesus were a minority, often a persecuted minority. In a sense, they couldn't survive as disciples and believers without living the radical kind of lifestyle which Jesus had demanded. When Christianity later became the official religion of the empire, the temptation for disciples often took the form of a desire to conform and to receive the kind of honours that are the opposite of gospel values. The two-directional tendency to self-abnegation and to conform to 'the world' has been a central feature of the tensions of Christian living ever since. Christians have never been quite sure how far they should conform to conventional values and mores and when they should provide a kind of 'counter-culture', an 'alternative life-style', a 'contrast society'. In our age, so much characterised by the draw of consumerism and secularisation, this tension is stronger than ever. In this setting, it is significant that the best known modern-day book on discipleship is one that draws attention to its 'cost'. It may be significant also that religious life, many forms of which arose as expressions of radical discipleship, is today experiencing the kind of drinking of the cup of suffering that may be a call back to real discipleship of the one teacher of Christians. Those in ordained ministry are being called, time and again, to the austerity, asceticism and simple life-style which mirror the way of existence of the original followers of Jesus. It would appear that all disciples today are being really and urgently called to learn and re-learn; to learn from the 'signs of the times'; to learn from each other, on all levels; to learn from history; to learn, above all, the unchanging and uncompromising message of discipleship, presented once and for all by the only teacher that Christians can recognise.

The twelve
The most renowned of the disciples of Jesus were 'the twelve'. The twelve were disciples, special disciples. They were special in their symbolic relationship to the twelve tribes of Israel. The twelve, in turn, symbolised the totality of the people whom God had chosen as his own. The coming of Jesus was the beginning of the last times when God would restore and re-constitute his people. There is an inseparable connection between the preaching of Jesus, the reign of God, the coming into existence of the Church which resulted from the preaching of the kingdom and that would itself be an agent of the kingdom. The twelve were intimately involved with all three realities. According to Mark, Jesus appointed them for three reasons: to be with him; to be sent out to proclaim the message; to have authority to cast out demons (Mk 3:14-15). It was a call to be and to do: to be in an intimate relationship with him and to do what only he was authorised to do, by the power of God.

The full gospel profile of the twelve includes a rich variety of elements: preaching and teaching with the authority of Jesus himself; casting out demons; healing; leading the community at all levels; doing, in remembrance of Jesus, what he himself had done at the last meal with his disciples; forgiving sins; being witnesses of the resurrection; making disciples; baptising. Some of the elements of this profile reflect the Church situation that followed on the resurrection of Jesus. Some reflect the rather highly developed structures of some of the churches which were set up under the influence of some of the twelve. This is notably true of the church reflected in Matthew 16 and 18, with Peter, the rock person, authorised to bind and loose in a church that must be listened to and that can make strong decisions. It is not easy to indicate the stages in the coming into existence and the development of the full profile of the role of the twelve, from the earthly ministry of Jesus to all that took place after the resurrection. The important consideration is that this full profile was soon to become normative for the life and ministry of entire Church.

The special twelve disciples came to be known as the 'twelve apostles'. The title emphasises their 'being sent' after they had seen the risen Lord. The definitive sending of the twelve took place after the resurrection, but in the gospels as we have them the word 'apostle' is already linked with the historical ministry of Jesus. Even in his earthly lifetime, Jesus was sending out the twelve. The word 'apostle' has a special place in the developed usage of St Luke. It soon came to be associated also with disciples other than the twelve. Several times, Paul emphasises his own right to the title. It would appear that for him the two requirements for a claim to the name are to have seen the risen Christ and to have been sent on mission by him to preach the gospel. Others like Barnabas, Silvanus, Timothy, Apollos, James, Andronicus, seem to have come to be recognised as apostles. The same is true of Junia and the other women listed by St Paul towards the end of the letter to the Romans. It is clear that they had been close co-workers of Paul in his apostolic ministry.

Apostolic succession
As the group of twelve began to fade out of the memory of the disciples, the consciousness of the necessity of the continuing of the apostolic mission came to be more and more expressed. It was clear that the twelve had had a unique and unrepeatable role in

the coming into existence of the Church, but it was equally clear that the apostolic office should continue, because the Church for whose service Jesus commissioned the twelve must continue in existence. The beginnings of the questions about what came to be called 'apostolic succession' were emerging. Already in his life-time, Paul was aware of the crucial importance of those who were his co-workers in spreading the gospel (Phil 4:3) and of those who had received various named gifts of leadership in the Christian communities (Rom 12:4-7). The Pastoral Epistles reflect a further stage in the continuation of what the 'college' of the twelve stood for. The memory of the individual members of the twelve was be-coming dimmed, but the importance of their place as foundation members, and the apostolic office for which they stood, especially in the local churches which they had helped to found, retained their central importance. In the vision of the new heaven and the new earth, towards the end of the Book of Revelation, there is a prominent place for the twelve foundations for the wall of the city and the twelve names of the twelve apostles of the Lamb that 'are written on them' (21:1-14). This position of the twelve apostles of the Lamb as foundation people was itself the foundation for a continuing and growing conviction that just as the Church of Christ is one, holy, and catholic, it is also apostolic.

This conviction and this belief has been expressed in different ways throughout the centuries. It finds a place in the Church's creeds, including the one significantly called the Apostles' Creed. At the Second Vatican Council, it was well expressed in the state-ment that the divine mission entrusted by Christ to the apostles will last to the end of the world (Mt 28:20), since the gospel, which was to be handed down by them, is for all time the 'source of life for the Church' (LG 20). Christ who entrusted this mission to his apostles had himself been sent by his Father on a mission into the world. He himself was the great 'apostle' (Heb 3:1), the one sent. Having completed his work of doing and teaching, and having given 'instructions through the Holy Spirit to the apostles whom he had chosen' (Acts 1:1-3), he was taken up to heaven in the act of assuring the apostles that he would send them the Holy Spirit (v 8). This Spirit was the promised advocate whose mission it was to 'teach you everything, and remind you of all that I have said to you" (Jn 14:26). It is all these sendings, all these missions, that constitute and authenticate the ongoing apostolic character of the Church.

An apostolic programme

Of the four properties of the Church of Christ, apostolicity is the one that has generated most controversy among Christians. The topic of apostolic succession, with all its historical and theological ramifications, has been very sharply discussed in the course of and since the sixteenth century Reformation. The reason is that all that the apostles stand for touches the very nerve centres of all Christian life: the Church's faith, the Church's ministry, the Church's style of living the gospel. The great ecumenical searching that has been going on, on so many levels, in recent years, has had many good effects. It has helped Christians of all traditions to search even more deeply for the contents and meaning of the good news as witnessed by those who were with the Lord Jesus all the time that he 'went in and out' among them, 'from the baptism of John until the day when he was taken up' and who later became 'witnesses to his resurrection' (Acts 1:21-22). It has helped all the churches to see that the four properties of Christ's Church cannot be separated from each other. It is an incentive for all Christians to see that the Church's call to be apostolic is a programme not only for the Church's public leaders but for all the baptised.

All Christian ministry and leadership, ordained and baptismal, derives its inspiration from the calling and mission of the first disciples and apostles. It is a response to the call of the Lord who was himself the great disciple and the great apostle. He is always present in his Church, sending his Spirit and calling people to be disciples and apostles, and inviting them, in turn, to make new disciples and make new apostles.

Francis A. Sullivan, SJ, *The Church We Believe In, One, Holy, Catholic and Apostolic*, (Gill and Macmillan, 1988).

Avery Dulles, SJ, *Models of the Church* (Second Edition), Chap. 13 (Gill and Macmillan, 1988).

CHAPTER 3

A saving community

Jesus came to save. He announced the reign of the God who saves. The Church, the new community which was coming into existence through his life, death and resurrection, is called to be a people who are always saving. Over the centuries, she has been described in many ways. In recent years, after much reflection on her saving mission, she has come to see herself as the 'sacrament of salvation'. At the Second Vatican Council, the very first paragraph of the *Constitution on the Church* stated that 'By her relationship with Christ, the Church is a kind of sacrament, that is, sign and instrument of intimate union with God and of the unity of all mankind' (*LG* 1., Abbott trans.). Later the same Church is described as the visible sacrament of saving unity (*LG* 9), and the universal sacrament of salvation (*LG* 48; *GS* 45; *AG* 1).

Sacrament of saving
Hearing the Church described as the sacrament of salvation was new for most believers. They had been used to applying the word 'sacrament' to those special outward signs of inward grace that marked the seven highpoints of the Church's saving work. This had been the common way of speaking since the twelfth century, and it had been made official in Catholic teaching which says that there are seven sacraments, no more, no fewer. The teaching of the Second Vatican Council was not intended to be a reversal of that teaching. Instead, it was a reminder that the seven sacraments are sacraments of the Church, herself the sacrament of Christ her founder. This way of speaking draws heavily on an older Christian language of mystery and sacrament. In fact, it places all sacramental life in the context of the total mystery of God. The mystery of God is the whole richness of the inner life of the triune God and of the secret plan of God by which creation shares in that inner life. This secret plan and purpose is being continually disclosed in the mystery of Christ, since the fullness of time has already begun (Eph 1:9-10). Describing this mystery as a 'sacrament' is a reminder of the practice by which, in Roman

times, soldiers in enlisting for service took an oath, a *sacramentum* of faithful service. This, in turn, is a happy link with the covenant in which God himself has sworn his own oath of fidelity (Lk 1:73).

Containing and effecting

Over the centuries, many attempts were made to define accurately what it is that constitutes a sacrament. Best known are the statements that a sacrament is a visible sign of invisible grace; sacraments are efficacious signs of grace; sacraments contain and effect the divine realities of grace which they signify; sacraments signify what they contain and contain what they signify; sacraments are instruments of the saving work of Christ. With the widening of the use of the word sacrament today, these descriptions can be applied to the seven special ritual actions, to the whole life of the Church, to the total mystery of the incarnate Christ.

As we re-discover the riches of sacramental language, we are also re-discovering the Christian meaning of symbol. We are coming to realise that symbolic actions speak more effectively than mere words; that the best of symbols contain and draw us to the reality which they point to. This, in turn, is leading us to search for the kind of symbolic actions which best evoke the beliefs and values which the Church stands for and which call for the continual conversion of the human heart. In all of this, there is an emphasis on the place of the human body, as a symbol of and expression of the depths of the human spirit. A result of this continual exploring of sacraments and symbols is the enriching of our understanding of the Church in her saving mission. Christ himself, in his humanity, is seen as the fundamental or primordial sacrament of God's continual saving action in the world. In his body he contains and diffuses all the qualities of the God of the covenant. In him, we experience God by what we hear with our ears, what we see with our eyes, what we touch with our hands (cf 1 Jn 1:1). He is the living symbol, containing and effecting the whole saving plan of God. The Church, in turn, is the body of Christ. Because she is his body, she is his sacrament. Because the life of Christ flows through her, she contains within herself and she makes effective the workings of God's grace. Even with her many sins, divisions, and human limitations, she is an agent of the unity for which Christ prayed (Jn 17:22); of the holiness of those called to be saints, and sanctified in

Christ Jesus (1 Cor 1:2); of the catholicity which reaches out to all, because God wishes all to be saved (1 Tim 2:4); of the apostolicity which is a sure and necessary foundation for the household of God (Eph 2:20). The individual sacraments highlight and celebrate the limitless riches hidden in the body of Christ.

Intimacy and unity

The Church is the sacrament of salvation. The Second Vatican Council saw this salvation in terms of two realities. The first is that of intimate union with God. The second is the unity of the whole human race (*LG* 1, 9). Intimate union with God is made possible by the grace of Jesus Christ continually empowering us to be in a son or daughter relationship to God (Jn 1:12). The unity of the whole human race is the fruit of the action by which Jesus died 'not for the nation only, but to gather into one the dispersed children of God' (Jn 11:52). The intimate union with God and the unity of the whole human race are not separate aspects of the saving work of Jesus Christ and of his Church which is his sacrament. Both are aspects of the one mystery of Jesus Christ who came with one mission of saving. The name he was given by the angel of God was a saving name: 'You are to name him Jesus, for he will save his people from their sins' (Mt 1:21). As his mission unfolded, people found endless saving riches in the name of Jesus; the people to be saved by Jesus turned out to be the whole human family; the sins by which they had been damaged comprise whatever had contributed to the damaging of the relationships of people with each other and with God. As Jesus himself sowed the seed of the word of God (Mt 13:37), he was like the farmer whose great desire it is to 'save' into a ripe harvest the fruits of all the seeds that he has sown.

There can be no counting the number of good seeds of salvation which were sown by Jesus during his earthly ministry. In turn, we can say that every act of faith in Jesus Christ, by anybody, at any stage in history, is a recognition in some form of his saving mission. The cry of Bartimaeus, the blind beggar, was the expression of what goes on in the heart of anybody who recognises the saving power of the name of Jesus and who 'springs up and comes to him' (cf Mk 10:50), shouting 'Jesus, have mercy on me' (v 47). It was out of shouts like this, and of Jesus' responses to them, that the faith-filled conviction grew that 'there is salvation in no one else, for there is no other name under heaven given among mortals by which we must be saved' (Acts 4:12). It is the same conviction that gives the preacher of the gospel the confidence to keep saying 'I have no silver or gold, but what I have I give you; in the name of Jesus Christ of Nazareth, stand up and walk' (Acts 3:6).

Vertical and horizontal

It is convenient to distinguish the 'vertical' aspects of salvation from the 'horizontal' aspects. The vertical would comprise one's personal faith relationship with God, what the *Constitution of the Church* (par 1) describes as intimate union with God. This intimate union is based on the continual action of the God who was and is 'in Christ, reconciling the world to himself' (2 Cor 5:19). Flowing from this continual process of reconciliation is the graced relationship of friendship with Father, Son and Spirit, during the whole course of one's life on this earth. The final flowering of this graced relationship is what has come to be called the beatific vision, the seeing that is the final gift of the God who declares and makes people blessed. The horizontal aspects of salvation would comprise all those temporal gifts that enrich our lives on this earth in our cultural, economic, political, and social relationships.

It is possible to speak of the vertical and horizontal aspects of salvation in a misleading way that would not merely distinguish between them but would somehow separate them. It could be said that much of the Church's thinking since the Second Vatican Council has been a search for ways of showing the relationship between and unity of the two aspects of salvation. The Council itself had laid much of the foundation for this work. Its vision of human life helps us to see the interconnectedness of what constitutes 'grace' and what constitutes 'nature'. It helps us to re-discover a holistic approach to all the needs and aspirations of every human person. In Synod documents and in other expressions of the Church's teaching, this holistic approach has been more and more in evidence. Action on behalf of justice and participation in the transformation of the world have come to be recognised as a constituent dimension of the preaching of the gospel (Synod, 1971: *Justice and Peace*). The ongoing debates about what constitutes authentic liberation theology are not between those who wish to free human beings from whatever oppresses them and those who do not so wish. Behind them all is a recognition that human efforts towards liberation need to be continually purified and uplifted, lest they lead to new forms of servitude and human bondage. But the Church has no option but to keep saving.

Universal sacrament of salvation

The Church is a sacrament. The Church is a sacrament of salvation. The Church is the universal sacrament of salvation. The word 'universal' is a variation on the 'catholic' aspect of the Church's mission. This universality is rooted in the original command of Jesus to go into all the world, to proclaim the good news to the whole of creation, to make disciples of all nations (Mk 16:15; Mt 28:19). The call to universalism generated its own tensions in the early years of the Church's life. It was never entirely absent from the Church's consciousness over the centuries. It has come very much to the fore in the Church's recent understanding of herself. It is expressed very powerfully in two teachings of the Second Vatican Council. The first is the conviction that since Christ died for all, and since all are called to one and the same destiny, 'we must hold that the Holy Spirit offers to all the possibility of being made partners in a way known only to God, in the paschal mystery' (GS 22). This is supported by the equally strong conviction that the Church is called to be 'for each and all' the 'visible sacrament' of the 'saving unity' of which Jesus is author and source (LG 9).

These two strong convictions have many implications. One is that the only grace that brings salvation to anybody is the grace of Jesus Christ. That grace has been at work in the world since the beginning. It has been communicated to different people, at different stages in history, in different ways. Another implication is that the Church of Christ, being the body of which Christ is the head, is the great communion of grace. Out of that communion and out of the network of the workings of grace, comes the instrumentality of the Church in bringing the grace of Christ to the whole human race. The one Church of Christ, which does not exclude any of the churches and ecclesial communities on various levels of communion, is, at all times and for all, a sign and living instrument of God's saving activity.

It is easy enough to see how Christians are instruments of salvation for each other. It also makes sense that since the people of other world religions are in various ways 'related to' the people of God (*LG* 16), they must in some way benefit from the saving mystery of the Church. Bearing in mind that God designed an economy of salvation that is social and sacramental, it is not so easy to see how the life of the Church can have any bearing on the very large numbers whom the proclamation of the word and the celebration of the sacraments never reach in a visible, audible, tangible way. In the same setting, one could ask whether the resources of the created universe, the multiple benefits provided by the great variety of human cultures and civilisations, and the advances in science, contribute anything to human salvation.

A partial light on these great questions is to be found by searching for the endless implications of the doctrine of the one body of Christ. In Christ, 'the whole fullness of deity dwells bodily' (Col 2:9). The Church, as body of Christ, has a unique sharing in that fullness. In the continual celebration of the eucharist, in which the all-sufficient sacrifice of Christ is made present, God is asked that what is now taking place will advance the peace and salvation not just of the community which is celebrating but of 'all the world' (*Eucharistic Prayer 3*). And, since it is through Christ and for Christ that 'all things in heaven and earth were created' (Col 1:16), we cannot separate the workings of the mystery of Christ from the workings of the created universe and of whatever comes from the hands and hearts of all those made in the image of God (Gen 1:27) and re-made in the image of his Son (1 Cor 15:49).

Integral salvation
The Church is committed to a programme of 'integral salvation', 'full liberation', 'total salvation' (*Declaration of the Fourth Synod of Bishops, 1974*). She can never lose sight of the fact that there is only one mediator of that salvation. There are still many unanswered questions about the ways in which different religions, different cultures, and different movements in history participate in the workings of that mediation. The questions must be continually set in the context of the related words 'catholic', 'universal', 'integ-

ral'. Salvation is for all that makes up the whole person, the whole of the human family, the whole of the created universe, the whole of human activity.

The call to be agents of universal salvation goes out to each member of the human family. In the sacramental world which God has designed, a special mission of saving is given to those baptised into the one body of Christ. Each of the seven sacraments is a focusing on some aspect of the Church's call to signify what it contains and contain what it signifies. This is the setting for the call to ministry of all the baptised. One of the seven sacraments is called the sacrament of 'holy orders'. In the efforts to understand this sacrament, the word 'order' has, over the centuries, come to be loaded with many meanings. It is best understood as a sharing in the task of Wisdom which 'orders all things well' (Wis 8:1). The work of promoting holy order must always be carried out in a saving way that is truly integral, catholic, universal. The call to a human being to be a sign of holy order within the universal sacrament of salvation is a gift of God. It is a life-long programme for being and doing.

Bernard Cooke, *Sacraments and Sacramentality*, (Twenty-third Publications, 1983).

Francis A. Sullivan, SJ, *The Church We Believe In*, Chaps. 6, 7 (Gill and Macmillan, 1988).

CHAPTER 4

A prophetic people

A prophet, as the original biblical name suggests, is one who is called and one who calls; because he is himself called by God, he calls God's people to a new way of life. A prophet is one who goes to bring an urgent message; he goes because he is sent by God. A prophet is one who speaks to God's people, not in his own name, but in the name of the God who has spoken to him. The prophetic calling, the prophetic going, and the prophetic speaking have taken a great variety of forms in the course of history. As we come more and more to realise that God has always offered his grace to every man and woman of goodwill, we have no difficulty in recognising the prophetic phenomenon outside the Judaeo-Christian tradition. In the tradition itself, prophetic elements can be recognised as far back as the religious memory can go. The events that helped the development of prophecy were the call of the patriarchs, the Exodus and the covenant, the emergence of the monarchy, the building of the first temple, the division of the kingdom, the destruction of the temple, the exile, the growing prophetic conviction of the coming of a new covenant, and the eventual emergence of that covenant.

From many backgrounds

The prophets came from a variety of backgrounds. Some were very much part of the political and religious institutions of their time. Some came from less privileged positions in society. In the northern kingdom, the prophetic emphasis was on calling the people to be faithful to the requirements of the Sinai covenant which had its own connections with the covenant made with Abraham. In this setting, Moses emerged as the perfect exemplar of the prophetic call, the prophetic mission, the prophetic message. His call, his being sent, his message, were not of his own designing. They were the call, the being sent and the message of one who, on God's initiative, had spoken to God 'face to face' (Ex 33:11). Out of the experience of the one who had this unique face to face communication with God arose his own conviction and the

31

conviction of the believing, hoping people that God would one day raise up the ideal prophet to whom people must listen (Deut 18:10 ff). In the southern kingdom, the context is more the promises made to David and the messianic hopes that kept growing out of these promises. The two emphases did not, in fact, exclude each other. In both, the prophetic voice felt free to critique the existing approaches to law, to political and religious institutions, to moral attitudes, to ways of worshipping.

In all authentic prophecy, the prophet looked to the future and recalled the past in a way that would focus attention on what God wants from his people now, in the present. The prophets preferred to illumine the present rather than predict the future. A test of the true prophet was the way he could interpret accurately and throw light on current happenings and call people here and now to live the religious implications of these. In the symbolic actions characteristic of some of the prophets, people were able to recognise the power of God working through the prophetic word-actions. As the prophet held a mirror up to people's consciences, and they saw both what they were and what God wanted them to be, the prophetic word generated either comfort and consolation or anger as people saw the yawning gap between ideal and reality in their lives. The prophet either became a hero or somebody who deserved rejection, even death.

For many prophets, a test of true religion was one's attitudes to the poor. There were prophets like Amos who railed against the sheer maltreatment of the poor, symbolised in the treatment of the widow and orphan, and prophets like Zephaniah who went beyond material poverty and called for and encouraged an attitude of poverty of spirit which expressed the ideal attitude of a grateful heart before a merciful God.

In these and in the many other variations on the prophetic themes, the emphasis was not on human wisdom but on the word of the living God. The true prophet was the personal recipient of that word. The word was destined to transform his own life and the lives of those who listened to it. How exactly the prophet received and experienced the word of God before he announced it to the people it is not always easy to see. The God who always took the initiative could use any medium of human communication and experience to alert the prophet. Sometimes God had to deal with reluctant prophets, as is clear in the call of Jeremiah. Always it was his message, not the private views of the prophet, that must be communicated. The believing community helped to write down, to edit, to interpret and re-interpret the message once given.

A new covenant

It is one thing to draw people's attention to the limitations of laws, of institutions, of moral behaviour, of ways of worshipping, and of the ways in which political leadership is exercised. It is quite another to say that the laws, the institutions and the ways of worshipping and behaving are intrinsically inadequate and that the present system will one day have to be dismantled. This was the conviction that ultimately arose in the consciousness of some of the prophets and that came to be articulated in a variety of ways. Though prophecy concerns the present rather than the future, it is never without implications for the future. Though the prophets of Israel hoped for the salvation rather than the destruction of their people, they became more and more concerned about the state of a covenant that continued to be broken, about a people demoralised by the destruction of the temple and the ensuing exile. Even then, they remained sure that God would be faithful to his side of the covenant, and that his loving-kindness would somehow be victorious. But they became convinced that there was need of an entirely new covenant. God would, as always, take the initiative. He still remained the loving husband of his people. He would write his law not on tablets of stone but right inside his people, in their hearts. In the symbol of the intimate relationship of husband to wife, he would be the people's God and they would be his people. All his people would know him and he would remember their sin no more. That is how Jeremiah saw it (31:31-34). Ezekiel saw the new covenant in terms of a new heart. God would gather his exiled people. He would sprinkle clean water on them. He would give them a new heart and a new spirit. He would remove their heart of stone and give them a heart of flesh. He would put his own spirit within them and make them to observe his statutes and ordinances (Ezek 36:25-27). In Second-Isaiah there is the assurance of God that he would make an everlasting covenant with his people (Is 55:3). This would be the work of the loving husband who with 'everlasting love' has compassion for the wife from whom he had hid his face for a while (54:1-10).

All these and similar prophetic assurances could be looked at as a kind of poetic exuberance, but, at a time of depression and uncertainty, which didn't cease with the return from exile, they came to be seen by many as the strong promise of something entirely new. What precisely that new situation would entail was not clear. What was certain was that at some stage there would be a break in continuity. God himself would visit his people. The day of the Lord, which in the mouth of some prophets had been a term of judgment, came more and more to be seen as the day when God would bring full salvation. It is not surprising that, when Jesus came to preach the good news of the reign of God, and when they saw that reign unfolding, those who believed in him saw the prophetic promises as forming one pattern with all that had been foreshadowed in the law of Moses and with the aspirations of those who had orchestrated the best hopes of Israel in the words of the psalms (Lk 24:44). In a sense, the whole of the scriptures came to be seen as 'the prophetic message' (2 Pet 1:19ff) to which Jesus now was the key.

Jesus and prophecy

Jesus came to call God's people to repentance and salvation. He came because he was sent by his Father. The words that he spoke were spirit and life (Jn 6:63). He had all the best qualities of the prophets. He fulfilled the promise of God that in the last days he would raise up a special prophet, the final Moses. The coming of Jesus is presented as having been particularly welcomed by people who were shaped in a prophetic way of thinking; Zechariah saw the birth of the precursor as the fulfilment of prophecy (Lk 1:70). Simeon and Anna praised God in the same prophetic spirit (Lk 2:25ff; 36). Jesus began his public ministry under the clear influence of John who spoke and acted in the way of the prophets. He saw John as putting into focus all that was good in the prophets and the law (Mt 11:13).

It is clear that Jesus showed a great respect and esteem for the prophets. In his way of preaching, he had many of their characteristics. But he never directly called himself a prophet, just as he did not take the initiative in applying to himself the language of priesthood and kingship. His prophetic mission was but one dimension of the many-faceted mystery of the Son who alone knew the Father and who was fully known only by the Father (Mt 11:27). As his disciples saw him in action, they were quick to recognise him as a great prophet (Mt 16:14; Lk 7:16; Jn 4:19; 9:17). Jesus saw himself as at the same time sharing the worst aspects of the lot of the prophets (Mt 23:37) and being confident that this lot would, by the designs of his Father, lead to the very salvation for which the prophets hoped (Mt 21:42). But he spoke and acted as one who was greater than any of the prophets (Mt 12:41). He spoke, at the same time, with the Father's authority and with his own authority. Whatever word had been spoken in the past was superseded by his authoritative word. Without apology, he could say 'but I say to you' (Mt 5:44). He could introduce his radical teaching not with the prophetic 'thus says Yahweh' but with the definitive 'Amen, amen' (Jn 1:51; 3:3-11). Like the prophets, Jesus spoke saving words, but his words have a unique force since they come from the Word made flesh (Jn 1:14). The prophets had promised salvation. But they did not live to see that salvation. They desired to see what the disciples of Jesus saw but they did not see it (Lk 10:24). By contrast with them, the disciples of Jesus were specially blessed. They saw, in live action, the salvation for which the prophets had hoped (v 23).

Though the title prophet had the limitations of all the titles which people wished to use in connection with Jesus, it remains a very powerful key to an understanding of his person and ministry. It combines the elements of calling, sending, and announcing which were at the heart of the ministry of Jesus. It links him with all the best expectations of a people who knew that in the final stage of God's plan of salvation he would speak through the perfect prophet. It provided a starting point for the formulation of much of the Church's belief and preaching. For his disciples, it illumined the events of the death and resurrection of Jesus in a way that made some of them come to see him as 'a prophet mighty in deed and word before God and all the people' (Lk 24:19). It helped them to link him with figures like Moses, Elijah, John the

Baptist and other prophets (Lk 9:8; Jn 1:25). It helped them to find a focus for all that God had promised. Above all, it helped them to see Jesus as the one to whom they should listen (Mk 9:2-9).

A prophetic Church

Though Jesus was the last of the prophets, the gift of prophecy has always remained alive in his Church. Indeed one can say that, because Jesus was a prophet, his Church must be prophetic. In the early Christian communities, in places like Corinth and Antioch, the charism of prophecy flourished. It was exercised by men and women in a variety of positions of leadership. Essentially the prophet was seen in such communities as a person of inspired insight into the meaning of the paschal mystery at a time when people very much felt the need of such insight. The prophetic person spoke in a way that showed understanding of mystery (1 Cor 13:2). Moses, in his time, had expressed a wish 'that all the people might prophesy' (Num 11:29). In the events of Pentecost, St Peter saw the fulfilment of this wish and of the prediction of the prophet Joel that in the last days God would pour out his Spirit 'on all flesh' and that 'your sons and daughters shall prophesy' (Acts 2:17). The charism of prophecy was one expression of this pentecostal outpouring. St Paul showed a high regard for the charism (1 Thess 5:20). Like all charisms, it exists for the good of the community (1 Cor 14:29-32). Those who use it rightly speak to other people 'for their upbuilding and encouragement and consolation' (v 3). In his vision of the body of Christ, Paul places the prophetic gift second after the gift of apostleship (1 Cor 12:28). Like all the other gifts, even these two must be lived out in the 'more excellent way', the way of love (v 31; chap. 13:1). In the exercise of leadership in the Church, Paul saw a close inter-relation between apostle and prophet. The line of demarcation between the two roles would be difficult to draw. The role of apostle suggests foundation and order; the role of prophet suggests insight and interpretation. But the role of both apostle and prophet is foundational (Eph 2:20).

Throughout the ages, the Church has remained prophetic, just as it has remained apostolic. No generation has been entirely lacking in prophetic people. The true Christian prophet experiences God, often at a time when many believers seem to have lost their way.

He or she is generous in opening up that experience to others in a way that will help them to interpret the apparent contradictions in their own experience. The prophet helps people to see that the truth, as well as the beauty, of God is ever new as well as ever ancient. The prophet shows the way for renewal and for new religious movements at times when the Church is confused or at a crossroads. The prophetic insight opens up possibilities that seem to have been unnoticed. This has always been the way of prophecy.

In our own day, there have been many expressions of a yearning for a strong re-emergence of prophecy, especially where there are burning issues of justice and peace. One expression of the desire for prophecy has been an appeal for the fostering of the 'prophetic imagination'. Out of this gift, it is claimed, the whole of our dormant religious memory can be made come alive again; a way of living which is an alternative to that of the dominant culture can be made possible; new symbols can be devised to help people to live the alternative lifestyle; people will be energised to live in a way that is truly new and fully human; the Church herself will be alerted to her mission by voices from outside her own confines.

Priesthood and prophecy
There is an inseparable link between Christian prophecy and Christian priesthood. All the baptised are called to be prophets. Christian ministerial priesthood is a priesthood of the living word. There are good grounds for saying that the first call of the ordained priest today is the call to be a prophet, to be a prophetic voice and to proclaim the word of God in the prophetic way. It is a call to live by the word and to have the insight and inspiration to help the priestly and prophetic people to interpret their lives in the light of the word and to be made new by the word. The call is not confined to priests with rare charismatic gifts. It is part of the mission of every priest.

Bruce Vawter, CM, 'Introduction to Prophetic Literature', in *The New Jerome Biblical Commentary*, pp. 186-200.

Walter Brueggemann, *The Prophetic Imagination*, (Fortress Press, 1978).

CHAPTER 5

Priests and presbyters

The English word 'priest' is an abbreviation of the Greek *presbyteros*. In itself, this word has no religious connotations. Literally, it stands for somebody who is an elder, by age or by some reason of status in a community. But the word has come to have strong religious connotations. In practice, it has come to be used as the equivalent of the Latin *sacerdos*, the Greek *hiereus*, the Hebrew *kohen*. All these suggest religious, sacred, cultic functions, meanings that have been captured in the Gaelic *sagart* and related words. This ambivalence in the 'presbyteral' and 'sacerdotal' aspects of priestly ministry can be a source of confusion. It can also be a help to provide a continual and creative tension between the secular and religious aspects of the ministry of ordained priests in a changing society. In this context, it is interesting that the Second Vatican Council promulgated a decree on the ministry and life of presbyters; but its title in English is the Decree on the Ministry and Life of Priests. In this chapter, the word 'priest' will be used with its religious connotations, rather than as an equivalent of the more neutral word 'elder'.

A long history

The world has known a variety of expressions of priesthood. With their various understandings of the gods, of worship, and of sacrifice, each of the peoples that surrounded Israel contributed something to the shaping of an understanding of the priestly function. Each had had its influence on the society of the patriarchs who had no official priesthood and for whom the offering of sacrifice was more a family experience than a sanctuary event. In the Exodus happenings, the priesthood received a central prominence for the people of Israel. It is not easy to determine what derived directly from the initiative of Moses and what was the result of later developments. The end result was that the tribe of Levi, of which Moses was a member, emerged as having a special responsibility for the functions of priesthood. It is not clear whether Moses himself functioned as a priest. He certainly saw himself as responsible for the establishing and promoting of authentic sacrifice and authentic priesthood. His brother Aaron was to become a symbol of all that priesthood stood for.

The emergence of the monarchy had important implications for priesthood. In the cultures surrounding Israel, the phenomenon of priest-kings was familiar enough. Already in Gen 14:18 ff there is an account of an event involving the priest-king Melchisedech, an event of which the letter to the Hebrews was to make much in describing the priestly credentials of Jesus Christ (chap. 7). The kings of Israel saw themselves as having a responsibility for the organisation of worship. Some of them are on record as having actually performed priestly functions. But the priests of the Levite tradition continued to lead worship and to consult the Lord at the various sanctuaries throughout the land, and especially at the sanctuary of Jerusalem.

With the building of Solomon's temple, the city of Jerusalem came to be seen as the special place of special worship, of special priestly activity. In the course of time, there was conflict between the Levitical priests and the Zadokite priests who saw themselves as the official Jerusalem priests, and who controlled temple worship for several centuries. Some subtle interpretation of genealogies was needed in the various attempts to link the two priesthoods. By the reforms of Josiah in 621 BC, foundations were laid for the distinction between the priestly functions of those who were descended from Zadok and other sanctuary functions exercised by the Levites.

The Levitical priests were among those who benefited from the destruction of the temple (587 BC). In the daily worship connected with the new temple, they came to exercise a cultic monopoly and they made significant contributions to the contents of the Pentateuch in what came to be called the 'priestly' sections. The details of priestly 'hierarchy' were traced back to and ascribed to the influence of Aaron. According to this hierarchy, the pride of place went to the head priest, the high-priest, who, at least in post-exilic times, had exclusive annual access to the Holy of Holies, that special dwelling place of God in the re-built temple. Next in rank came the college of priests, the sons of Aaron. Next were those called Levites, with various subordinate roles. All were in various ways involved in the offering of sacrifice, in temple worship. This was to become the pattern and paradigm of all priestly activity. The Hellenistic and Roman influences on temple life did not substantially weaken the priestly and Levitical influence. Appointment to and deposition from the higher forms of priestly office tended to come directly from political initiative. But the basic position of priests remained secure. The high-priest especially remained a figure of exceptional prominence and power.

If one were to rely solely on the letter to the Hebrews, the function of priesthood could be seen as, in effect, confined to the offering of sacrifice: 'Every high priest chosen from among mortals is put in charge of things pertaining to God on their behalf, to offer gifts and sacrifices for sins' (Heb 5:1). This describes accurately what was perceived to be at the heart of priesthood, and the situation obtaining at the time of the writing of the letter. But, in earlier centuries, the work of interpreting the divine will and of explaining and proclaiming the implications of the Law of God (cf Deut 33:8-10) were seen as an important part of the priestly task. As time went on, the work of interpreting the divine will tended to become more associated with the prophets; expertise in elucidating the implications of the Law went to those special teachers of Israel who were called scribes. In both developments, the growth of synagogue worship played a prominent part. The text in the letter to the Hebrews is an accurate expression of the situation at the time of the destruction of the second temple. In spite of its restrictiveness, it captures the essence of Israelite priesthood: priestly activity was orientated towards God; it dealt with the realm of the holy; it was designed to mediate access to God; it was most characteristically expressed by offering to God, on an altar, the sacrificial blood that was identified with life. Each of these expressions was to get a new meaning in the person and ministry of Jesus Christ.

The priesthood of Jesus
There is no evidence that Jesus ever described himself as a priest. His identifying with the shepherd's role and with the prophetic role does not have a corresponding identification with the priestly role. Neither is there evidence that any of his hearers or immedi-

ate disciples thought of him in priestly terms. Yet if we look at what had been the three characteristic activities of the priest of Israel, in the heyday of the cultic life of Israel, it is clear that they were admirably embodied in his person and ministry. His body emerged as the real temple, the only place of true worship (cf Mt 12:6; Mk 14:58; Jn 2:19-21). His sole concern was to interpret and do the will of his Father and to motivate others to do that will. The words by which he interpreted and taught God's Law were all life-giving words. They came from the one who was himself God's Word made flesh. He expressed perfectly in his own life the highest prophetic ideals for true sacrifice for those who offer temple worship. He is, in fact, greater than the temple, above priesthood (cf Mt 12:4ff). When we read the gospels in this light, it is very easy to see how he soon came to be described in explicitly priestly and sacrificial terms. His death was seen by his enemies as a punishment for blasphemy (Mk 14:64). His own understanding of his coming death came to be expressed in the sacrificial terms of covenant blood poured out (Mk 14:24). With words that evoked the sacrifice that followed on the Sinai covenant, the coming death of Jesus is described as a life given in ransom by the one who is at the same time Son of Man and Suffering Servant (Mk 10:45). The timing of his death had obvious associations with the sacrificial offering of the paschal lamb (Ex 12:7, 13-22 ff). Though the sacrificial aspects of his death did not automatically make him into a priest, it became clear that he wished his suffering and dying to have saving effects for others. The way was being opened for interpreting his life and death in priestly terms. In spite of his human recoiling from the prospect of his suffering, the will of his Father predominated (Mk 14:36). Nobody took his life from him; he laid it down of his own free accord (Jn 10:18). He took ownership of his 'sacrifice'. In him, priestly attitudes and priestly function were one; there was no division between who he was and what he did.

It was these dispositions that led to his being seen as the priest offering the sacrifice that kept rising up to heaven from his own body. The fourth gospel and the other Johannine writings have various threads of priestly and sacrificial language. Some writers have seen priestly overtones in the account of the taking of the tunic of Jesus which was 'seamless, woven in one piece from the top' (Jn 19:23). The 'one like the Son of Man, clothed with a long robe and with a golden sash across his chest' (Rev 1:13) is clearly a high-priestly figure. The sacrificial motifs in the account of the passion in the fourth gospel are introduced by the 'priestly prayer' in chapter 17. The one who 'sanctifies' himself so that his disciples may be sanctified (v 19) is the one whom Jesus had earlier described, in sacrificial language, as having been sanctified by the Father and sent into the world (chap. 10:36). The same sacrificial, and therefore priestly, motif is often taken up by St Paul. His call to a new way of life, characterised by sincerity and truth, is based on the fact that 'our paschal lamb, Christ, has been sacrificed' (1 Cor 5:7). The Day of Atonement provides him with a way of interpreting Christ's death (Rom 3:24 ff). Communion in Christ's life-giving blood is communion in sacrificial blood, in redemptive blood (1 Cor 10:16-22; Rom 5:9). By implication, it is the blood poured out in priestly action, with priestly dispositions (cf Col 1:20; Eph 1:7; 2:13).

The nearest Paul comes to describing himself as a priest is when he says that he is a 'minister (*leitourgos*) of Jesus Christ to the Gentiles in the priestly service of the gospel of God'. This priestly service of proclaiming the gospel is to ensure that the offering of the Gentiles may be acceptable, sanctified by the Holy Spirit (Rom 15:16). There is a profound understanding here of the purpose of Christian priestly ministry: letting the good news go so deep into people's hearts that their lives well lived will be the kind of sacrifice that really pleases God. A similar sacrificial perspective lies behind seeing Christian death as 'being poured out as a libation' (2 Tim 4:6). As a variation on the theme of sacrifice, some early Christian preaching and catechesis centred on the death of the sacrificed servant (Act 3:13-26; 4:27-30). In 1 Peter, the message of redemption and the place of the blood of the lamb are expressed in the assurance that 'you were ransomed ... not with perishable things like silver and gold ... but with the precious blood of Christ, like that of a lamb without defect or blemish' (1 Pet 1:18-19).

Priesthood made perfect
The letter to the Hebrews makes explicit and develops all that the other New Testament books had to say about the priesthood and

sacrifice of Jesus Christ. The unknown author, writing around the time of the destruction of the temple, sees the work of Jesus Christ as, on every level, a work of perfecting, completing, fulfilling. The basic typology of the letter derives from what happened on the annual Day of Atonement. In the working out of that typology, all the great religious words are re-defined and re-situated: covenant, temple, priest, sacrifice, holy of holies, mercy-seat. Many of the great figures and events from the story of salvation are re-assessed in the light of what has happened in the life, death, and glorification of Jesus. The key to the uniqueness and superiority of Jesus Christ is the fact that he is the son and heir (chap. 1:2) through whom God has definitively spoken. This sonship places him above all angels (chap. 1:2), above Moses (chap. 3), above Joshua (chap. 4). As the perfect high-priest he has the tender mercy and fidelity associated with the God of the covenant and enriched by his own sinlessness (chap. 5:3-27). In his unique relationship with God, he relativises or makes redundant all other expressions of priesthood. His eternal call by his Father highlights the limitations of Levitical priesthood and gives a significance to otherwise minor figures like Melchisedech who, when seen as as priest-king of 'justice and peace', and as one who is somehow outside the normal ways of reckoning human genealogies, provides a glimpse of what God has done in Jesus Christ (chap. 7). With his pedigree as a high-priest fully established, Jesus has entered the holy of holies of heaven, offering, at the divine mercy-seat, the perfect once-for-all sacrifice. Jesus is the perfect priest who offers the perfect sacrifice. However, he has shifted the location of priestly ministry and sacrifice. The sacrifice is not in animal blood but in his own life-blood. The altar of sacrifice is not in a section of the temple, built by human hands. It is the living body of Jesus himself (chap. 9). The reason the sacrifice fully pleases God is that it rises up to God out of the body-temple of the one who had no other concern than, in the spirit of the promised new covenant, to keep doing his Father's will. In the heart of this living body-temple, are written the laws of the new covenant (10:16).

The ideal for all Christian living is to identify with the sacrifice of Jesus, in a spirit of faith and hope, a spirit anticipated in some way by each of the well-known men and women who feature in the story of salvation (chaps. 11, 12). For the Christian, following the supreme example of Jesus, true sacrifice is a sacrifice of praise, sacrifice that continually goes up to God from the human body, from lips that confess his name, and from hands that shape good deeds and that are reached out in sharing (chap. 13:15-16). It is the task of Christian leaders to keep watch, since they must give account to God for the quality of sacrifice in the daily lives of believers (v 17). A purpose of the meeting together of Christians is to 'provoke one another to love and good deeds' and to 'encourage one another' (chap. 10:24-25). It is a way of ensuring that all will keep their 'eyes fixed on Jesus' who is the 'pioneer and perfecter' of their faith (chap. 12:2).

The perfect sacrifice by the perfect priest established the new covenant, long since promised by the prophets (Heb 9:15; cf Mt 26:28). In describing Jesus as the 'mediator' of that covenant (chap. 9) the author of Hebrews draws on the dual meaning of the word 'covenant'. As with the first covenant, the new one involves a whole new set of relationships. It also has the characteristics of the making of a will. It involves both a testator and those who are beneficiaries of the will (9:16).

A priestly people
It is in relationship to the one sacrifice, the one priest, the one covenant, the one mediator, the one will, that all language of sacrifice and priesthood can be applied to the Christian priesthood and to Christian ministry. By calling his disciples to a life patterned on his own, Jesus brought into existence a priestly people, a sacrificing people. In this setting, Christian life can be seen in terms of a continual sacrifice, a continual offering, a continual libation (Phil 2:17). Even the giving of financial support for the work of the Church becomes a 'fragrant offering, a sacrifice acceptable and pleasing to God' (Phil 4:18). In every human situation, the offering up of the human body can become a priestly activity, bringing about 'a living sacrifice, holy and acceptable to God, which is your spiritual worship' (Rom 12:1). In tune with the godward movement of Christ's body, every activity of the living body of every Christian can be the makings of a continual sacrifice of praise. As the Church of Christ came to explore the limitless implications of his call to his disciples and apostles, sacrificial and

priestly language came to be applied more and more to the members of Christ's body and to those who exercise Christian ministry. This development has been fruitful to the extent to which it has helped Christians to keep their eyes fixed on Jesus (Heb 12:2), their only priest, their only mediator, of whose last will and testament they have all become beneficiaries. Whether we describe ordained Christian leaders as priests or as presbyters, their mission is clear: to keep unfolding the riches of that will and testament and to enable every one of the priestly people to be continually enriched by the continual offering of the one acceptable sacrifice.

Nathan Mitchell, OSB, *Mission and Ministry*, (Michael Glazier, 1982).

J.T. Forrestel, *As Ministers of Christ: The Christological Dimension of Ministry in the New Testament*, (Paulist Press, 1991).

CHAPTER 6

Kings, shepherds and servants

At first sight, it would be difficult to see any connection between royalty and pastoral ministry. Yet, in the experience of the people of Israel, there was an easy association between the image of the king and the image of the shepherd. In many of the countries that were neighbours to Israel, the king saw himself in terms of a shepherd caring for a flock. Before King David was anointed king over Israel, the tribes expressed their confidence in him by recognising him as suitable to be, at the same time, king, leader, ruler, shepherd: 'It was you who led out Israel and brought it in. The Lord said to you: "it is you who shall be shepherd of my people Israel, you who shall be ruler over Israel."' (2 Sam 5:2). David, in turn, spoke of his people as sheep entrusted to his care, and he begged the Lord to save them (24:17). Having himself been taken from the sheepfolds, to be shepherd of the people, he tended them 'with upright heart', and guided them 'with skilful hand' (Ps 78:70-72). The shepherd imagery was even more explicitly associated with such leaders as the judges whom God had commanded to shepherd and guide his people (2 Sam 7:7), with some public rulers (Jer 3:15) and even with the princes of the nations (Jer 25:34 ff; Is 44:28). At all times, though, it is the Lord himself who is the real shepherd of the people he has chosen (Ps 100:3; Mic 7:14).

Out of much experience of many good and bad forms of shepherding, the conviction arose that there was need for a new David who alone could adequately shepherd God's people, according to the designs of God's own heart (Jer 3:15; 23:3-4). This conviction was strengthened by the growth of messianic expectations and by the repeated exposing by men like Jeremiah, Ezekiel and Zephaniah of the gross neglect of the flock by leaders whose duty it was to guide and feed them. Drawing from their experience of observing shepherds who formed so much a part of their society, people were quick to recognise the good qualities of the men who led them and who walked beside them at history's difficult stages. The qualities of the ideal shepherd were embodied in the providence and care of the Lord himself who, when human shepherds failed, could be relied on to feed his flock, gather the lambs in his arms, carry them in his bosom, and gently lead the mother sheep (Is 40:11). It became clear that every true shepherding must be modeled on, and must draw life from, the Lord's own shepherding. The new David, the awaited messiah, would bring together in his person all these shepherding qualities. In some expectations, the promised shepherd came to be identified with the one who, in accordance with God's saving designs, would be 'pierced' (Zech 12:10) and with the mysterious suffering servant of Second Isaiah on whom the Lord would lay the iniquity of all the sheep who have strayed (Is 53:6).

Jesus the shepherd

Jesus lived in a society that had ambivalent attitudes towards shepherds. On the one hand, the people had inherited all the prophetic dissatisfaction with shepherd leaders. They were part of a society in which to be a shepherd was to belong to a well known category of 'sinners'. The shepherd's way of life was believed to encourage a variety of forms of thieving and dishonesty. There was a particular suspicion of those hireling workers for whom shepherding was merely a form of livelihood that did not generate any of the ideal shepherd qualities. On the other hand, in the light of prophetic promises about the coming of the ideal shepherd-king, of the ideal of shepherding expressed in Ps.23, and of the people's own experience of individual honest shepherds, the word 'shepherd' had many favourable associations and connotations as well. It may well be that Jesus was born in a stable owned by shepherds. In that setting a group of shepherds would understandably have been the first to welcome and recognise him. They represented, at the same time, both the lowly ones and the sinners who were to be at the centre of the ministry of Jesus.

It is easy to see that the descriptions of the mission of Jesus in shepherd imagery were drawing both on the day to day experience of the people and on the hope that had arisen out of the continual promises of God. The special mission of Jesus was to the sheep who were lost (Lk 19:10; Mt 10:6; 15:24). He was moved, with the compassion of God himself, by those who were 'harassed and helpless like sheep without a shepherd' (Mt 9:36). The God he preached was the God who is the first to rejoice at the return of the lost sheep (Lk 15:3-7). His disciple-apostles are the symbolic group that represent the coming into existence of an Israel made new. They are the 'little flock' (Lk 12:32). Through them, the whole flock is alerted to the fact that they can expect all the testings and trials that characterised the story of the original Israel, but they will be shepherded by the one who would be 'pierced', the one who at the same time serves and suffers. Out of his very piercing and suffering will come his strength to lead his people and go before them (Mt 26:31). The way they respond to the requirements of his shepherding will be the norm for the separation between those on the king's right and those on his left in his final return in glory (Mt 25:31ff).

From being experienced as the messiah, leader, servant who was the fulfilment of all God's promises, Jesus came to be recognised as the 'great shepherd of the sheep' (Heb 13:20). By his wounds came the healing of his flock, who were led back to him as their shepherd and guardian (1 Pet 2:24-25). In the words of Moses' ideal for a shepherd, he went out before them and came in before them; he led them out and brought them in (Num 27:17). As Risen Lord, he was at the same time the sacrificial lamb and the shepherd guiding his people to the springs of the water of life (Rev 7:17). The shepherd theme is taken up very strikingly in the fourth gospel. Jesus is presented as coming to a people damaged by all the forms of bad shepherding that had been denounced by the prophets. Every promise of God to send a good shepherd and every human dream of good leadership is captured in his person and ministry. He is the good shepherd (Jn 10:11). The shepherd image captures and sums up all that his mission is about. It is about unity (v 16); it is about giving life (v 10); it is about very personal knowing and loving (vv 14, 15, 17); it is about recognising and following a voice (vv 5, 16, 27); it is about not running away (v 13); it is about the kind of love that is ready to pay any cost, even to the point of laying down one's life (vv 15, 17, 18); it is about drawing people into the very intimacy of communication between Jesus and his Father (vv 15, 30).

Pastoral ministry
Because Jesus is the only gate of entry into the life of God (v 7), and

the only true shepherd, all pastoral ministry in his Church must be a sharing in the mission of the one shepherd and in terms of accountability to him. Jesus is generous in admitting people into that sharing. After repeated assurances of his love, Peter is given the charge of universal shepherding by the risen Christ (Jn 21:16). One of the gifts of the Spirit for the building up of the body of Christ and bringing all its members to full stature was to be the gift of being pastors (Eph 4:11-13). The 'oversight' exercised by those called to be elders in the Church is to be characterised by the full range of the qualities of the chief shepherd (1 Pet 5:1-4). The fact that the chief shepherd will come and will re-appear (v 4) is no guarantee that the flock will be spared from onslaughts by various kinds of savage wolves (Acts 20:29). But ultimate victory is assured. The human shepherd, called to be an example to the flock, can live in the full hope of winning 'the crown of glory that never fades away' (1 Pet 5:4).

Prophet, priest, shepherd – king

It is not surprising that, in the course of the centuries, the language and images connected with shepherding became very much part of the day to day life and ministry of the Church. Writers like John Calvin presented the mission of Christ, systematically, under the headings of priest, prophet and king (shepherd). John Henry Newman saw the advantages of envisaging Christ's Church in the same triple perspective. The Second Vatican Council fastened on this theme and taught that God sent his Son 'that he might be teacher, king and priest of all, the head of the new and universal people' (LG 13). The Council presented this threefold mission of Christ as being shared by all those who are baptised into his body. In turn, it presented all ordained ministry as deriving from the same threefold mission, and existing in order to enable the prophetic, kingly and priestly people to keep growing into the likeness of their Head. It would be difficult, indeed impossible, to draw exact lines between these three aspects of the mission of Christ, of the Church, of the Church's ministers. In practice, the tendency has been to link prophetic ministry with the work of preaching and teaching, kingly (pastoral) ministry with the care and concern for all the faithful at the various stages of life's journey, priestly ministry with all that concerns divine worship. This is a convenient division but, in practice, there is a continual over-lapping of the three areas. The Christian minister is at the same time, a prophetic priest, a priestly shepherd, a pastoral prophet.

All aspects of ministry are expressions of the central Christian work of salvation and reconciliation. Each is continually calling for the pastoral work of healing, supporting, and sustaining all one's brothers and sisters, at every stage of life's journey. This arises out of the very nature of the many-membered body of Christ. Those in official public pastoral ministry are in various public ways commissioned to keep promoting the call to all the members of the body to love both God and neighbour, to be the good Samaritan to anybody, anytime, in any need, to keep pro-moting the building up of that body which is 'joined and knit to-gether by every ligament with which it is equipped, as each part is working properly, promoting the body's growth in building itself up in love' (Eph 4:16). The ordained shepherd is authorised to represent the members of that body to the Good Shepherd who is their Head, and to represent him to the members, especially in the moments of interaction between sacramental worship and com-munity pastoral care.

Though the prophetic, pastoral, and priestly aspects of Church ministry are inseparably linked, there are some activities that par-ticularly call for the qualities of the good shepherd. These include the various forms of pastoral visitation, care of the sick, the im-prisoned, the dying, people at various stages of human 'passage', the promoting of justice and peace in the local and wider commu-nity. The Church's ministry of pastoral care moves towards and flows from her liturgical life and worship. Each of the sacraments, properly celebrated, is an expression of the shepherding of the whole flock of Christ, in some way awakening and activating the pastoral urges of the whole flock, and led by those authorised to represent the whole flock. The providing for the exercise of the spiritual and corporal works of mercy, which is so much part of the Church's pastoral mission, has been done in various ways at various stages of the Church's history. The quality of public pas-toral care has always varied considerably from local church to local church. One of the ways in which the Church has been alerted over the centuries to various forms of human poverty and need

has been the periodic emergence of charismatic leaders and
founders, men and women who recognised needs and started
new movements of pastoral caring. A characteristic of the whole
Church in recent decades has been the emphasis on adequate pastoral formation for all those in ministry. In a Church that sees herself as the universal sacrament of salvation, one can hope to see
the emergence of many new and creative forms of pastoral care,
as all the members of the body of Christ keep interacting with
each other and coming to realise that they are 'keepers' to their
brothers and sisters (Gen 4:9).

Pastoral care
In these times of specialisation, there is much emphasis on the development of suitable skills for those involved in various forms of
pastoral care. This applies especially as pastoral care works out its
connections with specialised forms of counselling and therapy.
Those in public pastoral care are learning to work in close collaboration with others who are concerned with the development of
the human person. For some, this can be a difficult learning process,but for all it can be a providential opportunity enabling the
Church to become the kind of sacrament that she is called to be. A
vision is already emerging of one human family, on one journey,
in one universe, with one ultimate destiny. St Irenaeus has told us
that the glory of God is a human being fully alive, and that to be
alive is to see God. The ultimate aim of all Christian pastoral ministry is to enable people to see God at every stage of life's journey,
and after.

Journeying together
There is always a possibility that pastoral caring could generate
an unconscious attitude of patronising condescension towards
those to whom one ministers. The very language of sheep and
shepherd is open to being misconstrued in this way. In this context, some pastoral attitudes, inherited from a less egalitarian
society, are quickly seen to be inadequate today. Those in pastoral
ministry must keep realising that they are on the same journey
and surrounded by the same human needs and limitations as the
people to whom they minister. In their attitudes, they must embody many of the paradoxes of Christianity. They must be, at the
same time, teachers and learners; walking ahead of and at the

same pace as those ministered to; strong in faith yet sharing all
human weakness; physicians in need of healing; leaders who are
always serving; guides who are always seeking the way. This is
the kind of pastoral perspective encouraged by the *Rite of
Christian Initiation of Adults* which is already having such a profound influence on the life of the Church. The vision it provides is
of people all together on a common journey, walking with each
other, accompanying each other, supporting each other. This
vision draws continual encouragement from the exquisite example of Jesus on the road to Emmaus (Lk 24:13-35): he walked with;
he journeyed; he listened and he illumined; he helped recognise;
he shared.

There is much emphasis today on the human and Christian development of those in pastoral ministry and of those to whom they
minister. One hopes that the Church of Christ will always welcome whatever promotes this integral human development. The
surest programme for the Christian side of development is being
immersed in the programme for shepherding drawn up in the
gospel portrait of the Good Shepherd; in the continual invitation
of the one who, in a setting of love, keeps saying 'feed my lambs,
feed my sheep' (Jn 21:15-17); in the daily call to be 'examples to the
flock' (1 Pet 5:3). In these scriptural perspectives, there is a fully
coherent programme for pastoral theology and pastoral care. It is
a programme that can gracefully absorb any advances from any
sources in the understanding of the human person and the skills
that promote these advances. The most important requirement
for anybody in pastoral ministry, and indeed in all priestly and
prophetic ministry, is the ability to express the tender mercy and
fidelity of the God of the covenant. The God of the covenant is
identical with the shepherd whose goodness and kindness keep
following people all the days of their life (Ps 23:6). All his qualities
come together in 'the great shepherd of the sheep' (Heb 13:20).
This Great Shepherd is also priest, prophet, and suffering servant,
the one who took the risk of being fully pierced, out of a love than
which there is no greater (Jn 15:13).

Shepherding, service, ministry
The language of ministry is at a transition stage in the Church
today. In some usage, the word 'ministry' is reserved for those

who are authorised to carry out some form of public function or office in the Christian community. Some prefer to use the word in a more generic way and to speak of the call to ministry as applying to all of the baptised. It is likely that this way of speaking will prevail. Either way, all ministry must keep trying to find its meaning and its model in the person and ministry of the Good Shepherd who was in the midst of his disciples as one who serves (Lk 22:27). In his unique way of ministering, he was, at the same time, slave, servant and leader.

Alistair V. Campbell (ed), *A Dictionary of Pastoral Care*, (S.P.C.K., 1987).

John N. Collins, *Are All Christians Ministers?*, (E.J. Dwyer, 1992).

PART II

Alive in the Trinity

CHAPTER 7

In the name of the Father

At the heart of the good news of Jesus Christ is the assurance of the fatherhood of God and the related topic of the reign of God. In the synoptic gospels, Jesus is presented as announcing the coming of God's reign; in St John, this is transposed into the message of 'eternal life'. God's reign is the horizon in which it is possible for every human being to have and exercise the qualities that are characteristic of God the Father, and to have eternal life. The preaching and the parables of Jesus were a continual disclosure of the qualities of God the Father. He invited his hearers to put no limit to their practice of goodness, as their heavenly Father's goodness knew no bounds (Mt 5:48). He refined and drew out the rich implications of the message of divine fatherhood which was already known through the Hebrew scriptures. Jesus assured his hearers that God is a Father who is, above all, loving and forgiving (Lk 15:11-32). He cares and he provides (Mt 6:26-32). He makes his sun rise on those who deserve it and those who do not (Mt 5:45). He thus turns accepted human wisdom inside out and gives the motive for loving even one's enemies (Mt 5:43). The same reversal of accepted values allows the pagans to share in his reign (Mt 8:12), even to the extent of displacing those who think they have a right to it by their own merits. In spite of any human unworthiness, he gives the Holy Spirit to those who ask him (Lk 11:13). Because he is not tied to any human programme, he chooses and calls whom he wills. His special choice goes out to the 'little ones'; it is to them that he reveals his secrets (Mt 11:25).

Like children

Because the Father chooses 'little ones', Jesus himself has a uniquely intimate relationship with the Father. Only the Father knows him thoroughly and he is the only one who knows the Father; he, in turn, reveals the Father to anybody he wishes to choose (Mt 11:28). It is out of this mutual knowing and loving, and out of this revealing of the Father by the Son, that the call to be Christians derives. To our generation, which is particularly sensi-

tive to ways of imaging God, the naming and addressing of God
as Father can be an awkward experience. For some people, it suggests an approach that is paternalistic and condescending. But
even the most sophisticated of generations cannot get away from
the elementary experience of fatherhood and the relationships
which it implies. There is a close link between the teaching of Jesus
on the fatherhood of God and his assertion that unless we 'turn
round and become like children' we will never enter the kingdom
of heaven (Mt 18:3). The invitation to discipleship is an invitation
to become as children are. It is more than an invitation; it is the
statement of a requirement for admission to God's reign. Jesus il-
lustrates his message from the various states of childhood, from
the state of the child whom he called and set in front of him back to
the helpless state of childhood at and after the time of human birth
(Jn 3:3). The state of the small infant, in particular, is a state of need
and dependency. The small infant has to be washed by another,
fed by another, clothed by another. In the light of the full Christian
revelation, this is how we all stand before God when it comes to
talking about salvation and the meaning of the Church's sacramental life. This is the meaning, in particular, of the washing of
baptism, the feeding that takes place in the eucharist, the re-cloth-
ing that takes place in the sacrament of reconciliation. All this en-
hances rather than diminishes our humanness. It places us safely
in the hands of a personal power greater than ourselves.

Childhood and growth
It may be that we do not like what this dependency entails.
Indeed, there are aspects of child-ness that could diminish us
rather than promote our growth. St Paul, who so much appreciated the fatherhood of God and knew well that 'every family in
heaven and on earth' takes its name from him (Eph 3:15), was
clear that becoming fully human in Christ required the putting
away of the things of a child (1 Cor 13:11). In our society, the image
of children has often been sentimentalised, and, somewhere
along the line, we have succumbed to the myth of the total innocence of children. But those sons and daughters of God who have
grasped the message of spiritual childhood know that it has nothing to do with sentiment or with a romanticised innocence. St
Thérèse of Lisieux, that great teacher of the 'little way' to God, has

left it on record that one of the great graces she received in her early adolescent years was the realisation, on a memorable Christmas night, that it was time for her to grow out of childhood. The message of spiritual childhood is an invitation to full growth. Nothing delights loving parents more than the realisation that their child is growing. At every stage of growth, there is a new enriching and deepening of the parent-child relationship and of the loving language in which it is expressed. Part of the attractiveness of a growing child is the unclouded vision which enables it to communicate with a loving parent. For the grown-up believer, the ability to keep saying 'father' to earthly father and heavenly father is an assertion of a wholesome sense of creaturehood and a continual reminder that God is the one to whom we are in all things ultimately accountable, with an accountability that is life-giving and growth-giving. It is also an assurance that we are continually learning to pray, in the wholesome way that a child speaks to its father. The fatherhood of God provides the right perspective about life and death, about time and eternity. In the light of it, there is no contradiction between praying for earthly food and for heavenly food, for bread for today and bread for tomorrow. It creates a spirit of appreciation of and wonder at the gifts that God keeps giving to all his family. It does not take away the enigma of suffering, but it enables us to cope with suffering. It teaches us to distinguish between the suffering that is degrading and de-humanising and the suffering that is truly redemptive. It alerts us to the benign providence of a father who disciplines his children, precisely because he loves them (Heb 12:7-11).

Abba, Father

It would appear that the Son of God experienced the fatherhood of the One whose will he came to do best of all at the very time when the Father seemed most far away from him. This is the one time in the gospels in which he is recorded as crying 'Abba, Father' (Mk 14:36). In two of his greatest letters, St Paul was to pick up that cry and assure us that we can make it our own, as we come to realise that we are sons and daughters of the same God to whom Jesus prayed (Rom 8:15; Gal 4:6). There is some disagreement as to whether 'Abba' is essentially a child's word, somewhat like 'daddy' in English, or a more neutral word, suited equally for child or grown-up. The question is largely theoretical. The centrality of God's fatherhood in the teaching of Jesus is clear. Equally clear is his radical call to become as little children. His own agony cry to the Father, as recorded in St Mark's gospel, is both an expression of intimacy and a cry out of the depths. In the three contexts in which the word appears in the New Testament, we are dealing with the most basic of human experiences and needs. In the gospel context, Jesus was 'overwhelmed by horror and anguish' (Mk 14:33). His heart was ready to 'break with grief' (v 34). He was throwing himself on the ground and praying that 'if it were possible, this hour might pass him by' (v 35). He was at the same time coping with undeserved suffering, a situation which raises the most anguishing questions on earth; he was facing a violent death in all its rawness; he was praying and concentrating, in circumstances that make both difficult. Out of this totally vulnerable situation came his 'Abba, Father, take this cup from me' (v 36). It came 'with loud cries and tears' (Heb 5:7). But it came in submission to the will (Mk 14:36) of him about whom he had said 'the Son can do nothing by himself; he does only what he sees the Father doing' (Jn 5:19).

The Letter to the Romans deals with the great topics of law, grace and salvation. For St Paul, the key to the ways these three are related is the fact that we have received the Spirit of God himself. Led by this Spirit, we are enabled to cry 'Abba! Father!' (Rom 8:15). And Paul assures us that this is the cry which links us with the sufferings of the one who himself had cried (v 17; cf Hebr 5:7) and who makes us children growing in the spirit of the gospel, children who are heirs (vv 16, 17). The same message is given by Paul to the Galatians. They had been made free by the gospel. But they were falling back into a wretched slavery. The only way they could be made free again would be by crying 'Abba, Father', the cry of sons and heirs (Gal 4:6-7).

Whether 'Abba, Father' is primarily the cry of the small child or of the child who has reached full adulthood, it is the cry from the depths of the human condition to the personal, loving power greater than oneself. On various levels and at various stages, it is a cry of anguish, of grief, of one facing suffering, of one facing death. It is the cry of one learning to pray. It is the cry of one trying to concentrate on God and to find out and do his will. It is the cry of one in human bondage. It is the cry of one experiencing the joy and the freedom that only the Spirit of God can give, and that are continually there for the asking.

Priesthood and fatherhood

For many centuries, there has been a close connection between Christians' understanding of priesthood and their understanding of the fatherhood of God. Those who exercise ministerial priesthood have, like St Paul, the mission to 'beget' (cf 1 Cor 4:15) a believing community, by the proclamation of the gospel. Bearing in mind the riches of the fatherhood of God revealed in Jesus Christ, this is a daunting task. Moreover, the linking of priesthood and fatherhood would seem to contradict the clear command of Jesus not to call any man a father on earth (Mt 23:9). In St Matthew, this invitation is expressed in terms of being perfect (Mt 5:48). This, in turn, sums up the qualities of the Father which Jesus highlighted so much in the sermon on the mount: his graciousness, his generosity, his wholeness, his sheer goodness. St Luke, in his version, focuses on the strong but loving imperative to be compassionate like the heavenly Father (Lk 6:36). If priests are to continue to be called by the name of father, the justification will be in the fact that their ministry is an enabling ministry – enabling people to absorb into their lives the qualities of the Father. Only this, too, can justify their being called by words like 'good' and 'teacher', in apparent contradiction to the command of Jesus (Mt 19:17; 23:9). For both priests themselves, and for those by whom they are called father, teacher, and good, the sermon on the mount is a stimulus for an examination of conscience and an ever new programme for action. It is a continual call to conversion and a command to become more transparent with the qualities of the Father. It is a continual reminder to be in the Father's house, concerned with the Father's affairs (Lk 2:49).

Father and mother

In past centuries, the implications of the fatherhood of God were worked out in terms of what we would now call a patriarchal society. That situation has changed. We are faced with people's sensibilities about male-female language and male-female relationships. These must be integrated with the best of what we have inherited from the past. For this work of integration, help can come from various sources. We are becoming more aware that God is beyond gender and beyond any of our images, analogies and concepts. We are becoming aware that Jesus drew his images of God from observing the woman of the house as well as the man of the house. We are looking again at such biblical images of God's mothering as are found in the Book of Isaiah (49:15; 66:13), and at the almost forgotten but highly sacramental notion of 'our holy mother the Church'. In the full Christian perspective, the Church should be, at the same time, a fathering church and a mothering church, drawing its resources from the communion which is the Trinity. We know that Jesus revolutionised all familial language and thereby revolutionised all relations and relationships between men, women and children. He wants each of us to keep asking who is our brother and sister and mother (cf Mk 3:35); and he revealed to us the real meaning of fatherhood in telling us about the prodigal father (Lk 15:11-32), the God who is 'my Father and your Father, my God and your God' (Jn 20:17). It would appear that the urgent task for us is not so much to change any biblical God-words and God-images as to keep overturning our own understanding of all of them, in ways that are beyond gender, beyond limit.

The love of the Abba Father is a creative, dynamic love. It is also a devouring fire (Heb 12:29). The same fire of the Father's love can be warming, or purifying, or destroying. It all depends on how we choose to relate to it. It is the task of all in Church ministry to enable all people to choose at all times to benefit from the saving aspects of the fire which is the love of the Abba Father, ever alive and ever active.

Dermot A. Lane, *Christ at the Centre*, (Veritas, 1990).

Catherine Mowry LaCugna, *God for Us*, (Harper, 1991).

CHAPTER 8

Christ really present

The Church is the community of salvation, drawing life from Jesus whose very name spells salvation. The story of our salvation centres round the record of God's saving presence to a people whom he had chosen as his own. In praise of this intimacy of God with his people, Moses asked: 'What other great nation has a god so near to it as the Lord our God is whenever we call to him?' (Deut 4:7). The cloud and the fire of the Exodus, the tabernacle, the temple, were so many stages in God's approaching nearer to his people. Finally, God's own Word became flesh and tabernacled among us. The new and more worthy temple of God was the body of Christ. Henceforward it is in the temple of Christ's body that we must meet God. And when we have become united to God in Christ we ourselves become Christ's body and God's dwelling place (cf 1 Cor 3:16; 12:27).

During the earthly existence of Jesus Christ, his body was subject to the limitations of place and time. The resurrection saw the end of these limitations. Jesus became a 'life-giving spirit' (1 Cor 15:45) and he sent his Spirit into the hearts of those who believed in him. But the Spirit did not come in the place of an absent Jesus; rather he made Jesus himself present to the believers. Already Jesus had assured his disciples that he would be with them until the end of the age. As the most powerful expression of his presence, he had asked them to celebrate the eucharist as his 'memorial' and to eat his life-giving body and drink his blood.

Times of questioning

An over-riding conviction of the early believers was that though Jesus 'must remain in heaven' until 'the time of universal restoration' (Act 3:21) he remained ever present to his people, especially, but not exclusively, when they gathered to celebrate the eucharist. Systematic questioning about the exact mode of the eucharistic presence did not come until the Church had been believing in it for hundreds of years. Various eucharistic controversies, from the time of Berengarius in the eleventh century onwards, helped the

Church to develop an elaborate theology about the eucharistic presence. The twelfth century saw the emergence of the word 'transubstantiation', not as an explanation of Christ's presence but rather as an expression of the change which takes place in the innermost being of the bread and wine in the eucharistic celebration.

Part of the very considerable contribution of St Thomas Aquinas in the thirteenth century was his expressing of aspects of the eucharistic mystery in the metaphysical and cosmological language which was later to be taken for granted in orthodox Catholic teaching (substance and accident; matter and form; quality; quantity, etc). Later, the Fathers of the Council of Trent, countering what they saw as the over symbolic eucharistic teaching of some of the Reformers, were to draw heavily on St Thomas' theology. They defined, for instance, that, in the eucharist, Jesus is really, truly and substantially present; that the entire substance of bread is changed into his body and the entire substance of wine into his blood, a change which the Church 'suitably and properly' entitles transubstantiation. They condemned the view that the body and blood of Christ are present only in the use of the sacrament, while it is being received.

Recent concerns
There was little real development in the theology of the presence of Christ in the eucharist from the time of Trent until the present century. In recent decades we have seen many attempts to restate the existing theology and to develop new lines of approach. The promptings for these attempts came from many sources.

From investigations into the history of theology came a clearer realisation that the eucharist, like the rest of the sacraments, is a sign as well as a reality; that it is a sign of Christ's presence as well as being Christ present. Allied with the study of signs was an exploring of the meaning of religious symbols in the context of Christian sacraments. To those who saw an opposition between the symbolic and the real, theologians gave the reminder that in the sacramental theology of some of the Church Fathers, symbol and reality, far from being opposed to one another, were rather mutually complementary.

From philosophy and disciplines related to philosophy came a questioning of the value of continuing to apply the substance-accident language to the eucharist. Some maintained that the Fathers of Trent, in defining transubstantiation, had deliberately refrained from tying themselves to the Aristotelian notion of substance and accident; hence their avoiding the more philosophical word 'accident' and speaking instead of 'species' i.e. appearances.

From liturgical study, especially, came a new understanding of the 'real presences' of Christ. In recent centuries the term 'real presence' had tended to be restricted to the eucharist. Drawing heavily on an older Christian tradition, theologians in this century have been speaking of a hierarchy of ways in which the one active presence of the risen Christ manifests itself in the baptised Christian and in the Christian community.

The *Constitution on the Liturgy* has provided us with a great programme for entering into the mystery of the presence of Christ. It states that Christ is always present in the Church, especially in her liturgical celebrations. Within the liturgical context, it specifies the presence of Christ in the worshipping assembly, in the celebrating minister, in the proclaimed word, in the sacramental action and under the eucharistic species (*SC* 7). The teaching is re-affirmed in the *General Instruction on the Roman Missal* (1970, par 7). All the presences in question are real presences. Such a rich teaching has, in the last few decades, been providing a fine basis for understanding such topics as the interplay of baptismal priesthood and ordained priesthood. The special presence of Christ in the celebrating priest is a key to his sacramental and leadership role in the Christian community.

The eucharist is the most all-embracing sign of the multiple presence of Christ and of his complete self-giving to his Church. It gets all the other presences into one focus. Pope Paul VI's *The Mystery of Faith* (1965) speaks of the presence in the eucharistic species as the 'most remarkable presence – the presence in the fullest sense; because it is a substantial presence by which the whole and complete Christ, God and man, is present'. The same encyclical states that the eucharistic presence 'is called real, by which it is not intended to exclude all other types of presence, as if they were not real'. Among the presences of Christ listed in the letter are his presence in the Church's works of mercy, in its pilgrimage struggle, in the governing of the people of God.

Within the framework of seeing the eucharistic presence of Christ in relation to the other forms of his presence, many theologians in this century have preferred to describe the presence of Christ in terms of a person communicating with persons within a believing community rather than in the less personal language of substance, accident, matter, form, etc. They explored the change in *meaning* and *purpose* of the bread and wine rather than the change in the *substance* of bread and wine. In this search, new words like 'trans-signification', 'trans-finalisation' and 'trans-elementation' began to emerge in the 1950s and 1960s. These were attempts to express the change in meaning and purpose, just as transubstantiation expresses and emphasises the change of substance.

It has been argued that this emphasis on the change of meaning and purpose weakens the objectivity of the change. But this argument would seem to be based on a rather superficial understanding of meaning. That a change in meaning can involve a change in reality can be seen in the background in the Hebrew bible to the revealing of the mystery of the eucharist. Over a period of several centuries the ritual of celebrating the Passover remained basically the same. But, as a result of God's continual saving activity, and the prophetic insistence on the need of a new covenant, the Passover accumulated new meanings which eventually indicated an entire change of reality. Thus the Last Supper, which had many elements of the Passover ritual, was a reality different from the former Passovers, because it had received a new, God-given meaning.

The language of Christian devotion and preaching has always emphasised the meaning and purpose of the eucharistic mystery. Much of the theology before the Council of Trent had a similar emphasis. For practical reasons, Trent shifted the emphasis to the nature of the presence of Christ and the manner of that presence, from the 'why' of Christ's presence to the 'how'. With the shift away from polemics, more recent theology has been trying to reverse the emphasis. The change gave rise to some confusion and not a little apprehension. The publication of *The Mystery of Faith* was not intended as an end to discussion and development. But it provided a salutary reminder that the new words were not an adequate expression of the change which takes place in the eucharist, and that the reason why bread and wine take on a new significance and a new finality is because they contain a new reality. It is significant that a later Roman instruction, *The Eucharistic Mystery* (1967) drew attention to the fact that the substantial presence of Christ in the eucharist must be seen in the context of the other forms of Christ's presence.

Christ the sacrament

In the last few decades the presence of Christ in the eucharist has been placed more and more in the still wider context of the topic of the sacramentality of the humanness of Christ. Theologians have been exploring the humanness of Christ as the 'primordial sacrament'. This way of speaking has not yet received a place in official Church teaching, but it would seem to be presupposed in such descriptions of the Church as being 'in Christ ... a kind of sacrament, that is sign and instrument of intimate union with God and of the unity of all mankind" (*LG* 1, cf par.9 and par.48). In the Incarnation, the humanness of Jesus became the sacrament of God's real presence to the world. The eternal Word of God became really present in Jesus Christ, living among us (cf Jn 1:14). In that mystery, we are in touch with the source of all real presence. The humanness of Jesus is the primordial sacrament. The whole Church, in turn, is the basic sacrament of the real presence of Christ. To say that it is a sacrament is to say that it is a 'mystery', putting us in direct touch with the mystery of Christ which is expressed especially in baptism and in the eucharist to which baptism leads. Because the Church is a sacrament, the eucharist is a sacrament. Because the Word of God is really present in the humanness of Jesus Christ, Jesus Christ is really present in the Christian community. Because he is really present in the Christian community, he is really present in each of the individual sacraments. Because the eucharist is the sacrament of his body and blood and since its celebration is 'the summit toward which the activity of the Church is directed' and 'the fount from which all her power flows' (SC 10), he is present in a unique way in the eucharist.

Recognising the presence

It will take some time before this new context for looking at the presence of Christ in the eucharist will be absorbed into the consciousness of the whole Church. In the process, it may need some further refining of language, but it cannot but be enriching for our appreciation of the mystery for which, up to recently, we reserved the description 'real presence'. It should, for example, help us to link the eucharistic mystery with the growing awareness in the Church that the grace of the Risen Christ is offered to every man and woman. It should help us to find a context for understanding the presence and action of the Risen Lord in all of human history, for 'in him all things in heaven and on earth were created ... and in him all things hold together' (Col 1:16-17). It also reminds us that the real presence of Christ in all its forms is a constant invitation to better communication, and that it is the real foundation for all Christian ministry. His real presence to us is not a static presence but rather an invitation to be really present to him, to all the members of his body and to ourselves. It is, above all, an invitation to recognise him as our only Lord wherever, whenever and through whomsoever he manifests his presence. It is an invitation to beg him to keep 'making himself known' to us 'in the breaking of bread' (Lk 24:35). It is an invitation to have the mentality of the 'beloved disciple'. It was he who had the eye, ear and heart that enabled him to say 'It is the Lord' (Jn 21:7). In the gospel, many people witnessed the miraculous deeds of Jesus and they heard his preaching, but not all of them recognised him as the one in whom God was really present. He stood in their midst and they did not know him (Jn 1:26). Thereby they ran the risk of being told 'I do not know where you come from' (Lk 13:25). In the meantime, he has given us the one sure criterion of how we can recognise him and he will recognise us: 'Those who love me will keep my word and my Father will love them, and we will come to them and make our home with them' (Jn 14:23).

Presence and worship

The real presence of Christ in the eucharist gathers into one focus all the other expressions of the real presence of Christ in the

Church and in the world. The celebration of the eucharist is both 'summit' and 'fount'. The Lord gives himself in the very basic signs of living body and living blood, in the very elementary but profound setting of all that is involved in eating and drinking. Those doing the eating and drinking are in a privileged way in touch with the glorified humanity of Christ. In the Western Catholic Church, this experience has given rise to many expressions of faith and devotion. One of these is the worship of the reserved sacrament. The history of this form of worship is simple enough. First came a period in history in which the total emphasis was on eucharistic celebration. Then came the practice of reserving the sacrament for the benefit of the sick. Then came the cult of the reserved sacrament, first in terms of personal private devotion and later in such forms of devotion as public adoration, processions, benediction. Over the centuries, there have been many variations on these. Sometimes, the emphasis was on seeing and adoring the sacred host rather than on eating it as the bread of life. The practice of the worship of the reserved sacrament has continued to be encouraged by the voice of the magisterium, not least in the teaching of Pope John Paul II (cf *Of The Lord's Supper*, 1980). Today, as Christians of all traditions try to learn from each other in their appreciation of the great mystery of faith, one hopes that any further decisions or developments concerning extra-sacramental eucharistic devotion will continue to foster private, prayerful devotion before the reserved sacrament. As to the public forms of worship, a test of the quality of any celebration centring on the eucharist is the extent to which it leads to and follows from the very explicit wish of Christ that we should 'take and eat' and 'take and drink', and grow in loving appreciation of the mystery of the Incarnate Word who keeps giving us signs of his real presence in every one of life's experiences and at every stage of life's journey.

Kenan B. Osborne, OFM, *The Christian Sacraments of Initiation*, (Paulist Press, 1987).

Luis M. Bermejo, SJ, *Body Broken and Blood Shed*, (Gujarat Sahitya Prakash, 1989)

CHAPTER 9

The breath of God

While I breathe, I hope; as long as I keep breathing, I keep hoping; *dum spiro, spero*. The very first pages of the bible introduce us to the breath of God and the hope it has continued to engender wherever there is the breath of human life. In a great variety of ways, the rest of the bible keeps telling us about God's life-giving breath. Sometimes, the spirit of God is spoken of in highly personal ways, sometimes as a hidden force and energy. The line of demarcation is not always easy to draw and it would be wiser not to attempt to draw it too finely. In Christian times, the divine breath of life, the divine Spirit, eventually came to be recognised as a distinct divine person who, in the words of the Council of Constantinople, 381 AD, 'proceeds from the Father', and 'together with the Father and the Son is adored and glorified'. Later, the teaching of the Western Church was amplified in a way that presented the Holy Spirit as proceeding from the Father 'and the Son'. The development obtained final approval in the Council of Florence, 1439 AD. The Eastern Church saw this as in some way derogating from the special place of the Father and subordinating the Spirit to Jesus Christ. The topic has remained a source of division. A search for a basis for agreement goes on. Among suggested formulae are 'who proceeds from the Father through the Son', 'who proceeds from the Father and shines out through the Son'. All are agreed that, as well as proceeding from the Father, the Spirit was, from the beginning, uniquely at work in the person and ministry of the Son, and that his action pervades all God's economy of salvation. In the continual search for how we are to think of the person of the Holy Spirit, perhaps the most notable contribution was made by St Augustine who saw the Spirit as the love which binds the Father and the Son. The search for suitable images continues in our own generation. One of today's concerns is to image the Holy Spirit in ways that transcend all gender, and that contribute to our recognising the truth and beauty of the living God.

Breath, breeze, wind

The approach to the Spirit as the breath of God has immediate appeal to people of every generation and culture. It needs no explanation. Breathing is in every sense basic. In the account of creation, the breathing of God reached a high point in the coming into existence of the first human being: 'The Lord God formed a human being from the dust of the ground and breathed into his nostrils the breath of life, so that he became a living creature' (Gen 2:7). Later, a psalmist was to portray the life-giving Spirit of God as being continually at work in the whole of living creation: 'When you take away their spirit, they die and return to the dust from which they came. When you send forth your spirit, they are created, and you give new life to the earth' (Ps 104:29-30).

There is an easy connection between the breath of God and the wind as a symbol of the creative power of God. Already in the first line of Genesis, the wind blowing over the original abyss evokes the creative action of the spirit (*ruach*) of God sweeping over the face of the waters (Gen 1:1-2). In the conversation of Jesus with Nicodemus, in which he invites him to be born again of water and the Spirit (Jn 3:5), the symbolism of the wind gets a prominent place: 'The wind blows where it chooses, and you hear the sound of it, but you do not know where it comes from or where it goes. So it is with everyone who is born of the Spirit' (v 8). In his poem *Ode to the West Wind*, Percy Bysshe Shelley provides some insights into how the symbol of the wind can help us see the action of God, nurturing what is life-giving and destroying what is life-taking. The wind is seen as the 'breath of autumn's being'; it chariots 'to their dark wintry bed the winged seeds ... until thine azure sister of the spring shall blow'; it is seen as the 'wild spirit ... moving everywhere; destroyer and preserver'; it is invited to 'make me thy lyre', to 'drive my dead thoughts over the universe, like withered leaves to quicken a new birth'.

Somewhere between the symbol of human breath and the symbol of the wind is the symbol of the air and the breeze as representing the action of the Spirit of God. Elijah must have been used to expecting God to manifest himself in storm, earthquake and lightening as he had done in times past (cf Ex 19). Instead he experienced God in the 'faint murmuring sound' (1 Kgs 19:12). The faint murmuring sound was presumably the domesticated wind, the air, the breeze in which God chose to speak, in an atmosphere of intimacy, but with a message that was strong. The action of God's spirit was no less powerful in the faint, murmuring sound than it had been in the stronger forces. This dual action, in the strong and startling way as well as in the quieter rhythms of the air and the breeze, has always remained characteristic of the action of the Spirit of God who refuses to be predicted and programmed. Once again, the imagery of a poet can help us here. Reflecting on the life of Mary on whom the Holy Spirit came and who was overshadowed by the power of the Most High (Lk 1:35), G.M. Hopkins wrote his poem, *The Blessed Virgin compared to the air we breathe*. In praising Mary, he praised the Spirit of God at work in her. He addressed the air as 'wild air, world-mothering air, nestling me everywhere'; as 'this needful, never spent, and nursing element'; he praised the air 'which, by life's law, my lung must draw and draw, now but to breathe its praise'; he was sure that 'we are wound, with mercy round and round, as if with air'; he asked Mary to be 'O thou dear mother, my atmosphere'.

Elementary and elemental

Breath, wind, and air. In these three symbols of the Holy Spirit we are dealing with, in many senses, the elementary and the elemental. These, and all the other great symbols of the Holy Spirit, keep bringing us back to the creative actions of God and the various manifestations of the power of God in creation, and in God's continual nurturing and sustaining of the world. The basic elements of the universe have often been said to be earth, air, fire and water. All four have provided powerful images for the person and activity of God's Spirit. The Spirit was active in the shaping of the earth (Gen 1:1-2) and in renewing its face (Ps 104:29-30). The action of the Spirit is manifested in the movements of the air we breathe and in its sisters, wind and breath. The most notable manifestation of God's Spirit in the form of fire was at the first Pentecost (Acts 2:3). The Spirit moved over the waters of creation (Gen 1:2) and of the baptismal waters of re-creation (Mt 3:16). Because he is the Spirit of the Father, his action is always an expression of the creative power and energy of God.

The creative Spirit

In the pages of the bible, this creative power and energy takes many forms. In one instance, it is the action of the creative spirit that gave a man 'skill, intelligence, and knowledge in every kind of craft … to devise artistic designs' (Ex 35:31-33). In another, it is the Spirit of the Lord that enabled another man to do daring deeds and to rally others to pursue a challenging cause (Jdgs 6:34-35). Prophets were enriched by power of the Spirit and they were inspired to follow the path of justice (Mic 3:8). Isaiah's ideal messianic king would be anointed with the Spirit of the Lord (Is 11:2). It is the Spirit who enabled Ezekiel to prophesy over the dried bones (Ezek 37:1-14) and open up new vistas of hope. The Suffering Servant was essentially a Spirit-person (Is 42:1; 61:1.2). In the power of the Spirit, he would be a bearer of justice to the nations and of hope to the poor.

In due time, these and many other activities of the Spirit were to be fully orchestrated in the person and ministry of Jesus. The Spirit prepared the temple of Mary's body to give the world the new temple (cf Lk 1:35). He was highly active at the baptism of Jesus (Mt 3:16). It was the Spirit, with whom he was filled, that led Jesus into the desert (Lk 4:1). It was the Spirit who anointed him for his messianic mission (Lk 4:18). Discipleship of Jesus, in turn, must come by rebirth 'of water and the Spirit' (Jn 3:5). The Spirit was active in all the ministry of Jesus until he was eventually raised up and he gave up his Spirit (Jn 19:30). On the evening of the Resurrection, Jesus breathed his own life and power into his disciples. In that breathing, he gave them his peace. He sent them as the Father had sent him. He gave them the Holy Spirit, enabling them to forgive sins (Jn 20:21-23). At the completion of resurrection time, when the day of Pentecost had come (Acts 2:1), the Spirit came in power and filled all of the disciples who were waiting for his coming (vv 1-4). The Church had come alive.

Life in the Spirit

The result of this great coming of God's power was that life for all disciples would be life in the Spirit of Jesus. St Paul saw this clearly. More than once, Paul spoke of the Christian's body as the temple of the Spirit (1 Cor 6:19). The body in all its aspects is to be treated with all the wonder and the reverence that the new and lasting temple deserves. It is in this body, this temple, that God is glorified (1 Cor 6:20). This is, in a variety of ways, a great recurring theme in the first letter to the Corinthians. The ways in which the Spirit has endowed and enriched all Christians, who together form one body, one spirit with the Lord (cf vv 13-20), is the basis for Paul's great resurrection teaching in chapter 15. This body-to-body relationship with Christ becomes the basis for all Christian living. It enables us to be built into a 'spiritual' house (1 Pet 2:5); to pray (Rom 8:26), to love (Rom 5:5), to be free and to cry 'Abba, Father' (Rom 8:15), to say 'Jesus is Lord' (1 Cor 12:3), to have access to the Father (Eph 2:18), to be assured in our own spirit that we are children of God (Rom 8:16), to receive a variety of gifts and exercise a variety of services (1 Cor 12:4-5), to be strengthened in our inner being (Eph 3:16), to sow seeds that will ripen (Gal 6:8), to be alive by putting to death the deeds of the body (Rom 8:13), to live a life in the grace of the Lord Jesus Christ, the love of God, and the communion of the Holy Spirit (2 Cor 13:13). In short, the Spirit who makes us one body with Christ enables us to be 'partakers in the divine nature', to be 'deified'.

Fruits and gifts

Partaking in the divine nature is not an abstract idea. It is the gift we receive of having the same 'nature', the same dispositions, the same loving and merciful outlook as Jesus possessed in his unique relationship with his Father. Thus, the list of the 'fruits' of the Spirit in Gal 5:22-23 (love, joy, peace, patience, kindness, goodness, faithfulness, gentleness and self-control) are really a list of the most cherished inner dispositions of Jesus Christ, who did nothing except what he saw his Father doing (Jn 5:19). The Spirit who was so active in Jesus keeps sowing in us seeds which produce fruits that make us more and more like Christ and like his Father. Each of the 'fruits' is a programme for a whole life, touching and transforming every area of our own 'nature' and our many relationships. The peace of Christ, for example, is a direct consequence of a loving trust in the Lord. It is not incompatible with uncertainties and insecurities. It is not a euphoria or a superficial persuading oneself that all is well. Jesus was a man of peace and yet he was straightened and strained (Lk 12:50) and he even showed signs of sudden fear and great distress (Mk 14:33). He was also a man who declared war on the two enemies of his peace – sin and death in all their forms.

What is true of the fruits of the Spirit is also true of his 'gifts'. All these describe relationships with God and with all his creatures. They transform our attitudes and the way we use all our senses, and they keep facilitating a continual change of heart. They enable us to see with our eyes, hear with our ears, be in touch with God (cf Mt 13:15), be the aroma of Christ (2 Cor 2:15), have a taste for what is of God (Ps 34:8). They bring about the gift of a new heart and a new spirit (Ez 11:19), a heart ready to receive the message of God whenever, however, wherever, by whomsoever God communicates. In the fruits and gifts of the Spirit is the full programme for any Christian spirituality. All authentic spiritualities are based on variations of the great basic themes of the fruits and gifts of the Spirit.

The second paraclete

Perhaps the most illuminating name for the person and 'nature' of the Holy Spirit is the 'Paraclete'. Jesus promised to send another paraclete (Jn 14:16). Presumably he himself was the first paraclete. When Jesus would become a 'life-giving spirit' (1 Cor 15:45) the Father would send the second paraclete. The Paraclete is the advocate, the counsellor, the consoler, who is, in every sense, like Jesus himself, always 'on our side'. The Paraclete has all the characteristics of Jesus himself. He is praised by this comforting name in the best-known hymn to the Holy Spirit, *Veni Creator*; in this same hymn, he is seen as Creator Spirit; visiting our minds; getting right into the depths of our being; being a fount of life, a fire, love itself, an anointer; being both gift and gift-giver; enlightening all our senses; strengthening us in our frailty; bringing us right into a share in the inner mystery of life of the Father and the Son, out of which flows God's saving action in the world.

The renewing Spirit

The Second Vatican Council was prepared for and inaugurated by many invocations to the pentecostal Spirit. In the course of the Council, the bishops became painfully aware of the inadequate prominence which the Spirit had been receiving in the life and worship of the Western Church. In a variety of ways, they set about remedying that situation. In the renewal of the liturgy of nearly all of the sacraments, an emphasis came to be placed on the role of the Spirit. Among other ways in which the role of the Spirit has continued to receive a prominence in the Church's consciousness since the Council are Pope Paul VI's call for a new and deeper study of the Spirit's place in the Church, and Pope John Paul II's encyclical, *The Lord and Giver of Life*. In papal and synodal documents, awareness of the call of the Spirit is more and more seen to be the real basis for the Church's involvement in all kinds of social ministry.

The re-discovery of the person and action of the Holy Spirit has been leading to a new appreciation of the mystery of the triune God, Father, Son, and Spirit. However we envisage that mystery, it must ultimately be in terms of knowing and loving, of communication, of fruitful self-giving, of perfect relationships, of three persons fully in tune. Christian life is a calling to intimate sharing in every aspect of that divine mystery. Christian priesthood gets all its resources from this sharing which enables it to offer the perfect sacrifice in the perfect temple.

In his great priestly action, Jesus 'through the eternal Spirit offered himself without blemish to God' (Heb 9:14). It is the task of all priestly ministry to enable people to enter more deeply into that offering, since it continues forever. As the message of baptismal priesthood, which comes from our being plunged into the mystery of Father, Son, and Spirit, sinks into the consciousness of the whole Church, one can confidently hope that we are at the dawn of a new age in the life of the Church when baptismal priesthood and ordained priesthood will enrich each other and throw light on each other powerfully. This, indeed, will be a great gift which only the Spirit of God can give.

Brian Gaybba, *The Spirit of Love*, (Geoffrey Chapman, 1987).

John J. O'Donnell, *The Mystery of the Triune God*, (Sheed and Ward, 1988).

CHAPTER 10

A network of relationships

For centuries, in many schools of theology, the three divine persons were described in terms of relations. Each of these relations was so perfect that it existed as a distinct divine person; it 'subsisted'. The relation of the Father to the Son was called paternity; the relation of the Son to the Father was called sonship; the relation of the Father and Son who breathed forth the Holy Spirit was called active spiration; the relation of the Spirit to Father and Son was called passive spiration.

A relational God

This way of speaking owed much to the philosophy of Aristotle who saw relation as being 'towards another'. It was refined and elaborated on by many teachers of theology. In recent decades it has been largely abandoned as too abstract, too arid. Efforts have been made to replace it with a more personal language, a language more connected with human experience. But already there are second thoughts. In the very attempt to find a more personal language for talking about the nature of God, many are finding that there is no more satisfying source than the language of relations. The only God we know is the God from whom all things come, the God who sustains all things in being, the God who is continually guiding all things to their final destination. This is surely the God of relations. We know God in relation to creation before we know God in his own inner mystery. And the secret disclosed in Christian revelation is that God's own inner nature is a relational one. In the disclosure that God is love (1 Jn 4:16) we have the key to both what God is in relation to the universe and to what is going on inside God's own inner world of knowing and loving. It would be good to think that we are about to experience an integration of the older abstract language of relations and the newer, warmer, and more personal language of relationships.

Covenant relationships

At the centre of the revelation of God, as described in the pages of the Hebrew bible, is the experience of the covenant. The God there disclosed was the God who kept offering a covenant to his people. In that continual offering, he remained the God of 'loving kindness' who is 'true' to his name forever. This 'mercy and truth' are the makings of the kind of relationships into which he kept inviting his people. They are the source of his continual invitation to love with heart, soul, strength and mind. They are the only motivation he provided for making the great choice between 'life and good' and 'death and evil' (Deut 30:15). The God of the covenant is also the God who reveals himself in the highly relational imagery of marriage, the God who is not afraid to reveal God's self in the intimately sensual imagery of the Song of Songs, in the marriage experience of Hosea whose fidelity was tested, and in the loving nuptial imagery of Isaiah.

A relational Church

The covenant and nuptial relationships were brought to fulfilment in the relationship between Jesus Christ and his Church whom he loved and for whom he gave himself up (Eph 5:25). This loving and this giving up of himself enriched and blessed every human relationship. The gospel according to St Luke portrays him as having been brought up in a setting of loving and supportive relationships. No wonder that at the time of his disappearance in the temple precincts, the first instinct of Mary and Joseph was to assume that he was safe 'among their friends and relations' (Lk 2:44). Yet when he had fully taken in the message which he had learned in his Father's house where he was 'bound to be' (Lk 2:49) he changed the whole meaning of familial language. He completely changed the meaning of words like brother, sister, mother (Mk 3:35). It is out of the change of the meaning of basic family words like these that the community which is the Church emerged. In his body which is the Church, all the members are related to each other and to him who is the head, in links of mutual dependency and intimacy. The life of the body, in turn, overflows into the whole human family. With echoes of the once familiar language describing the trinitarian relations, the *Constitution on the Church* described the Church of Christ as subsisting in the Church which has its visible centre in the See of Peter (par 8). It indicated the various relationships between this Church and other Christians, people of other religions, and people of goodwill who have not yet come to believe in a saving God (par 16). Since the Second Vatican Council, Christian churches and ecclesial communities have been trying to articulate further and give body to these relationships. One recalls that in days past many families delighted to 'trace' the relationships that linked them to other families and to individuals of distinction, living and dead. In many ways, this tracing has become a lost art. Yet the efforts to map out the 'family tree' is an occupation that has a growing fascination for many people today. This seems to have a very close bearing on what it is to be human. It is the mission of the Church and the special responsibility of those who exercise a teaching and preaching ministry in the Church, to 'trace' relations, to discover and re-discover all the relationships that link Christians with each other, with the rest of the human race, with the whole created universe, with the whole communion of saints, with Father, Son and Spirit. This arises out of the very nature of the Church as the 'universal sacrament of salvation'. Each of the three words that constitute that description is a call to every Christian to be alert to the endless riches of the relationships which are possible for each one of us, in Christ. It is an invitation to promote the mission of the Church which is a share in the mission of the Son who was sent by the Father, and the mission of the Spirit who is sent by Father and Son.

A relational priesthood

The members of Christ's body which is the Church do their tracing of relationships in union with Christ their Head. The one head of the Church is also the one mediator in the continual two-way communication between God and humankind. He is the one priest who alone is able to exercise that mediation. He offered the one sacrifice which made that mediation possible. And still we can speak of Mary as mediatrix of graces; indeed we speak of all the members of the communion of saints as mediators. The mother of the one Mediator and the other members of the communion of saints do exercise a real mediation on various levels. But it is a mediation that is relative. It is mediation dependent on, and resourced by, the mediation of Jesus Christ. Similarly the whole people of God exercise a real priesthood, by virtue of their baptism. Those ordained to ministerial priesthood exercise a priesthood that is real. But it is a priesthood that is relative. It is the priesthood of those who are living instruments of the headship of the one high-priest, Jesus Christ. The same applies to an understanding of sacrifice. Catholic Christians have continued to cherish and insist on the sacrificial nature of the eucharist. The eucharist is indeed a sacrifice, but it is a relative sacrifice. And, in the Letter to the Hebrews, the daily living of genuine Christians is also seen as a true sacrifice. This daily living and the eucharist which is its sacrament are relative sacrifices. They draw their meaning and efficacy from the one sacrifice of the one priest who said 'sacrifice and offering you did not desire, but you have prepared a body for me' (Heb 10:5). He said this to his Father who is our one Father in heaven and in whose name all those who are called father on earth exercise a relative fatherhood.

Damaged relationships

The best of relationships can go wrong, and in the sinful human condition they do continually go wrong. Sin and alienation are the breakdown of right relationships. St Paul knew and appreciated the difference between Jew and Greek but he rejected the breakdown of attitudes whereby anybody could believe that people of any nationality had any prior rights in the eyes of the God of Jesus Christ (Gal 3:28). Similarly he appreciated the differences in giftedness and in human characteristics between man and woman, but he was clear that, in the estimation of God, male and female were equal in value and in destiny. And, though he did not get around to teaching that slavery should be abolished, he laid the foundations for such a teaching: slave and free person are equally human and equally lovable in the eyes of Jesus Christ whom Paul praised for himself taking the form of a slave (Phil 2:7). These are only three of the areas in which Paul saw a great breakdown between God's way of reckoning and the faulty human way of reckoning. Hence his seeing the great need for the continual 'ministry of reconciliation' (2 Cor 5:18) and his heartfelt appeal to be 'reconciled to God' (5:20). The world he experienced was a world of broken relationships, a world continually in need of mending and healing.

Building and repairing

Every Christian life must be a daily search for ways of building up relationships and of repairing damaged relationships. In our day, there has been a wonderful flowering of a great variety of forms of Christian spirituality. But there is a sense in which there is only one Christian spirituality. Every approach to spirituality must keep testing itself against the spirit of the beatitudes, the exercise of faith, hope and charity, and the desire to glorify God. The beatitudes are a programme of attitudes and relationships to God, to other people and to the good things of creation. Living them involves a continual jolt to the conventional values which can control our lives. Since they are 'theological' virtues, the virtues of faith, hope and charity are a continual reminder that all relationships must lead us and others to the vision of God. Faith keeps our eyes fixed on the God who spoke 'in many and varied ways' in the past, and in the 'final age' has spoken to us 'in his Son' (Heb 1:1-2). Hope keeps us continually 'anchored, safe and secure, where Jesus has entered on our behalf as forerunner' (Heb 6:19-20). Charity keeps us continually probing into and drawing from the mystery of the inner life of Father, Son and Spirit. In one sense that innermost life of the divine persons is a closed world to us. In another very real sense, it has been broken open for us. In fact, the news that 'God is love' is the heart and soul of Christian revelation. From the love that is the inner life of the divine persons comes the overflowing of love that is the creation of the universe. The emergence of human beings within that creation was the nearest thing to an 'image and likeness' on earth of what is going on within the Trinity. Human beings, in turn, are like the divine persons, made to be relational by their very essence. They disclose that essence most of all when they love with heart, soul, strength and mind. They are continually invited to let that love reach out to the Lord God and to neighbour, and into themselves. That reaching out brings us in contact with every level of the whole of creation which is God's loving handiwork. In that contact, that touching, the plan that God has in mind is achieved. It is a plan of glory to God, a glory that is given by the whole of creation and voiced by the only creature on earth who can really give it voice. If the glory of God is a human being fully alive, and being fully alive consists in seeing God (St Irenaeus), one can see that the glory given by human beings to God is a 'relational' glory, a glory that comes from recognising the relatedness of all created beings and that reflects the relational life of Father, Son, and Spirit. The man or woman who truly gives glory to God is in a state of grace, since grace is the state of a growing friendship with each of the divine persons. Graced persons are conscious of living in a graced world. They are continually being 'surprised by grace' since every thing and every person in God's creation is the fruit of God's creative love, alive with seeds of glory.

At the closing of the Second Vatican Council, Pope Paul VI described the Church, the community of believers, as Christ himself working in and through human relationships. The call to Church ministry in any of its many forms is a call to a continual enriching of human relationships on every level. Ordination is a call to a ministry of word, sacrament, and pastoral care, that enables people to grow in all their relationships. Each of the ingredients of ordained ministry is relational by its very definition. Ordination is a call to being a disciple, to being an apostle, to being an 'elder' in the Christian community, to being a man of the word, to being a minister of reconciliation, to being the president of the eucharistic community, to a continual exercise of pastoral charity. Each of these is a call to be, to enable others to be, and to become. It is in this daily being and becoming that the relations which are the divine persons meet the whole range of created human relationships. This daily meeting reaches its high point in the sacramental signs that are laden with divine love. Those who celebrate these signs are helped to live towards others and towards God.

Readings: As for chapters 7, 8, 9

PART III

Baptised and Ordained

CHAPTER 11

Baptised into priesthood

The First Letter of Peter was written some time before the destruction of the temple of Jerusalem. It was addressed to converts from paganism for whom persecution was always a real possibility and who were always in danger of returning to their pagan ways. The letter is an attractive portrayal of the life worthy of those baptised into Christ, sharing in his sufferings, and letting his light shine through them in a pagan world. It is possible that much of the material is a baptismal homily on these themes. It is addressed to people whom the writer congratulated as having got a 'new birth into a living hope' (1:3), 'born again, not of mortal but of immortal parentage' (1:23), 'like newborn infants, craving for pure spiritual milk' (2:2), people 'brought to safety' through baptism (3:21). The baptised are addressed as 'a chosen race, a royal priesthood, a dedicated nation, a people claimed by God for his own' (2:9). In this description, four well-known titles of God's chosen people are applied to those he has now chosen in Christ. The central image of the letter is the image of a house, modeled on the temple itself. Christians who comprise this house, this temple, are like a group of priests continually offering sacrifice in the temple. They themselves are the living stones of the temple. Though, in one sense, they are houseless and 'homeless' (2:11), 'visiting strangers' (1:1) and 'resident aliens' (2:11), they are members of the best household in the best-built house on earth. That house is the spiritual temple into which they are being continually built (2:5). This vision of baptised Christians as living stones in a living temple, out of which sacrifice is continually rising up to God, links the letter to the mystery of Christ himself who, in his unique relationship with the temple, revealed the priestly and sacrificial work which he was always carrying out in his own body. It is worthwhile to delay on what that unique relationship was. As the author of the letter to the Hebrews saw, the temple imagery is a splendid basis for understanding the priesthood of Christ and of all his members.

Old temple, new temple

The temple occupied a very central place in the story of the people of God. In their history, they at various stages encountered God in places they came to regard as sacred, in the surroundings of the tabernacle, and then in the temple. The last of the prophets spoke of the Lord coming to his temple, purifying and refining the levites (Mal 3:1-3). At the Annunciation, the mother of the Lord was greeted in temple language (Lk 1:35). The Lord's precursor came from a family with a temple and priestly background. The only recorded priestly act of his father in the sanctuary of the old temple made way for the new temple and the new priest (cf Lk 1:5-80). Later, the presentation of Jesus in the temple was made memorable by the prophetic and thankful utterances of a temple man and a temple woman (Lk 2:25-39). Every year his parents brought him to the temple at Passover time (Lk 2:42). It was at the time of such a visit that he had the experience of his heavenly Father which both bewildered his earthly parents and set him resolutely on his own mission. His many temple visits were to form the backdrop for some of his greatest preaching (Lk 18:9ff; 21:1-14; Mt 5:23). He must have been present at many sacrifices and observed many priests in action; and he sensed that all was not well with either the sacrifices or the priests. His relationship with the temple seems to have been, at once, one of affection and of distancing, of fascination and of detachment. His temple experiences must have kept him searching for what was at the heart of true religion. He participated faithfully and lovingly in the temple festivals. It was at a temple festival that he spoke of the rivers of living water that can flow from the heart (Jn 7:38). He knew that the temple was where countless generations had seen the strength and the glory of God (Ps 63:2). He knew that many good people had sought reconciliation with his Father there on the Day of Atonement. He was angered by those who didn't recognise the temple as essentially a house of prayer (Lk 19:45).

And still Jesus had the prophetic insight to recognise that the temple was inadequate for worship and would become redundant. He told the woman of Samaria that true worship had nothing to do with temple buildings (Jn 4:21ff). He was to go further and talk about the destroying of the temple and its rebuilding in three days

(Jn 2:13ff). No wonder that the chief priests and others sought to destroy him (Lk 19:45-47). No wonder that he was eventually arrested in the temple precincts. His death had repercussions in the temple: the curtain of the temple was torn in two (Lk 23:45). In three days came the re-building. It then became clear that he himself was the temple, that his living body was the temple, that his 'heart' was the temple. In this temple, body, heart, the perfect sacrifice of praise is offered by the perfect priest. The essence of this message was taken up and developed by St Paul in his linking of the temple and the human body. For him, Christians are the temple of God (1 Cor 3:16), a holy temple (v 17), temples of the living God (2 Cor 6:16). Their members are temples of the Holy Spirit (1 Cor 6:19). Those who comprise the temple of the living God can make no agreements with idols (2 Cor 6:16). Any destroying of the real temple which consists of the bodies of Christians will have dire consequences (1 Cor 3:17). The central message of the Letter to the Hebrews, in turn, is built around the temple theme. The letter sees the real temple as the body of Christ in which the real sacrifice took place, offered by the real priest whose one concern, as he came into the world and after, was to do his Father's will (10:5-10). In his body, priest, altar and sacrifice are perfectly unified. The exhortation that concludes the letter follows clearly from this union. In Jesus Christ we have our own altar (13:10); let us go to him outside the camp and bear the abuse he endured (v 13); through him let us continually offer a sacrifice of praise to God (v 15); in short, the real sacrifice takes place in Christ's body, our body, my body. In Christian terms, these are all one body, one temple.

The First Letter of Peter

It is in this context of the new temple, which is the living body of Christ the priest, that we must see the baptismal exhortations in the First Letter of Peter. Christians are called to be priestly and sacrificial in the way that Christ was priestly and sacrificial. They are called by none other than the Father of Jesus Christ. Like him who is holy, they must be holy in all their conduct (1:15), separated from the pagan world, yet a light to it. Though they are classified as aliens, they belong to God's household; they have the full run of God's own house which has the perfect cornerstone (2:6-8). Out of that house, spiritual sacrifices, sacrifices offered in the life-giving Spirit of Christ, must continually go up to God (2:5). That is why there is no doubt about what should comprise these sacrifices. The sacrifices of Christians comprise all the attitudes and activities demanded by Christian living. They include everything Christians do and endure, in a pagan world that does not understand their values. At no stage does the letter get round to questioning the existing structures of the society of the time and its cultural assumptions, structures and assumptions that Christians were to criticise and even overturn in later centuries. The Christian virtues of faith, hope, love, and obedience were to be practised even in the setting of the faultiest of structures. Slaves are to be slaves in a way that befits Christians (2:18-25). The gospel has a bearing on every area of domestic life (3:1-7). Though Christians are servants and, in a sense, slaves of God they must live as free people (2:16). Accepting the 'authority of every human institution' (2:13) provides opportunities to 'honour everyone' (2:17). The letter continually makes connections between ransom with the precious blood of Christ, confidence in Christ in whom God's mighty deeds have reached their height, sharing Christ's suffering, enduring persecution, renouncing sin. All the topics are suffused with Christian joy and hope based on the resurrection of Jesus Christ from the dead and leading us into 'an inheritance that is imperishable' (1:4).

The liturgy of life
The First Letter of Peter and the Letter to the Hebrews place their emphasis on the saving role of Christ and the priestly and sacrificial qualities which should characterise those who believe in him. In neither letter is there an emphasis on either the role of those we describe as exercising ministerial priesthood or on the place of the eucharist in Christian life. Yet both authors must have been well aware of the legacy which Christ left to his Church on the night before he suffered; and the eucharist must have been celebrated in the communities to which they were writing. It would appear that the authors saw a greater urgency in concentrating on the liturgy of life rather than on the liturgy of the Christian assembly, on the temple of the human body rather than on the building where Christians met. Indeed one could say that St Paul too, though he was at great pains to hand on what he had received from the Lord

(1 Cor 11:27-32), saw a special urgency in imploring his readers to offer their very selves to God, a living sacrifice, the worship offered by mind and heart (Rom 12:1-2; Eph 5:2; Phil 4:18).

At the time of the writing of these and similar letters, the sacrificial nature of the eucharist, the exact nature of Christian priestly ministry, the linkings between Christian life and Christian liturgy, had not yet received the careful attention that they were later to receive. Yet each of the letters in question was to make a powerful contribution to later developments in all these areas. The First Letter of Peter sets a high and demanding ideal for the elders who are to tend the flock of God as shepherds who are an example to be followed (5:2-3). The author of Hebrews emphasised the importance of obeying the religious leaders and submitting to their authority (13:17) and the seriousness of staying away from the meetings of Christians (10:25). The very writing of these two letters and the concern in them for the sacrificial quality of the daily lives of believers was to be a precious contribution to the development of an understanding of both eucharist and of ministerial priesthood.

Baptismal and ordained

Over the centuries, the Church has gradually come to a clearer articulation of the meaning of the priesthood of the whole people of God:

1) It is a royal priesthood for the offering of spiritual sacrifice. It is royal because it is exercised by people who are in a special way agents and beneficiaries of the reign of God; a people whose roots are in the people who produced the kings who so much shaped the destiny of God's people. It exists for the offering of sacrifice in the way desired by the prophets and especially by the prophet of prophets – sacrifice that would be less about ritual details than about promoting a true communion of life between God and us, 'in spirit and truth' (Jn 4:23);

2) It has its source in baptism which is our total insertion into the life of Christ who is the source of all priesthood, prophecy and kingship, and in confirmation which is a further 'confirming' of the process begun in baptism, leading to the eucharist. It has received names like the 'common priesthood' and 'priesthood of

the people of God' which are variations on the very rich name of 'baptismal priesthood';

3) It is the source and resource for all Christian activity in the world, and in the Church which is the sacrament of the world. As the understanding of the eucharist and of the sacramental life of the Church grew over the centuries, it was to be expected that baptismal priesthood would make more and more connections with the sacraments and with various forms of liturgical and other Church ministries. While this development was good, it is important to keep remembering that baptismal priesthood was and is first of all about the Christian's daily living outside of the liturgical assembly. This daily living leads to public worship and is further resourced by it. The ongoing search for integrating personal living, family living, living in society, sacramental life, and involvement in various forms of ministry is expressed in such Church documents as Pope John Paul II's *The Vocation and Mission of the Lay Faithful in the Church and in the World* (1988).

From the Church's growing understanding of the eucharist and of its presidency, there emerged the conviction and teaching that baptismal priesthood and ordained priesthood differ not only in degree but in essence. Whatever way we understand this teaching, it must be continually set in the context of the teaching in the First Letter of Peter that each of the baptised has received a special grace, to be put at the service of others (4:10). The meaning of ordained priesthood comes to light in the special relationship with word, sacrament and pastoral care that is expressed especially in the celebration of the eucharist and in the sacrament of reconciliation. It is only one of the many gifts of the risen Lord to his body, the Church. But it is a gift for the performing of a unique service to and function in the body. It is not derived from or reducible to any other gift or grace. It is a service of headship and leadership that consists in representing Christ, the Head of the body, to the rest of the members of the body, and representing the members to the Head. But it exists only for the sake of the whole of the baptised priestly people, and it must be continually put at their service.

Signs of baptismal priesthood
Those sharing in the baptismal priesthood should never cease to

explore the mystery of their baptism into Christ. In the sacrament as we have it, there are seven actions which are full of significance and meaning. The 'baptismal' letter of St Peter throws light on the meaning of each of these actions. The pouring of water is 'not the washing away of bodily impurities but the appeal made to God' (3:21). The anointings are messianic signs plunging us into the mystery and mission of the one whom the Letter of Peter keeps calling 'the anointed one' and whom we know to be priest, prophet and king. The lighting of the candle is the call out of darkness into God's wonderful light (2:9). The clothing is our being wrapped in the humility of Christ to be servants of each other (5:5). The signing with the cross is the sign of the one who 'was bearing our faults in his own body on the cross' (2:24). The giving of a name brings us into communion with all the women and men who have helped to promote the reign of God (3:5-6; 18-20). The prayers and actions over ears and mouth are an appeal to hear and speak the word of God in the spirit of the prophets who lived by 'the everlasting word of the living and eternal God' (1:23; cf 1:10-12). There is a programme here for a very full life of both baptismal priesthood and of ordained priesthood in the building up of the only temple that matters.

William J. Dalton, SJ, 'The First Epistle of Peter' in *The New Jerome Biblical Commentary*, pp 903-908.

Kenan B. Osborne, OFM, *Priesthood*, esp. pp 25-29; 315-324.

CHAPTER 12

In the person of Christ – by baptism

If there is one key to the teaching of the Second Vatican Council on the role of the ordained priest, it is the attention to the fact that priests act 'in the person of Christ'. This expression comes from St Paul in 2 Cor 2:10. The context there is a delicate pastoral work of reconciliation in which Paul was involved. After a longish appeal to the Corinthian community for the forgiving of an unnamed offender, he states that he himself was forgiving him, for the community's sake, in the *persona* of Christ. In these days, in which the exact meaning of the expression is being explored, it is interesting that translators do not opt for 'in the person of'. Versions include 'in the presence', 'before', 'in the sight of' Christ; 'by Christ's authority'; 'as the representative of' Christ.

When St Jerome chose to translate Paul by the words 'in the person of Christ', the word person was already showing signs of developing a very high profile in Western theological discussion, a profile that was to reach one great highpoint at the Council of Chalcedon (451), and that got many further refinements according as the Word of God in hypostatic union with a human nature came to be seen as the one subject of divine-human actions; a profile that led St Thomas Aquinas to say that a person means that which is most perfect in nature. The word that St Paul had used was the word for the human face. He had forgiven in the *prosopon* of Christ, literally before/in front of/on the side of/in the presence of, the *face*, the *countenance*, the *eye* of Christ.

In Greek drama, especially religious drama, the *prosopon* was the actor's mask. The Latin *persona* had basically the same meaning. It had the extra nuance of emphasising the place of the voice, the sound that came through the mask which was somehow his face. The one who was being portrayed 'sounded through', spoke through, 'sonated' and 'personated' through the mask which was somehow his face. This seems to be the most accepted explanation of the origin of the word 'person'. In passing, it is worth noting that, though we associate the use of masks largely with bygone cultures, their proper use was, and still is, a very powerful medium of communication. This being true to, becoming, and making present the person we portray and represent is an admirable summary of the call of every baptised person. And still the bishops at the Second Vatican Council deliberately decided to apply the expression 'in the person of Christ' to no other sacrament but orders. But, as we explore the riches of the expression, we find that it is, in fact, a very fruitful source for points of contact between ordained and non-ordained ministry.

In a very real sense, all the baptised are called to act in the person of Christ. In another sense, only the ordained person acts in the person of Christ. Church teaching is insistent on the 'essential difference' between these two expressions of priesthood, but the difference must not give the impression of an iron wall of separation. The meeting points are far more important than the differences, since the two are 'by their very nature related to one another' (*LG* 10) and together they manifest the one priesthood of our one high-priest; the candles of both are lit from the one Paschal Candle and, in turn, they help to light each other. A continual exploring of the *persona* expression can throw light on how they are related. In fact, as we see the many ways in which baptismal priesthood and ordained priesthood intersect, the clearer we can become on what is distinctive about each.

Every ministry in the name of Jesus Christ and of his Church is a manifestation of the face, the presence, the voice of Christ. This is particularly apt at a time of universal yearning for all that is authentically personal and what promotes the inter-personal. Our Christian religion is proud to be a religion of persons, divine and human, and proud that it is ever seeking to unfold the riches of the Incarnation, in which a divine person identified in a unique way with our humanness. Is it any wonder that as spirituality today draws on the resources of psychology, we are more aware than before of the many personas which we all wear and the implications of our many masks? Our personas are authentic to the extent to which they reflect the person of Christ. Baptism calls us to be his face, his presence, his voice.

His face

The face reveals the person. In a sense, the face is the person. It speaks the whole range of our thoughts, our feelings, our affections. Every language has its 'face vocabulary': we save face, we lose face, we show face, we face issues. The bible has severe things to say about those who made graven images. The basic reason was that the Creator's face is beyond depicting. And still there was a tension. Though no one ever saw God (Jn 1:18), we are assured that the Lord used to speak to Moses face to face, as one 'speaks to a friend' (Ex 33:11). Whatever the exact nature of the experience of the first Moses, it was in the face of the second Moses, at whose transfiguration Moses and Elijah appeared, that the glory of God was finally and uniquely manifested. His disciples watched his face light up while he prayed to his Father. It must have been the same attraction of the same face that drew people to discipleship and that touched hearts with compunction. From the eyes of that face came the tears which disclosed the Lord's heartbreak and his compassion. We might ask is it any wonder that the stories of the 'shroud of Turin' and of the 'towel of Veronica' have had such a haunting fascination; there was far more involved in these than the search for two pieces of cloth.

There have been many attempts to express the final destination of the human race. None has been more successful than 'beatific vision' the seeing that will make us fully blessed and that is the final blossoming of all the ways that God has 'blessed' us, before and in creation, in the movement started by the call of Abraham who was assured that he would be a blessing, in the charter of blessedness in the beatitudes which are about 'seeing God', and in the anticipation of the final 'Come you that are blessed by my Father' (Mt 25:34). The assurance of God is that the crown of all his blessing will be seeing him 'as he is'(1 Jn 3:2), 'face to face' (1 Cor 13:12). The purpose of all pastoral ministry is to enable people to have 'beatific vision', even in this life, to help them 'count their blessings', and see how God is blessing them in every event in life and in death and beyond; to keep their eyes 'fixed on Jesus' (Heb 12:2); to make their faces 'light up', even when all odds seem stacked against them. In the same spirit, all pastoral ministry is a work of removing: helping to remove from people whatever is closing their eyes to the vision that is beatific, since we all tend to see in a sin-damaged way. This opening of the eyes requires a continual range of conversions if we are to keep seeing people and events not with the 'eyes of the foolish' (Wis 3:2) but 'with far-seeing eyes' (Num 24:3).

All those called by God in Christ are invited to mirror to the world something of the infinite riches of the face of God. A man who has an eye and a heart for the beautiful recently spent a whole day entranced before an El Greco painting of St Francis in ecstasy. This was the effect on unaided human eyes of a painting of a human face by human hands; it gives us some glimpse of the riches of the real face of God, fully disclosed. The face of God Incarnate uniquely disclosed that real face. The face of his mother disclosed it in a way that only a woman could. One would hope that it is this yearning to experience the feminine face of God that is behind much of the search for the feminine in Church ministry today. A man manifests the riches of God in one way, a woman in another way; each man, each woman, made, as they are, each one in the image and likeness of God, in their own way; the religious, faithful to the charism of his or her community, reflects it in one way, the lay person in another way; the ordained one way, the non-ordained another. At a time of some concern about Church numbers, we can take heart from the fact that one face can light up a whole universe. One has only to think of Pope John XXIII, Pope John Paul I, Mother Teresa of Calcutta ...

A phenomenon of recent Church life has been an emphasis on people's desire to see the 'human face' of God. This is more than a passing fashion. It underlines that what people yearn to receive from the Church and her ministers: 'Your face, Lord, do I seek. Do not hide your face from me' (Ps 27:8-9). Every generation voices its protests against what it perceives to be faceless people and faceless systems. Invariably we get a new hope when we find any leader in whom we recognise a face that is true in the way that the God of the covenant is true. We get a new conviction that God is still gracious, that he is still blessing us, that his face is still shedding its light upon us (Ps 67:1)

His presence

There is a close connection between the 'face' of God and the 'presence' of God, between the face of Jesus Christ and the presence of Jesus Christ. There are good grounds for saying that the most far-reaching teaching of the Second Vatican Council is what it had to say about the related topics of:

1) the presence of Christ in his Church;

2) the presence and action of his grace in every man and woman of goodwill;

3) the fact that belief in the kingdom of Christ should spur us on to develop this earth in the expectancy of a new earth – this earth which is already being enriched by his risen presence (*GS* 39). These three topics have many implications:

1) *The Constitution on the Liturgy* (par 7) taught that 'Christ is always present in his Church, especially in her liturgical celebrations. He is present in the sacrifice of the Mass ... in the person of the minister ... in the eucharistic species ... He is present in the sacraments ... in his word ... When the Church prays and sings ...' This realness of the presence of Christ has been re-affirmed in the *General Instruction on the Roman Missal* (chap 2, par 7) and elsewhere. It has, in turn, helped us to see Christ himself as the 'primordial' sacrament of God's presence in the world, and to see the Church as the basic sacrament of Christ's presence. It has enriched our whole understanding of the words 'real presence', as we look at the real presence of the Word in the human-ness of Jesus, in a union that is 'hypostatic', i.e. 'centred on a person', as the basis of his other presences. All this provides a fine context for our approach to that special refining of real presence which we recognise in the eucharistic celebration and the eucharistic species. It also suggests new ways of imaging his real presence in the peace which he left us and gives us (Jn 14:27), in the mission he gives us (Lk 10:16), in the power he gives us to do greater things than he did (Jn 14:12), in his suffering members (Mt 25:42-43; Acts 9:4), in the communications he provides us with him and his Father (Jn 14:20).

2) Closely related to the Council's teaching that the Lord is always present to his Church is the teaching on the action of his grace in all men and women of goodwill, not just those with a recognisable

Church affiliation. A foundation text here is in *LG* par.16: 'Those who, through no fault of their own, do not know the gospel of Christ or his Church, but who nevertheless seek God, with a sincere heart, and moved by grace ... Nor shall divine providence deny the assistance necessary for salvation to those who ... have not yet arrived at an explicit knowledge of God, and who, not without grace, strive to lead a good life.' The same conviction is expressed in the teaching that the Holy Spirit, in a manner known only to God, offers to everybody the possibility of being associated with the paschal mystery (*GS* 22).

The implications of these teachings are far-reaching. They have been providing a rich foundation for inter-faith dialogue, and they have had a prominent place in the teaching of Pope John Paul II, notably in his encyclicals on Redemption, Divine Mercy, and Mission.

3) The teaching on the presence of Christ and on the grace of Christ is inseparable from the Council's teaching on the Lord as the alpha and omega: 'The goal of human history, the focal point of the desires of history and civilisation, the centre of mankind, the joy of all hearts and the fulfilment of all aspirations.' (*GS* 45). This, in turn, links closely with the teaching on the relationship between this earth and the new earth to which we look forward. The presence, the grace, and the transforming action of the risen Christ help us to see the whole universe as one house, the whole human family as one household, with the Lord himself as the householder, an image provided by more than one gospel parable (e.g. Lk 14:21).

As we look at the ways that the risen Lord is always present in his Church, at the workings of his grace in all hearts of goodwill, at the fact that he is the focal point of the desires of history and civilisation, we can say that there are many real presences of Christ in the world. In another sense, we can say that there are many manifestations of his one real presence, for 'in him all things hold together' (Col 1:17). The mission of all those who minister in the name of Christ is to be alert to and to alert others to the whole range of the manifestations of the presence of Christ in each person's life and in each event that has a bearing on that life. It must aim at helping each person to see how Christ's real presence is compatible with his 'absence', since only heaven can properly 'keep' him 'till the universal restoration comes' (Acts 3:21). The ideal for everybody in Christian ministry is to be fully present to each person in the whole range of their experiences, especially in the ones that appear to be absurd and senseless; to help each person to be 'really present' to him/herself, his/her neighbour, to Christ, to the Father; in all human seasons, especially when a human heart tends to cry: 'How like a Winter has my absence been, from thee ...' (Shakespeare, *Sonnet 97*).

His voice

Through the persona comes the voice. The one who speaks 'personates' (L. *sonare*, to sound) through the mask. The Christian application is clear. God speaks through people and through events involving people. He has spoken many words, notably in the creation of the world and in introducing the new creation: 'Long ago God spoke to our ancestors in many and various ways ... in these last days he has spoken to us by a Son' (Heb 1:1-2). In the psalmist's vision 'Day to day pours forth speech ... their voice goes out through all the earth, and their words to the end of the world' (Ps 19:2-4). All God's ways of speaking are summed up in the Word who was from the beginning and who became flesh and lived among us (Jn 1:14), and caused amazement by the gracious words that came from his mouth (Lk 4:22).

With this background, the task of all ministry is to bring the living word of God into every area of people's lives and to allow it to 'become flesh'. From the beginning, this has been the great thrust of the proclamation of the gospel. The voice that went out to all the earth (Rom 10:18) became the living word of the apostles. As far as God is concerned, his word never returns to him empty (Is 55:11). In our age when people listen more willingly to witnesses rather than to teachers and listen to teachers only because they are witnesses (Pope Paul VI, *Evangelisation Today*, par 41), the Church of the Word made flesh must make sure that it does not become a wordy Church. It must learn to keep 're-sonating' with the heart and voice of Christ. And in these days of 'preferential options', especially for the poor, all those in Church ministry should be providing a voice for those who have no voice. There is a very real sense in which power today is in voice.

Through the voice of the baptised person, people come to hear the voice of Jesus Christ. As they hear the voice of Christ, they come to recognise his presence. As they experience his presence, they get a glimpse of his face. As they see his face, they come to know and love him in a personal way. In this knowing and loving, they are drawn into the life of the three divine persons.

Bd. Marliangeas, *Clés pour une Théologie du Ministère,* (Beauchesne, 1978).

Articles on 'In the Person of Christ' in *Worship,* January, May, November 1991; November 1992.

CHAPTER 13

In the person of Christ
– by ordination

The Second Vatican Council taught that ordained priests act 'in the person of Christ'. The fullest expression of the teaching is in the *Decree on the Ministry and Life of Priests*, where it is closely linked with anointing, character and headship: 'Priests by the anointing of the Holy Spirit are signed with a special character and so are configured to Christ the priest in such a way that they are able to act in the person of Christ the Head' (par 2). In all, the expression 'in the person of Christ', or its equivalent, occurs five times in the *Constitution on the Church*, three times in *The Decree on the Ministry and Life of Priests*, and once in the *Constitution on the Liturgy*. Since the Council, the expression has had a continual, indeed a growing prominence in official Church pronouncements. Pope Paul VI used it often. It has an important place in the *General Instruction on the Roman Missal* (1970), and in the Apostolic Exhortation following on the 1971 Synod. It is given a key importance in the 1976 *Declaration on the Question of the Admission of Women to the Ministerial Priesthood*. Among the many contexts in which Pope John Paul II has used it is in articulating the *Dignity of Women* and the *Role of the Lay Faithful*. The Congregation for the Doctrine of the Faith has been using it quite a lot since 1973. The new *Code of Canon Law* uses the expression three times, notably in the nearest it comes to a definition of the sacrament of orders (899, 2; 900, 1; 1008). It features in Pope John Paul II's Apostolic Exhortation on the *Formation of Priests*, 1992.

The decision of the bishops at the Second Vatican Council to use the expression 'in the person of Christ' to describe the place only of those baptised who are called to ordained ministry has led to its further use to illumine such topics as the relationship between ordained and non-ordained ministry, the 'essential difference' between baptismal priesthood and ordained priesthood, the ministry of women in the Church. Recent study of the expression 'in the person of Christ' has shown some interesting developments over the centuries. In patristic writing generally, the Church rather than the ordained minister was seen as acting 'in the person of Christ'. The shift of emphasis seems to have come with Aquinas. His use of the expressions 'in the person of Christ' and 'in the person of the Church' is highly nuanced. In the celebration of the eucharist, he saw the priest as acting 'in the person of Christ' because it is here that Christ acts in a unique way through him. Similar use of the expression in describing the role of the priest is found in such writers as Albert the Great, Scotus, Bellarmine, and Suarez. The Council of Florence took up the teaching: the priest speaks in the person of Christ in effecting the eucharist. The Council of Trent did not use the expression. It was used by Cardinal de Berulle who so much influenced the French School of spirituality. A phrase like 'in the person of Christ' was used by Pope Pius XI in his encyclical on *Catholic Priesthood*. In *Mediator Dei*, Pope Pius XII made strong connections between the person of Jesus Christ and the person of the priestly minister.

It is clear that the Second Vatican Council was not using a new expression in teaching that priests act 'in the person of Christ'. The implication of the teaching is that a man is ordained to be a face, a presence, a voice, in the name and with the authority of Jesus Christ who is

* The shepherd who reveals the Father's merciful and faithful face, and knows his own and is known by them (Jn 10:14);
* The priest who by his perfect sacrifice has gained entry to the presence of God in the heavenly holy of holies (Heb 9:24);
* The prophet who heard the Father's voice and spoke only what he heard from his Father.

The ordained person can never afford to forget that he has no monopoly of sharing in this triple mission of Christ. His special ministry is to promote the exercise of this triple sharing by all the baptised, who in their own way are called to the face, presence and voice of Christ. His ministry is special in seven principal ways:

* In his work of unifying;
* In the way he is authorised by the Church;
* In his relationship with the word;
* In his exercise of headship;

* In his exercise of pastoral charity;
* In the way he represents Christ and the Church;
* In the way he is a living instrument of Christ the priest.

Unifying: The body of Christ on earth is the whole community of the baptised. It is to this whole body, this whole community, that Christ has passed on his mission in the form of shepherding, priesthood, and prophecy. The whole of the baptised people is called to be a ministering people. But in a Church which has one Lord, one faith, one baptism (Eph 4:5) and which must keep moving towards the ideal 'that they may all be one' (Jn 17:21), ordination provides a sacrament of one-ness. The gift of ordination helps to disclose, make blossom, and unite the gifts of all the baptised. All Christian ministry, pastoral, priestly and prophetic, exists to reflect the face of God and in that sense must be exercised 'face to face' with people and with God. This is true of the eucharist, of the celebration of every sacrament, and indeed of every act of pastoral ministry. The ordained priest brings all these 'facings' into one focus, especially when the Church is most characteristically herself, in the celebration of the eucharist. As a sacramental person, he becomes one face for the myriad faces of the people who comprise the sacrament which is the Church. He is ordained to be a sign and maker of unity for the local Christian community. He is also a sign of the unity that links the local eucharistic community with the rest of the believing and celebrating Church.

Authorised: Jesus in his lifetime did not answer the very important question 'by what authority?'. He let the answer unfold in his deeds and in the handing on of apostolic office which was to be an integral part of his many-gifted Church. By ordination, the Church, in turn, through her already authorised leaders, assures her members that she is authorising and empowering the person being ordained, for the building up of the whole Church. This authorising and empowering is done by the sacramental word, by the imposition of hands, by anointing and by the conferring of the 'character' of ordination (cf PO 2). When this character, this sealing, is seen not as a personal gift for the ordained but as a special gift for the further enriching of the whole community of those sealed in baptism and confirmation, the priesthood of the ordained and the priesthood of all the baptised blend harmoniously with the priesthood of our one High Priest. To continue the image of per-sonating, the voices of praise from priest, people and the interceding Christ (cf Heb 7:25) together shape a 'sonata' of praise that glorifies God. The ordained priest is the 'guarantor' for the community of the baptised that each eucharistic celebration is an authentic 'appearing' of the crucified and risen Lord who has 'entered into heaven itself, now to appear in the presence of God on our behalf' (Heb 9:24). This is the significance of the fact that, in the list of the ways in which Christ is present in liturgical celebrations, a special presence is linked with the person of the minister. This presence is for the gathering and lifting up of the gifts of all the members of the body and the guaranteeing that the once-for-all sacrifice of Christ is being made sacramentally present, for this congregation, in this celebration.

The word: There have been many attempts to answer the question 'What is the theological starting point for a definition of the priestly ministry?' Some like to start with pastoral leadership. Some start with the preaching of the word of God. Some start with the celebration of the eucharist. The three are, in fact, inseparable. What unifies all three is seeing priestly ministry in terms of a relationship with the Word of God and with the proclaiming of his word. This was put very effectively by Karl Rahner when he stated that 'the priest is he who, related to an at least potential community, preaches the word of God by mandate of the Church as a whole and therefore officially, and in such a way that he is entrusted with the highest levels of sacramental intensity of this word ... (*Concilium* Vol 3, No 5). The priest's special relationship with the word must never be isolated from his community leadership, liturgical and pastoral. This is why Rahner was careful to emphasise that 'the proclaiming of the word and the administering of the sacraments have therefore a common root and are ultimately one in nature'. Pastoral ministry, in turn, is the bringing of the word of God into every human situation. Pastoral leadership is a function of the word. The preached word, the word proclaimed in sacrament, and the pastoral word, are one. In all three the 'flock of God' are 'fed' by the one word (cf 1 Pet 5:2).

Headship: When the word of God is proclaimed at its highest level of sacramental intensity, especially in the sacraments of eucharist and reconciliation, the priest exercises a unique sharing of Christ's headship of the Church. In the eucharist, he is presiding at the celebration which is the summit and source of the whole Church's existence (*SC* 10). In the sacrament of reconciliation, he is speaking words which are the high sacramental point of a process that should be going on all the time in all the Christian community. In both, the headship of the ordained person is the sacramental assurance of the saving presence of Christ to all the members of his body. This is why the fuller description of priesthood in the teaching of the Second Vatican Council is in terms of acting in the person of Christ 'the Head' (PO 2). This headship and leadership is not confined to sacramental activity. It overflows into every expression of pastoral care, by those called to be 'examples to the flock' (1 Pet 5:3). Those ordained to priesthood act in the person of Christ who is at the same time Head and Shepherd. They are 'a sacramental representation of Jesus Christ, the Head and Shepherd' (*I Will Give You Shepherds*, par 15). In the biblical imagery, the head expresses authority, but, at the same time and inseparably, it expresses the giving of life and the encouraging of life.

The headship of Christ is never a headship of domination or mastery since Christian power is the exact opposite of worldly power. The only headship which Christ recognises as exercised in his name is a headship of love, a headship of self-giving, a headship of self-sacrifice, a headship of service, a headship in which the head is in continual life-giving organic interaction with all the members of the body, all of whom share his kingly, priestly and prophetic mission. It is the headship of the one who 'loved the Church and gave himself up for her ... that she may be holy and without blemish' (Eph 5:25-27). It is the headship of the one who taught '... with you this must not happen. No, the greatest among you must behave as if he were the youngest, the leader as if he were the one who serves ...' (Lk 22:24-27). Any day on which ministerial priesthood is perceived as domination or monopoly is a day on which what should be light has been turned into darkness. It is for the same reason that the ordained person should see no threat in sharing many of the elements of 'in the person of Christ' with the rest of the baptised. The fact that, in official Church usage, the expression is applied only to the ordained is a continual reminder of that 'head-ship' and unique relationship to the word that is proper to those exercising ordained pastoral leadership.

Pastoral charity: In the continual cycle of ministries in which the preached Word leads up to its highest level of sacramental intensity and out to pastoral care and back again to sacrament, the priest must be truly a man of face, a face that reflects the heart and voice of the Good Shepherd. It is in line with this vision that the Second Vatican Council spoke about that quality of pastoral charity that flows from ordained leadership (*PO* 16). Pastoral charity is the fruit of the mutual love between the ordained person and the Good Shepherd, whose charity he helps to mediate. In the man of true pastoral charity, word, sacrament and pastoral headship become one and they authenticate each other. This is the ministry of unifying, in action. Sunday celebration will be unreal without weekday pastoral concern; the real meaning and purpose of pastoral concern will be unfolded on Sunday.

All this will show in the face of one who is always strongly present to the Christian community, and who is not just one who puts in appearances. True to the mystery of the Incarnation, his ministry will always be 'embodied' in the day to day realities of the lives of people. The details as to how pastoral charity and pastoral unifying are to relate to and overflow into and intersect with educational, economical, political and social interests will vary in different human situations, in different cultures.

Representing: All priestly ministry, whether baptismal or ordained, is an exercise in presence. In the sacramental life of the Church, every aspect of the mystery of Christ is continually being made present. One expression of presence is re-presenting. A man is ordained to represent Christ and to represent the Christian community. Does he directly represent Christ, or does he directly represent the priestly people, and through them represent Christ, the Head of the body, thus acting 'in the person of the Church?' It has always been a strong conviction of the Christian churches that it is the risen Lord himself who, through his Spirit, calls and commissions for ministry. In this context, one must say that the ordained person directly represents Christ, the living and life-giving Head of his body the Church. But from the perspective of Christ's handing over his whole mission to his whole body, and bearing in mind the inseparable union between Head, members and minister, the second approach has many attractive elements. The ordained person's ministry finds its meaning only in the heart of the people whose faith, devotion and worship he represents, and in whose name he presides. The priest's unique way of imaging Christ is by representing Christ the Head to the members of the living body, all of whom themselves represent and image Christ in unique and irreplaceable ways.

Representing is a key word in contemporary approaches to ordained priesthood, as it has been in various ways in the past. As well as being prominent in Catholic thought, it has an important place in the ARCIC and Lima ecumenical statements. The priest represents Christ who is the one Head of the whole mission-filled body. This re-presenting means that he is an effective sign of the continual active presence of Christ, the Head, to the members of his body. He is sacramentally authorised to represent Christ, the 'sacrament' of God's saving work, in the middle of the Church which is Christ's sacrament. There are times, even in the eucharist, when his words are in the form of reported speech. In addressing the Father about the work accomplished by his Son, he speaks of the Son in the third person: 'He took bread ... he blessed ...' But what is special to his sacramental role is that he speaks in the name and person of Christ, the Head of the body of the faithful, in the celebration in which Head and body are uniquely united. He is both related to the Head through the Church and through the Head to the Church. The ideal is that his ministry in the person of Christ the Head and his ministry in the person of the Church should form a harmonious unity.

Instrument: Over seven centuries ago, St Thomas described ordained priesthood in terms of instrumental causality. In these days of the primacy of persons, the language of instruments may seem strange and arid. But there is a perennial appeal in the image of the good musician playing on a well-tuned instrument and in the thought of what an instrument can become in the hands of a master-craftsman. Nobody has written more sensitively about what human instruments can become than did Aquinas. In the eucharist especially, he saw the whole priestly people as raised to a special level of instrumentality. In this setting, he pointed out the necessity that there be only one minister who is specially empowered by God to represent Christ. His understanding of instrumentality is closely linked with his understanding of sacramental character and its place in the special participation of the ordained person in the priesthood of Christ. In that participation, every one of the priest's human qualities can become a living instrument of salvation.

The language of instrumentality continues to be used in official Church teaching. For the ordained person, it is a salutary reminder to keep looking to the One in whose hands he is an instrument and to keep renewing his desire to be a willing and loving agent of the Church's one Head.

In-personating
Does the language of 'in the person of Christ', *in persona Christi*, suggest acting a part and impersonation? As always, we are dealing here with the limitations of all human language and imagery. There certainly is an ambivalence in the mask image, in particular. The man who wears a mask or persona can become a caricature or a phantom person. A persona can conceal and distort, as well as reveal. The suggestion of 'masked men' can have hideous connotations. The hardest thing Jesus said about the Pharisees was that they were 'hypocrites', literally stage-actors. But being 'in persona' is a programme and a life-long process. All through his life, the ordained person is invited to grow into the persona of Christ, grow up into the Head (Eph 4:15). Instead of seeing him as 'impersonating' Christ, perhaps we should say that he is called to a daily conversion that will enable him to be an authentic image, 'in-personating' Christ. In this, he is beyond acting; he is exercising a ministry of transparency.

Robert M. Schwartz, *Servant Leaders of the People of God*,

Daniel Donovan, *What are they saying about Ministerial Priesthood?*, (Paulist Press, 1992).

CHAPTER 14

The shaping of priestly ministry

Christians recognise only one priest. Any attempt at understanding and renewing priestly ministry must be done with 'eyes fixed' (Heb 12:2) on this one priest. It is a commonplace to say that, in the pages of the New Testament, while all believers are seen as a priestly people, no individual Christian is called by the name of priest. Yet, in the course of the centuries, the word 'priest', in the cultic sense, came to describe the role of the leader of the priestly people. The story of how this came about and of the various ways in which the priestly role has been seen over the centuries has been well told in a number of recent scholarly works. Reading them, one could single out nine major influences in the ongoing shaping of the priestly role. These are 1) the call of the disciples and apostles; 2) the emergence of a language of Christian ministry; 3) the stabilising of sacerdotal and sacrificial language; 4) different ways of seeing ordained ministry and non-ordained ministry; 5) different ways of understanding vocation and the call of God; 6) different approaches to authority and power; 7) different ways of understanding the call to be set apart; 8) different ways of understanding Church and world; 9) different ways of relating prophecy, priesthood, and shepherding.

Disciples and apostles: The primary call to every Christian is the call to be a disciple of Jesus Christ. The whole Church is a community of disciples, a community of learners. The one teacher of all disciples is the Christ who himself learned from his Father and from every one of his human experiences, including those in which he was 'tested as we are' (Heb 4:15). Christian priestly ministry must always be seen as a ministry by which disciples make disciples, after the example of the disciple-teacher who said 'proclaim the good news' (Mk 16:15) and 'make disciples' (Mt 28:19). The place of the teaching aspect of ministry, through the proclaiming of the word of God, was expressed forcibly by men like St Augustine who saw his preaching work as feeding people with the word of God. It was highlighted in the Reformation controversies about word and sacrament, and in the undeveloped teaching by the Council of Trent that the preaching of the gospel is the primary function of bishops. It was stressed in the way the Second Vatican Council saw the primacy of the proclaiming of the word of God in the description of the roles of bishop and presbyter. The fact that the Christian teacher-preacher must first of all be a disciple, always trying to absorb the message of the word, is supported by contemporary ways of seeing the whole Church as a 'community of disciples'. Since the apostle is primarily a disciple, all that applies to disciples applies to apostles. The original twelve were a strong symbol of the coming into existence of a renewed Israel. Already in the pages of the New Testament, the name apostle was applied to a wider group than the twelve. Somehow the word came to capture the notions of foundation membership, of being sent to set up new Christian communities, of being the ultimate human authorities in Christ's Church, of being the inspiration for all future initiatives in teaching, in ways of worshipping, and in Church order. The whole history of Christian ministry, and especially of ordained ministry, is a history of different kinds of emphasis on the different elements of what it is to be a disciple and what it is to be an apostle and to continue the mission of the first disciples and the first apostles.

The emergence of a fixed language of ministry: The early Christian Church knew a great variety of words describing Christian leadership and ministry. We read of apostles, prophets, evangelists, teachers, pastors, presidents, and leaders. Among these, pride of place seems to have gone to the apostles and prophets. Both groups were seen as, in a special way, foundation people (Eph 2:20). The preaching of the word and the setting up of churches by the original 'twelve' and by those who shared their name had an obvious foundational character. The prophets were inspired charismatic preacher-leaders who emerged in the Church as the prophecy of Joel (Acts 2:16-17) came to be fulfilled at Pentecost time. Their leadership took many forms in the life of the early Church, including, as the *Didaché* informs us, the presidency of the eucharist.

The names which were to stay with official Church ministry when a tripartite division of ministry became the norm were bishops, priests and deacons. Literally, these three words mean overseers, elders and assistants. It would appear that, in this terminology, the early Christians adopted some of the institutions of the society of the time. Having a college of presbyter-elders was an established feature of Jewish life. The language of 'oversight' reflects hellenistic and other influences. In the first century Christian communities, the line of demarcation between overseer and presbyter is not always easy to draw. In many instances, at least, the words seem to have been used interchangeably. The Jerusalem Church was at first ruled by the 'apostles and presbyters', under the presidency of James the brother of the Lord (Acts 15). A presbyteral leadership of the Church seems to have existed in various parts of Asia Minor (Acts 14:21-23). This is also the way in which St Luke presents St Paul's setting up of Church leaders. It is reflected most clearly in the account of Paul's farewell to the elders of the Church at Ephesus. He asks them to watch over all the flock, 'of which the Holy Spirit has made you overseers' (Acts 20:28). Apart from the attention to 'overseers and deacons' in Phil 1:1, there is, in fact, no mention of either overseers or elders in any of the letters which are of undisputed Pauline authorship. The Pastoral Letters reflect a situation in which Paul's 'apostolic delegates' appoint overseers, elders and deacons, responsible together for every aspect of the wellbeing of the Church. It is clear that the various forms of ministry in the life of the apostolic Church were attempts to develop and continue the apostolic mission itself. There is, as yet, little or no exact definition of roles. There is no clear indication, for example, as to what kind of leaders would qualify for presiding at the eucharist. There is no clear indication as to the role of deacons, apart from the obvious helping and agency roles which the name suggests. But sure foundations were being laid for the emergence of a later Church order which was to become normative for the whole Church: one bishop, many presbyters, deacons. It was already in place in the letters of St Ignatius of Antioch at the beginning of the second century. By the third century, it had become universal. It was seen as assuring the continuation of what the apostles stood for.

Sacerdotal and sacrificial language: In the apostolic and sub-apostolic church, the celebration of the eucharist was not explicitly described in terms of the offering of sacrifice; the person presiding was not described in sacerdotal terms. This fact has been interpreted in a variety of ways. What is clear is that the Lord's Supper continued to be celebrated in a domestic and familial setting, in a way that evoked the atmosphere of a meal rather than that of a sacrifice. In this, the eucharist was in line with the Passover meal which, though it followed on the offering of sacrifice, was not itself looked on as a sacrifice. With the destruction of the temple of Jerusalem and the growing conviction of Christians that they had their own religious autonomy, the language of priesthood and sacrifice came to be applied directly and explicitly to the celebration of the eucharist. This way of speaking became more and more explicit in the course of the third century. There are strong indications of it in the writings of Hippolytus and Tertullian. It becomes very explicit in the writings of St Cyprian (c 200-258). For Cyprian, the bishop is the cultic person, the *sacerdos;* he symbolises Christ; he presides at the eucharist 'in the place of Christ'; the Old Testament sacrificial rites have been replaced by the sacrifice of Christ. Cyprian envisages the possibility of the eucharist being celebrated by presbyters. But he rules out any question of a eucharist without the authorisation of the bishop. Over the following two centuries, eucharists presided over by presbyters became more and more common. In time, with the development of Frankish influences in the structuring of the Church, this became the norm. The ministry of reconciliation also came to be more and more exercised by presbyters. Though men like St Augustine had reservations about applying sacerdotal language to the ministry of bishops and presbyters, the way was set for seeing both offices in primarily sacerdotal and cultic terms.

Ordained and non-ordained: 'Ordination' has for long been the word that expresses the official commissioning of bishops, priests and deacons. Until the publication of Pope Paul VI's *Certain Ministries* (1972) we also spoke of people receiving various minor orders. The word 'order' expresses a very simple and very basic human desire and experience. It concerns the assuring of harmony in every area of human life. In this sense, the word 'order' occurs a lot in Christian usage from the beginning. St Paul saw the unfolding of the Christian mystery in terms of order: first-fruits leading, stage by stage, to full harvest, with everything happening in its own 'order', Christ himself being the 'first-fruits' (1 Cor 15:23). Those leading the community were to ensure the promotion of this God-willed order. This, in fact, may have been the original understanding of the role of presbyters, those who were the 'first fruits' of the preaching of the gospel and who, in turn, should promote its 'orderly' spread. The idea of 'ordering' was further promoted by the Roman system of appointing people to perform various public civil functions. The sixth-century Syrian writer who came to be called Dionysius the Areopagite worked out an elaborate scheme in which he saw everything and everybody, in heaven and on earth, in terms of various orders and ranks. The developing Christian notion of holy orders drew on all of these approaches to order and holy orders. While the words 'laity' and 'clergy', in their literal meaning, were originally applied to all the baptised, rituals were soon devised for the authorisation and installation of various office holders in the Church. These came to be recognised as people in 'holy orders'. Some detect the existence of an 'ordination' rite in the Pastoral Letters, 1 and 2 Timothy. Certainly, we have some foundations here for later rituals of ordination. From the beginning of the third century comes the detailed ordination rite of bishops, presbyters and deacons in Hippolytus' *Apostolic Tradition.* Since then, ordination rituals have reflected the various stages of the evolution of the understanding of Church ministry. As well as expressing something of the mystery of the Church, each inevitably reflects something of the society and culture of its time. Each reflects its own approach to an understanding of the 'hierarchy' i.e. the sacred order, of the Church.

Different approaches to vocation: The assertion in the letter to the Hebrews that 'one does not presume to take this honour, but takes it only when called by God' (Heb 5:4) and the way in which Jesus called his disciples has always had a profound influence on the Church's understanding of ministry. The conviction that it is the Lord who calls to ministry and that ministry is not by self-choice or by the community's choice has always been accepted by all of the Christian churches. But the understanding of the ways in which the Lord's call is mediated has varied at different stages of history. This is true of both Levitical priesthood and Christian priestly ministry. Though the Levitical priest was called by God, the call came through being born into a particular tribe. In the choice of bishops in the centuries after the monarchic episcopate became normative for the Church, the voice of the people and of the presbyters was very powerful. Our contemporary ordination rite envisages ordination as the culmination of a process in which people say yes to the leadership of somebody they have come to trust and whose call they have come to authenticate. There is an ongoing search for ways in which full justice can be done to the call of God, the inner conviction and sense of calling on the part of the person to be ordained, election by the people, and the sacramental laying on of hands by the episcopate. The emphasis on inner calling and on the call of God has always been strong in the tradition of the religious orders. In the diocesan priesthood, the emphasis has been on the public and ecclesial aspects of the call. There is still room for further integration of the two appoaches.

Authority and power: Jesus was recognised and admired as one with authority (*exousia*) and power (*dynamis*) (Lk 4:36). He acted with the authority and power of God himself. In several pages of the gospels, he is represented as giving his disciples a share in the same authority and power. Like all authority, gospel authority is a right to be and a freedom and approval to do. Power is a being able, being competent. Gospel power is a sharing in the creative energy of God. The key to the proper exercise of gospel authority and gospel power is in the contrast Jesus made between the ruling style of the kings of the Gentiles and the model he set for his own disciples: 'the greatest among you must become like the youngest, and the leader like one who serves' (Lk 22:26). Over the centuries, leaders of Christ's Church have at times imitated the Gentiles in the way they have exercised authority and power, especially when Church and State became closely identified. Renewal of ministerial priesthood must always begin with imitation of the leader who said 'I am among you as one who serves' (v 27).

The call to be set apart: The description of the ordained minister as a person set apart has had much prominence in Church tradition: 'Apart' from whom and from what? The question is closely related to an understanding of the holy and the sacred. The holiness of

God makes him separate from the limitation and imperfection that characterise creatures. But the real holiness of God and the holiness to which he calls those made in his image and likeness is moral holiness, a sharing in his own covenant qualities. There were times in the Church's history when those in ministry were somehow seen as outside and separate from the people they were ordained to lead. It happened, for example, at times when much of the pastoral and liturgical service to the local church was provided by monasteries; it happened whenever priestly spirituality was seen as somehow different from the spirituality of the rest of the baptised. Any renewal of an understanding of ministerial holiness must see the minister as one who is fully a member of the baptised people and, at the same time, in tune with the holiness of the God, who though he is 'not far from each one of us' (Acts 17:28), 'dwells in unapproachable light' (1 Tim 6:16).

Church and world: There is a sense in which Christians must love the world. The reason is that God himself loved the world at a great cost (Jn 3:16). There is a sense in which Christians should not pray for the world. The reason is that Jesus refused to pray for the world (Jn 17:9). This tension has always been reflected in the life of the Church and in church ministry. Sometimes, those in church ministry seem to have been encouraged to live a life that is other-worldly in a way that denies the goodness of creation. The Church's present understanding of herself as the universal sacrament of salvation, and her drawing from the perspective of the *Constitution on the Church in the Modern World*, should provide a good context for re-defining what is healthily worldly and what is unhealthily other-worldly.

Prophecy, priesthood and shepherding: The vision of church ministry as at the service of the Church which shares in the triple mission of Christ as prophet, priest and king, is central to the teaching of the Second Vatican Council on Church and ministry. It brings together much of what was dispersed in various areas of the consciousness of the Church from the beginning. However, in official Catholic teaching, it is a new way of imaging together the mission of Christ, the mission of the whole Church, and the mission of the ordained. It will take a long time before its rich implications are absorbed by the Church. It has implications especially for those in ordained ministry. The ordained person is, at the same time, a prophet, a cultic person, and a pastor. There are many authentic ways of combining these three callings.

B. Cooke, *Ministry to Word and Sacraments,*

Paul Bernier, SSS, *Ministry in the Church,* (Twenty-Third Publications, 1992).

CHAPTER 15

Bishops, priests, deacons, other ministries

Priestly ministry must be seen in the context of the mission of the whole Church. The Church, in turn, exists as the community of the baptised, in a wide-reaching network of relationships. All the members of the Church are related to the Father who has blessed us with every spiritual blessing (Eph 1:3). They are related to their Lord Jesus Christ in whom the Father has blessed them (v 3). They are related to the Holy Spirit with whose seal they were all marked when they received the gospel of their salvation (v 13). They are related to each other as members of one body in which each was given a grace according to the measure of Christ's gift (4:7), equipping them 'for the work of ministry, for the building up of the body of Christ' (4:12). They are related to all the members of the communion of saints and to all the rest of the human family, in tune with the will of Christ to 'create in himself one new humanity in place of the two' (2:15) and to 'break down the dividing wall' (v 14). They are related to the whole of creation, in tune with the plan of the Father in Christ, 'to gather up all things in him, things in heaven and things on earth' (1:10).

An enabling ministry
It is in the perspective of all these relationships that we must see the teaching of the Second Vatican Council on Church ministry, especially ordained ministry. Ministry is effective to the extent that it promotes all the relationships that comprise the Church. The teaching of the Council on ministry is spread throughout all its statements, and notably in the constitutions on the *Church*, on the *Liturgy*, on the *Church in the Modern World*, and in the decrees on the *Office of Bishops* and on the *Ministry and Life of Priests*. A special achievement of the Council was its perspectives on the one, yet triple, mission of Christ as prophet, priest, and shepherd-king. It saw this triple mission of Christ as percolating through to and involving every member of the Church. All official, public ministry was presented by the Council as an enabling ministry, enabling the whole Church to be prophetic, priestly and pastoral.

Presenting the mission of Christ and of the whole Church in this triple perspective contains many challenges for the Church in her understanding of herself. The triple perspective must in no way be seen as conflicting with the primacy of mission, and the call of all to be disciples and apostles in promoting that mission. All the baptised are all the time being sent on a mission that is prophetic, priestly and pastoral after the model of Jesus Christ who was sent by his Father to be prophet, priest and shepherd-king.

Overseers and presbyters

In dealing with their own role, the bishops at the Council knew that they had, at the same time, to be faithful to the fully developed teaching that has grown up over the centuries and to an understanding of the historical stages that went into the making of that teaching. The earliest use of episcopal language in the New Testament does not give a clear picture as to the exact kind of oversight that was then involved. Neither does it express a clear line of demarcation between the episcopal role and the presbyteral role. The letters of St Ignatius of Antioch (died c 107, AD) show the clear place of the monarchic episcopate in the churches in Asia Minor to whom he wrote. By the beginning of the third century, this pattern seems to have become universal. The bishop appeared primarily as the pastor of the local community of believers, the president of the eucharist, the minister of reconciliation. His presbyters acted largely as a consultative body.

In the course of time, as the presbyters became responsible for out-lying churches, they themselves were, in effect, the pastors, the presidents of the eucharist, the reconcilers of penitents. More and more, they came to be seen as the ones to whom the word 'priest' most obviously applied. The bishops came to be seen more as those responsible for the safeguarding of the tradition reaching back to the apostles and the communion of the churches reaching out through the whole known world. The priestly office came to be understood more in terms of the role of presbyters than in that of bishops. A consequence was that the episcopate as such was not seen as a sacrament. The bishop was seen as possessing a jurisdiction over and above what was entailed in priestly ordination. There were differing views as to the exact source of this jurisdiction. Hence the many medieval disputes about the relationship between the 'power of orders' and the 'power of jurisdiction'. In its concern with the challenges of the Reformers, the Council of Trent emphasised the institution of the priesthood and of the hierarchy by Christ; it defined the power of the priest to consecrate and offer sacrifice. With little historical nuancing, it defined the divine origin of the episcopacy. Concerned with the Reformers' emphasis on the common priesthood of all the baptised, it emphasised the differences between ordained priesthood and the priesthood of all the baptised. The precise relationship, sacramentally, between bishop and priest was not defined.

The college of bishops

The bishops at the Second Vatican Council were aware of the historical complexities that surrounded the origin and development of the tripartite ministry of bishop, priest and deacon. They clearly wished to present all three as being in continuity with the mission of the first apostles. They taught that 'amongst those various offices which have been exercised in the Church from earliest times the chief place, according to the witness of tradition, is held by the function of those who, through their appointment to the dignity and responsibility of bishop ... are regarded as transmitters of the apostolic line' (LG 20). It would be useful to read this and related teachings of the Council in conjunction with the ARCIC agreed Statement on Ministry and Ordination (1971): 'The full emergence of the threefold ministry of bishop, presbyter and deacon required a longer period than the apostolic age. Thereafter this threefold structure became universal in the Church' (par 6). Conscious of the implications of some evolution in this threefold structure, the bishops at the Council clearly taught the sacramental nature of the episcopacy. By episcopal consecration, the bishop receives the fulness of the sacrament of holy orders. He is thereby made a member of the college of bishops, a cohesive group with a common concern for all the good of all the Church. This college, with the Pope as its head, exists by divine will in the Church. Together it is responsible for every aspect of the wellbeing of the universal Church (LG 23) and for safeguarding the unity of the apostolic faith (LG 23). Sacramental ordination to the college is an empowering. In this empowering, orders and jurisdiction are sacramentally united. As hands are imposed and the words of consecration are prayed, the Holy Spirit is invoked. The grace of the same Holy Spirit is conferred. In the whole sacramental action, the bishop 'in an eminent and visible way' takes on Christ's own role as teacher, shepherd and high-priest and he is commissioned to act in the person of Christ (*LG* 21).

The emphasis on collegiality brings out the need of the bishop to be in full communion with the Pope as head of the college and with all the members of the college throughout the world. Through the bishop, in this full communion, the whole Church becomes present in the local Church (*LG* 25). By the preaching of the gospel of Christ and the celebration of the mystery of the Lord's Supper, the individual bishop is a visible principle of the unity of the local Church (*LG* 26). His membership of a college and his call to full communion point to the qualities that should characterise his relationships with the priests of his diocese and with all those who promote the welfare of the local Church. This topic receives special attention in the *Decree on the Office of Bishops* (par 16-18).

Priest and bishop

Since the episcopate expresses the fulness of the sacrament of orders, priests can be said to be the closest sharers with the bishops in the same sacrament. They are, in an older Church language, a language that is still in limited use, 'priests of the second order'. Together with their bishop, they constitute a 'unique sacerdotal college' (*presbyterium*) (*LG* 28). They are the 'support and mouthpiece' of the episcopal college. In each local assembly of the faithful, they are said to 'represent in a certain sense the bishop'. In practice, this 'representing' is a making sure that they are in a harmonious and creative communion with the bishop and with the universal Church. Under the authority of the bishop, they sanctify and govern that portion of the Lord's flock assigned to them. By doing so, they serve the welfare not only of the local Church but of the whole Church. There is a sense in which religious priests, too, belong to the diocesan clergy (*CD* 34). The charisms of their institutes are designed to enrich the local Church as well as the universal Church. Hence they are encouraged to find points of communion with the local presbyterate. The portrait of priesthood painted in the *Decree on the Ministry and Life of Priests* mirrors all the qualities that should characterise the bishops of the Church.

By definition, every priest is a member of a college, a man in communion, a collaborator. There is here a programme for a whole life's ministry. Like bishops, priests are, by the sacrament of ordination, authorised and empowered to proclaim the word of God, to celebrate the sacraments, and to exercise pastoral care. Like the bishops, they are visible and public signs of the prophetic, priestly and pastoral mission of Christ. Like the bishops they are so intimately related to Christ that they 'act in the person of Christ, the Head' (PO 2). In one sense priests receive their identity by their being collaborators with their bishop. There is a sense too in which their task is to make their bishop present (PO 5). There is also a sense in which they receive their identity from the community whom they serve in the particular Church for the service of which they were ordained. But the priest's full identity derives directly from the sacrament of ordination by the character of which he shares in the headship of Christ, who is prophet, priest and shepherd.

The Council's description of both bishop and priest puts a strong emphasis on the place of the word of God. 'Among the more important duties of bishops' the preaching of the gospel has 'pride of place' (LG 25). The exercise of the teaching role and the proclaiming of the gospel of Christ is 'one of the principal duties of bishops' (CD 12). The 'first task' of priests, as co-workers of the bishops, is to 'preach the gospel of God to all'; their ministry of the word is exercised 'in many different ways' (PO 4).

It would be an over-simplification to say that the Council regarded the proclamation of the word of God as the most important work of bishops and priests, but the prominence it gave to the word is a very satisfying starting point for a unifying approach to all priestly ministry. In the whole range of the priestly ministry of teaching, catechising and preaching, the word that God has spoken in the past is so presented that it illumines the present. People are alerted to the word that God himself is now speaking in their lives. In the celebration of the sacraments, the word is proclaimed in a way that expresses the highest power of words. In the variety of forms of pastoral care, the word of God is brought into every human situation. Emphasis on the word of God brings a continual new light on the topic of the relationship between word and sacrament which was such a live issue at the Reformation and has been ever since. In the search for a priestly spirituality, the word, with all its rich connotations, can be a strong starting point and a continual focal point.

Deacons

The Second Vatican Council made important statements about the diaconate. The most important of these was the clear indication that it should be restored 'as a proper and permanent rank of the hierarchy' (*LG* 29). The word 'deacon' is an eloquent expression of what all the Church is called to be, a servant people, in the spirit of their founder who came 'not to be served but to serve' (Mk 10:45). Recent historical studies of the same word suggest that it can also connote the position of somebody who is authorised to implement the wishes of another. The history of the diaconate in the Church would suggest the interplay of these two approaches to the diaconate. It has been argued that the deacons in Phil 1:1 are on the same level as the bishops in that text. When the twelve, according to the account in Acts 6:1-6, were concerned with their neglect of the word of God in order to wait on tables, they prayed and laid hands on seven selected men of good standing. In popular understanding, this is seen as the setting up of the diaconate. But there is, in fact, no indication that any of the seven came to be associated with work related to waiting on tables. They are never called deacons. Two of their numbers, Stephen and Philip, became involved in the ministry of preaching and baptising. The history of the diaconate expresses a similar ambivalence. Sometimes, deacons were prominent in liturgical ministry. Sometimes the emphasis was on their social ministry and care for the poor. The diaconate has had its high points and its low points. In the fifth century it would appear that, in some places, the deacons, in their ministry of social care, occupied a position that was more prominent than that of the presbyters, and it was largely from them that bishops came to be chosen. The period preceding the Second Vatican Council could be described as a period of decline. In the Western Church, the diaconate had come to be merely a stepping-stone to priesthood.

In his introduction of the new ritual for the ordination of deacons in 1968, and in his norms for the order of diaconate in 1972, Pope

Paul VI, echoing the words of *LG* 29, presented diaconal involvement in the liturgy in terms of the sanctifying ministry; diaconal proclaiming of the word in terms of the preaching and teaching ministry; diaconal charity in terms of pastoral ministry. In a diaconate that is no longer merely a transitional stage in the preparation for ordination to priesthood and that is open to both married and celibate men, one can hope for many developments in the integration of the triple ministry envisaged by Pope Paul. A renewed diaconate can be a living challenge to all the Church to be both a serving community and a community that acts in the name of Christ. It can be a continual bridge between the liturgical life of the Church and the promotion of justice, peace and charity in the world for which the Church must be continually the sacrament of Christ's saving presence.

Many ministries
Until the Second Vatican Council, we spoke of major orders and minor orders. This continued a way of speaking that was common in the Church since the fourth century. In the course of the centuries, various 'minor orders' came into existence, in the Church's response to new situations and new needs. After a while, they settled down to be ritual stages towards ordination to priesthood. Since 1972, by a decision of Pope Paul VI, the minor orders and sub-diaconate have ceased to exist. Replacing them are the two ministries of lector and acolyte for the promotion of the reading of the word of God and for the service of the altar. Unlike diaconate, these two ministries are not part of the sacrament of orders and of the hierarchical dimension of the Church. Those commissioned for them are 'instituted', not ordained. As such, the two ministries are conferred on laymen, some of whom will later present themselves as candidates for holy orders. In introducing them, Pope Paul envisaged a great flowering of new ministries that would respond realistically to the ongoing needs of the Church. Those instituted into the public ministries of lector and acolyte comprise only a small percentage of those exercising ministry in the Church. One would hope that we have here the makings of another bridge, a bridge between the ministry of those in holy orders and the ministry of all the rest of the baptised for the building up of the one body of Christ.

CHAPTER 16

Ministry of reconciliation

At every level of human society, we are nowadays hearing many cries for reconciliation. Yet, until quite recently, 'reconciliation' was not a word in regular Catholic usage. We talked rather about penance, about repentance, about confession. All these are very precious words in our Christian tradition. Each of them expresses a continual Christian need. To set them in context, and to describe the work of Christ in revealing, restoring and repairing the kind of relationships that should link us with each other and with God, there is no more fitting word than reconciliation. The word has been re-instated by the two eucharistic prayers of reconciliation, by frequent use in the *Order of Penance* (1973), and by some use in the *Code of Canon Law* (1983).

A marriage word
Though it does occur in a gospel text, in the teaching of Jesus about leaving the gift in front of the altar and going to be reconciled (Mt 5:24), it is St Paul who opened up for us the possibilities in the word. His message to the Romans (5:10) is that we are reconciled by Christ's death and saved by his life. His message to the Corinthians (2 Cor 5:8-21) is an appeal to be reconciled to God, because God was in Christ, reconciling the world to himself, and because he has committed to his 'ambassadors' the ministry of reconciliation. The basic meaning of the word Paul used was 'to change', 'to alter'. It would appear that, in the Greek world, a familiar usage concerned the bringing together again of an estranged husband and wife. Paul himself explicitly uses the word in that sense (1 Cor 7:11). In the great reconciliation texts, he figuratively applies this usage to the bringing together again of human beings with each other and with the God from whom they have been estranged. This deep and continual need in estranged human hearts is the key to the Christian meaning of sin, repentance, and reconciliation. All of these find their proper context in the covenant. We know that the most cherished and intimate expression of the Sinai covenant relationship was in terms of the

husband-wife relationship and the father(mother)-child relationship. There are no more basic human relationships than these. They are the models that Christians must continually keep in mind as they try to live according to the new and everlasting covenant and when they fail to do so. The covenant, which is based on them, is our entry into the mystery of the triune God.

Father, Son, Spirit

The source of all the familial imagery of the covenant is the familial intimacy of Father, Son and Holy Spirit. This familial intimacy is the source of all the Church's life and mission. In his earthly existence, Jesus experienced his own intimate and unique relationship with his Father whom he addressed as 'Abba, Father' (Mk 14:36). He was also conscious of his unique relationship with the Spirit of his Father. As his disciples listened to his ways of expressing this double experience, and as they later reflected and prayed on them, in the light of his resurrection and glorification, the Christian doctrine of the Trinity came to be shaped and formulated. That doctrine will never find adequate human expression, but it keeps us focused on the mystery of three persons who are defined by the ways in which they know each other and love each other. This knowing and loving is self-giving, fruitful, creative, limitless. In that perspective, the creation of the world comes to be seen not as a divine afterthought but as the overflowing of the eternally fruitful life of the divine persons. The Incarnation is seen not as a last effort to salvage a plan that had gone wrong but as the great visible and personal expression in our earth of the bonds of intimacy between the Son who is the 'image of the invisible God, the first-born of all creation' and all persons and things that were created 'through him and for him' (Col 1:15-16). The covenant is seen as the disclosing and sharing of the mind and heart of the God who from eternity planned to make the world through his Son and for his Son. The relationships between the Father and the Son and with the Holy Spirit who is the fruit of their love become the programme for the whole life of the Church of the new covenant.

The members of the Church are called to be one body, one spirit, in Christ, with all the intimacy and communion which that image suggests. The covenant images of bridegroom-bride and parent-child yield up endlessly new possibilities for those called to be brothers and sisters of 'the only Son, who is close to the Father's bosom' (Jn 1:18). In this new intimacy with God, gender-language breaks down. God the Father loves with a mother's love (Is 49:14-15; 66:13). By the power of the Spirit whom Jesus breathed forth at his death (Jn 19:30), and who gives birth to the Church, the water and blood flow from the side of Christ (v 34). In this new creation, the woman who is to be both bride and mother comes forth from the side of the new man and becomes the mothering Church. The virgin-mother of God becomes the mother of the Church.

Inviting us

The riches of the relationships between Father, Son, and Spirit have been put at the full disposal of the Church. The Father and the Son, with the Spirit, are always ready to come and make their home in the heart of the disciple who loves (Jn 14:23). This divine coming and sharing is the atmosphere in which all Christian prayer must take place. It is the basis of all liturgical worship 'to the Father, through the Son, in the Holy Spirit'. It is the basis for all the Church's work of loving. It is the basis for all the Church's work for justice and peace which are so much part of all God's programmes for loving. It is the basis of the Church's being the universal sacrament of salvation. It is the basis for the Church's continual ministry of reconciliation. It must provide the agenda for all the Church's services of penance.

Salvation and reconciliation

Jesus came to proclaim the reign of his Father 'from whom every family in heaven and on earth takes its name' (Eph 3:15). In telling us about this Father, he revolutionised all familial language. Anyone who does the will of the Father is the brother and sister and mother of Jesus (Mk 3:31-35). This is the meeting point of all the covenant imagery and of the overflow into the human family of the qualities that comprise the community life of Father, Son, and Spirit. The whole work of Jesus consisted in calling the human family to share intimately in that community life. Two words, in particular, sum up his work: 'salvation' and 'reconciliation'. The two words are inseparable. Salvation could be described as the establishing for human beings of the richest possible relations with the Father, Son, and Holy Spirit, with each other, and with the whole of creation. Reconciliation is the continual repairing, restoring, and developing of these relationships, and lifting them beyond themselves to levels hitherto undreamt of. The seeds of salvation and reconciliation are continually being sown in every human heart by the Spirit of the One whose name is Jesus, the bringer of God's salvation (cf Mt 1:21). He is continually bringing these seeds to harvest, and preserving them from what might bring destruction and blight.

Ambassadors and reconcilers

We have inherited a rich variety of words to describe the work by which Jesus saved and reconciled us. These include atonement, expiation, and propitiation. With the Catholic emphasis on redemption and the Reformation emphasis on justification, no Christian can afford to forget that the first subject and first agent of all reconciliation is God himself. It is not a question of our trying to placate an angry God. It is he, the covenant God, who always takes the initiative; it is he who reconciles us; it is he who was in Christ, reconciling the world to himself (2 Cor 5:19). The reason is that he has loved us with an everlasting love and that he has kept on drawing us with loving-ekindness (Jer 31:3). We are invited to receive and welcome God's gracious gift of reconciliation, and to be, in turn, ambassadors of Christ, with a ministry of reconciliation (2 Cor 5:18-20). We are Christ's ambassadors because it was 'in Christ' that the God of the covenant did the work of reconciliation (v 19). It is Christ who has broken down the dividing wall (Eph 2:14). He himself is the place of expiation, the mercy-seat (Rom 3:25). The holy place where God is reaching out to reconcile us is the body of Christ from which the covenant blood flows out. In this divine reaching out, our guilt is continually removed; confidence is restored; love is begotten; victory is assured. This process is going on all the time. As God does his work of expiation in his Son's blood, faith and repentance come to life in us.

Though there is no question of our appeasing an angry God, the holiness of God cannot peacefully co-exist with the sin and deformity which it meets in the earthly members of his Son's body. The first letter of John provides a good meeting point for understanding human sin, the expiation achieved by Christ, and the transforming power of God's light: God is light; by living in the light, we share in the life of God's own Son; his blood keeps cleansing us from all sin (1 Jn 1:5-7). In this meeting of God's light, our sins, and the blood of Jesus, we continually experience God's surgery and therapy, repairing and restoring the areas of darkness and damage in our lives. By taking to himself our fallen humanness, Jesus has let God's light enter every area of our darkness, our alienation, our sin. He was 'made sin' for us; as a result we are 'made God's righteousness' in him (2 Cor 5:21).

The humanity through which Christ saved us is not an abstraction. Its saving action was at work at every stage of God's entering into our condition in the Incarnation. It started with the existence of the Word of God in Mary's womb. It continued with his being born in a situation that lacked many human securities, with his having to be clothed, with his receiving milk at his mother's breast, and being fed by human hands. It was at work in everything he did and allowed to be done to him in the whole course of his life. It reached its culmination in his dying and rising, which were the key to the reconciling action that was going on at every stage of his life; through his human experience, his saving and reconciling action had involved every movement of his hands, his feet, his head, his heart, his whole body. Since his glorification, the love of God has been continually poured into the heart of everybody who has communion with the glorified heart and body of Christ, 'through the Holy Spirit that has been given to us' (Rom 5:5). The response on our part should be the kind of walking according to the Spirit that makes us follow the Son's example and cry Abba, Father (Rom 8:1-17).

A Call to change
Reconciliation is a call to be at-one, a call to change, a call to alter what is out of tune with the life of the triune God. The loving-kindness and the fidelity of God do not change. They keep calling us to a change in our attitudes and relationships to him, to each other, to all creation. God's reconciling action is a calling back, a gentle beckoning to share in his trinitarian life of unity, truth, goodness and beauty. His call is an attraction, a drawing, in line with his everlasting love in which he draws us to himself (Jer 31:3) and keeps drawing us to his Son (Jn 6:44). In drawing us, he invites us to respond. Our response must be free, since the one thing

that God cannot do in our lives without our co-operation is to be intimate with us. It is in this context that we must see the fact that Christ is the sacrament of God's reconciling action. In the social and religious categories of his time, Jesus was a layman. But, led by the Spirit, his followers came to recognise him as the perfect priest-reconciler. He, and he alone, was 'able for all time to save completely those who approach God through him, since he always lives to make intercession for them' (Heb 7:25). He is the unique sign and instrument of the Father's loving-kindness and fidelity which are the source of his priestly and reconciling activity. The Church, in turn, is the sacrament of all of his priestly and reconciling activity. Her members do not have a monopoly of saving activity, since the kingdom of God is wider than the membership of the Church. But, since she is the body of which Christ is Head, all saving activity is in some way related to her mystery and mission.

A reconciling Church

The whole Church is, and should be seen to be, an agent of reconciliation in everything she is and everything she does. Since the Church exists for the sake of the whole human family, her reconciling action must be as evident in every area of human culture, and of social and political life, as it is in the daily life of her own members. This conviction was one of the inspirations behind the contents and the first words of the *Constitution on the Church in the Modern World*, expressing the yearning of the Church for solidarity with all human beings in all their needs. In her work of building up, the Church, like her founder, must keep breaking down any walls that separate and divide (cf Gal 3:28). All the Church's work of building up and breaking down calls continually for the exercise of the ministry of healing – the healing of minds and bodies, of relationships, of memories. Healing is a crucial part of the work of reconciliation. Each of the seven sacraments is, in its own way, a celebration of reconciliation and healing.

A special sacrament of reconciliation

The sacrament which is called the sacrament of reconciliation makes us particularly aware of Christ as the mercy-seat of God, and as the person in whom God's reconciling action is continually taking place. In recent years, our attention has been drawn to the many ways in which this sacrament has been celebrated over the centuries. It would appear that at present we are part of a new historical development in the shaping of the sacrament. Since the Second Vatican Council, the Church has given us the gift of a new *Order of Penance*. There is scope for much creative use of each of the three rites which are there envisaged, and for ways of combining elements from the three. For the ordained celebrant of the sacrament, a suitable examination of conscience would be the extent to which he is an agent and promoter of reconciliation in every area of the whole local community of which he is a leader. Each public celebration of the sacrament should reflect what is happening in all the community, all the time. It should bring to light the sins hidden in human hearts and in the structures of our society. It should be like a new appearance to the community of the risen and reconciling Christ.

The ministry of reconciliation

There is a very real sense in which all the baptised are called to be ministers of reconciliation in all their attitudes and in all their relationships. The daily life and interaction of Christians calls for the continual living and repairing of the bridegroom-bride qualities of the new covenant which are continually resourced by the community life of the divine persons. The work of reconciling and of forgiving sins had a special place in the call of Christ to the twelve founder members of the New Israel. St Paul saw the ministry of reconciliation as in a special way entrusted to those who, as ambassadors of Christ (2 Cor 5:20) continue the apostolic office. From the third century, especially, the public reconciliation of sinners came to be seen as very central to the office of those ordained as bishops. When the role of presbyters became more clearly defined, the sacramental ministry of reconciliation came to occupy a central place in their lives too. Bishop and priest receive the sacrament of orders to promote holy order in the Church and to repair and heal the dis-order of sin. They do this in the name and person of Christ, the head and shepherd.

A daily programme

Each priestly ministry of proclaiming the word, each celebration of a sacrament, each exercise of pastoral care, is an exercise of the ministry of reconciliation. Because each of these is an exercise in basic covenant relationships, each calls for an exquisitely sensitive approach. They all reach their highpoints in the celebration of the eucharist and in the celebration of the special sacrament of reconciliation. The two sacraments are inseparably connected. The two are concerned with the repairing and building up of the one body of Christ. In the two, there is a life-long programme for all priestly ministry. In the two, the great flow of life between the divine persons keeps moving into and through the members of the body who are 'growing up in every way into him who is the head, into Christ' (Eph 4:15). Through them, it touches the whole of creation. The sacrament of anointing of the sick is an eloquent meeting point between the two. The sick person is invited to be reconciled, anointed, and fed for the next stage of life's journey. Here is pastoral ministry at its deepest.

Pope John Paul II, Apostolic Exhortation, *Reconciliation & Penance*, (1984).

Catherine Mowry LaCugna, *God for Us*, (Harper, 1991) esp pp 292-304, 382-388, 400-410.

CHAPTER 17

Communion in the holy

The bishops at the Second Vatican Council spoke of the ministry and life of presbyters rather than about the ministry and life of priests. This is sometimes wrongly interpreted as a move away from a cultic, sacral understanding of priesthood to one which emphasises community leadership. In fact, the choice of words was dictated by the need to distinguish those in the second level of sacerdotal ministry from bishops, who exercise it in the first level. The ordained person must, of course, be, at the same time, community leader and an agent of sanctification and consecration. But it is this latter cultic and sacerdotal activity that is his title to leadership and that defines his leadership. His task is to alert people to the holy and to help people to live in the ambit of the holy. There is a sense in which, in the Christian view of things, the dividing wall between secular and sacred is the wall which Jesus Christ has broken down (Eph 2:14). Every place and every human experience can now be sacred, insofar as it is a possible point of contact with the holy. God's 'heaven', God's 'temple', the primary place where God calls for priestly worship, is now in our own hearts and in the hearts of the least of our brothers and sisters. These are the primary holy places for Christians. But our estranged faces can fail to recognise these holy places. This failure to recognise is the greatest tragedy for a Christian. It is still possible for Christians to fail to recognise the risen Christ in the myriad ways in which he is, literally, in their midst, inviting them to share in his own way of knowing and loving. The invitation to this sharing and to all that grows out of it is their call to holiness. Enabling them to be alert to and to recognise and answer this continual call is central to the work of ordained ministry. This ministry must continually help every son and daughter of God to worship God in every human heart. This continual worshipping reaches its highpoint in the eucharist which is the sacrament of the loving-kindness of the heart of our God, the sacrament of the communion of saints.

In the Western Church, the belief in the communion of saints has been an integral part of the Christian creed since the fifth century. In the communion of saints, we are part of a whole network of holy things, holy events, holy persons. This has been made possible because the all-holy God has kept entering our world in such a way that we keep discovering his activity in every area of his creation. Through everybody and everything in the created universe, we can enter into continual communication with God who is the source of all holiness. Those re-born in Christian baptism are in special contact with the holiness of God. In this sense, all the baptised are holy: they are all saints, forming one great holy communion. In a more restrictive usage, we apply the word 'saints' to those whose way of life has so expressed the holiness of God that the Church is sure that they now enjoy the vision of his face. But the word is more widely applied to the communion of all those on earth, 'under the earth', and in heaven, who are, in varying degrees, the beneficiaries of the holiness of God.

The saints on earth are continually enriched by contact with other holy persons and with holy things. This is particularly true in the celebrations we have come to call sacraments. We talk, for example, about holy baptism and holy orders. In a special way, we associate the word with the holy eucharist. It is in this celebration that, as one body, we are in living contact with the body of the Lord in whom 'the whole fulness of deity dwells bodily' (Col 2:9). In this sacrament, holy persons are in privileged contact with holy things and with Jesus Christ, the great bearer of God's holiness. It is not surprising that, in earlier Church usage, 'communion of saints' was seen as a communion in holy things as well as a communion between holy persons.

You alone are holy
The one who provides harmony between all holy things, holy events and holy persons is the third divine person whom we call the Holy Spirit. The conviction of Christians is that 'if the Spirit of him who raised Jesus from the dead dwells in you, he who raised Christ from the dead will give life to your mortal bodies also through his Spirit that dwells in you' (Rom 8:11). For a Christian, it is impossible to separate the action of the Holy Spirit, the mystery of Christ, the mystery of the Church, and the destiny which

God has in store for the human body. All are linked together in the communion of holy persons and holy things. This holy communion gets ever richer meaning for us as we come to recognise the incarnate and risen Christ as the alpha and omega of all creation and of all human history. There are profound implications in the ancient Christian teaching, highlighted for us by the Eastern Church, that what has not been assumed has not been saved; because he assumed human nature, Jesus, through his humanity, has a continually saving influence on all of humanity and indeed on the whole of creation.

More than ever in the course of its history, the Church today is teaching a doctrine of the multiple manifestations of the real presence of the risen Christ, in the Church herself, in all of human history, in the whole of creation. This real presence provides multiple points of contact for us with the holiness of God and it provides ever new perspectives on the meaning of the communion of holy persons and of holy things. The search for ways of exploring the riches of the word 'sacrament' is a continual search for the points of contact between the all-holy God and the whole of creation which his Son came to make new. In this search, we keep discovering that the kingdom of God is indeed wider than the Church, but that the Church is being continually called to become the universal sacrament of salvation for the whole of creation. We come to recognise and celebrate the expressions of the holiness of God in other Christians, in people of other world religions, in all people of good will.

Holy Trinity, holy Church
In searching for the many expressions of the holiness of God outside the recognisable boundaries of the communion of saints, we must keep returning to the source of all holiness, the communion between Father, Son, and Holy Spirit. Any holiness in the 'one, holy, catholic and apostolic Church', and outside it, is a participation in the holiness that unites Father, Son and Spirit. The Church is a 'holy nation', precisely because it is 'God's own people' (1 Pet 2:9) invited to share in God's own way of knowing and loving. On earth, Jesus was recognised by both the unclean spirits and by a believing disciple as the 'holy one of God' (Mk 1:24; Jn 6:69). He was full of the Holy Spirit who had come upon his mother and by

whose power he himself was holy (Lk 1:35; 3:22; Acts 10:38). Out of this fulness, he 'loved the Church and gave himself up for her, in order to make her holy … so as to present the Church to himself in splendour … so that she may be holy and without blemish' (Eph 5:25-27). By the same sanctifying action, he made the Church into 'a holy temple in the Lord' (Eph 2:21). This is why Christians must live a life worthy of their calling (Eph 4:1-3; Col 3:12-15). The unbroken and unbreakable union between Christ and the Church, which is a share in his own union with the Father and the Holy Spirit, is the basis for the continual act of faith by which Christians say 'I believe in the holy Church'. The Spirit of the risen Christ, who alone is holy, is continually poured into the Church. That Spirit is the 'Lord and giver of life'. The knowing and loving activity of the Father, the Son, and their Spirit keeps bringing into existence and sustaining the communion of saints, the communion of holy persons expressing their fellowship with the divine persons. The holiness expressed in the lives of the members of the communion of saints flows from their sharing in and response to the holiness of God.

Holy and sinful
In its pilgrim state, the Church is at the same time a community of saints and a community of sinners. The compatibility of these two ways of seeing the pilgrim Church has always been a live and even contentious question for the Church. Already in the time of the first letter of John, there was an awareness of the co-existence of the beautiful ideal and the harsh reality, and our need to be aware that there is a way of coping with the reality; the believer in Jesus should not sin, 'but if anyone does sin, we have an advocate with the Father, Jesus Christ the righteous; and he is the atoning sacrifice for our sins, and not for ours only but also for the sins of the whole world' (2:1-2). Later there were those who maintained that when Christians sin they cease to be members of the Church. The Donatist controversies raised major issues about the status of sacraments conferred by unworthy members and the question of re-ordaining or re-baptising those who, having apostasised, showed signs of repentance. Later, in the Reformation controversies, there were many variations on the topic of the co-existence in the human being of holiness and unholiness. One major issue was whether sinful human beings could in any sense be agents of

God's work of sanctification. This question, in turn, had implications for a whole range of questions on such topics as salvation, reconciliation, justification, the relationship between faith and good works. The controversies on all these topics went on and still go on in the 'holy Church of sinners', the community of people who are, at the very same time, just and sinning, a community of people in continual need of reform. Sometimes the Church learns this lesson in ways that are hard and humiliating.

Out of all the controversies has grown an ever clearer conviction, on the part of all the protagonists, that God alone is holy, that God alone is the source of any holiness that is to be found in persons, in events, in things, and that it is God who takes the initiative in making any of his creatures share in his holiness. There is also a growing conviction that it is the will of the all-holy God that his holiness be expressed in every area of human living and of human communication. Today's pressing questions about justice and peace, human liberation, the bettering of all human institutions, must be seen in the light of the mystery of God who wishes his holiness to be reflected wherever there is communication between human beings who are made in his image and likeness. The will of God, as expressed in Jesus Christ, is that human beings become a 'new creation' and that this new creation is 'everything' (Gal 6:15). In the bringing about of this new creation, the all-holy God has taken the bold initiative of somehow identifying with sinful human beings. The One who knew no sin he made to be sin 'so that in him we might become the righteousness of God' (2 Cor 5:21). It was in this unique identification of the sinless one with sinners that our reconciliation was achieved, because God was 'in Christ, reconciling the world to himself, not counting their trespasses against them' (v 19). Whatever way we envisage human beings as the ministers of that reconciliation, we must keep our eyes fixed on Christ Jesus who alone became for us 'wisdom from God, and righteousness and sanctification and redemption' (1 Cor 1:30).

Holy places, sacred places

There have been many attempts to define the holy and the sacred. Each of the great world religions has made its contribution: the holy is other; it is transcendent; it is beyond human reach; it generates awe and fascination; it is beyond and separated from the profane and limited world; it is the ultimate in goodness, truth and beauty; it is beyond what we can contact through our senses; it is the hidden and undisclosed source of all that there is. The sacred is whatever is our point of contact with the holy. All these partial attempts at capturing the mystery of the holy and the sacred have their value but they have given way before the unique manifestation of the holiness of God in the incarnation of the Son of God. The holiness of God dwells not in any tabernacle or temple made by human hands, but rather in the human hands themselves, in the human body, in the human heart. The holiness of God makes its home in the human flesh of his Son (cf Jn 1:14). The human flesh of his Son brings holiness to all human flesh. God wishes to share his holiness with us, in the intimacy of knowing and loving, not somewhere out there but in the human heart. Holiness is no longer about the totally 'other' and the totally transcendent. It is a continual touching of every human heart by the God who in the human heart of his Son yearns to share with us his own great covenant qualities of tender mercy and fidelity.

It is in this intimate sharing that we become merciful in the way that our Father is merciful (Lk 6:36), perfect as our heavenly Father is perfect (Mt 5:48). The holiness of God percolates through into all our moral attitudes, all our relationships. The holiness of God is his own unique and perfect way of knowing and loving; a knowing and loving that is without shadow, without limitation. The holiness of those made in his image and likeness becomes a very personal sharing in that knowing and loving. Holiness, communion and community come to have converging meanings. The reconciling action of Jesus Christ consisted in making possible this holy sharing. All his prophetic, priestly, and shepherding ministry was designed to make this sharing a reality. It is for this that, in the extended imagery of John 17, he 'consecrated' himself, that he made himself into a sacrificial victim. This consecration, this 'making holy' was the bringing of his whole body into total harmony with the will of his Father. In that sacrificial state he entered the heavenly holy of holies, offering the perfect sacrificial gift to the Father. In this he achieved reconciliation for all those for whom he died. He brought sinful human beings into a full communion with the all-holy God. This communion is the foundation and source of the communion of saints, of all inter-action of holy persons with each other, and with holy things. It is the foundation of the mission of the Church as universal sacra-ment of salvation; it is the continual bridging that all Christian priesthood should seek to achieve.

Ordained ministry is exercised in the person of Christ who is the living and life-giving head of a body. All proclaiming of the word, all leadership in the celebration of the sacraments, all pastoral care exists in order to enable all the members of the body to be in communion with their life-giving head, to be and remain 'holy in the truth' (Jn 17:17). The initiative in every act of priestly ministry is still taken by Christ himself who is the one priest, the one recon-ciler, the only one who deserves by right to be called the holy one of God. Those whom we have come to call Christian priests are agents, instruments, servants, in their relationship to the One Priest. Their proclamation of the word and their pastoral ministry is all orientated towards the work of sanctification, of making holy. The great summit and source of this work of sanctification is the holy eucharist. In this holy communion, the members of Christ's body celebrate the heart of the Christian call, the graced sharing in God's own way of knowing and loving, in a way that 'brings salvation to the whole world' (*Eucharistic Prayer* 4). This is the celebration of what holiness is about, that God has transferred the place of his trinitarian family life from the remote heavens into the intimacy of human hearts. The president of the eucharist stands as a sure sign of the presence of the all-holy Lord, in the midst of a holy people, for the making of a holy world. This is why, at priestly ordination, the bishop prays 'renew in him the spirit of holiness'. As a member of, and leader of, the community called to holiness, the priest-president continually calls people to holiness in the name of the Head of the community. He is primarily a man of the cultic, the sacral, the holy. But he must continually re-learn the meaning of true cult. He must continually re-discover the real sacred places. He must continually re-name the holy places. They must all be re-named after the real holy place, the human heart, the real temple of God.

Second Vatican Council, *Constitution on the Church*, chap. 6

John J. O'Donnell, *The Mystery of the Triune God*.

CHAPTER 18

Living to intercede

Jesus Christ is alive. He holds his priesthood permanently, because he continues forever. He is able for all time to save those who approach God through him. He can save them completely. The reason is that he always lives to make intercession for them. These assurances, from the letter to the Hebrews (7:24-25), show the inseparable links between Christian priesthood, sacrifice, and intercession. The ongoing intercession of Jesus is not an activity separate from his once-for-all sacrifice. On earth, his sacrifice took place continually in his human body. It began when that body came into existence. It continued through every stage of his earthly existence, and reached a high point at his death. In his exaltation to his Father's right hand, he entered into the heavenly holy of holies. In this entry into heaven, his sacrifice bridged time and eternity, earth and heaven, this age and the future age. His sacrifice remains eternally present, before the heavenly throne of grace (Heb 4:16) and it takes the form of continual intercession. This intercession provides us with the great assurance that God is truly 'for us' (Rom 8:31). We are dealing with the God who 'did not withhold his own Son but gave him up for all of us' (v 32). This Son is none other than Christ Jesus 'who died, yes, who was raised, who is at the right hand of God, who indeed intercedes for us' (v 34).

His intercession goes on
The ongoing reality of the priestly intercession of Jesus is the most satisfactory key for understanding the great prayer which has come to be called his 'priestly prayer' (Jn 17). In the gospel of John, it is not presented as the prayer of Christ in agony or of the dying Christ. It is the prayer of the Son who somehow is already in the realm of the Father's glory and who somehow is outside of the limitations of time. It expresses all the confidence of a person who has won the victory. Into his intimate communication and intercession with his Father, he draws his disciples and indeed all those 'who will believe in me through their word' (v 20). The lan-

guage has echoes of the priestly and sacrificial language which describes the mission of the Son whom 'the Father has sanctified and sent into the world' (Jn 10:36). Jesus prays that his disciples would be sanctified in that special 'truth' which is the word spoken by his Father (Jn 17:17); in his own continual sanctifying of himself, they too would be sanctified (v 19). All this work of sanctification and intercession makes Jesus fully suited to be at the same time the great intercessor, the great advocate, the great atoning sacrifice with the Father (1 Jn 2:1). It is in this position in heaven that he is the support and encouragement of all those who encounter difficulties on their journey to the Father. The courage of those trying to witness to Christ has always come from seeing 'the heavens opened and the Son of Man standing at the right hand of God' (Acts 7:55).

More than petition

The intercession of Jesus in heaven has all the qualities that we associate with the prayer of petition. But it is far more than prayer of petition. It is the continuation and crowning in heaven of all the attitudes which Jesus had towards his Father, and towards people, while he was on earth. It is the continuation of his attitudes in his many unforgettable 'blessings' to his Father, at the Last Supper, and at other times. It is the continuation of the attitude of the one who said 'my food is to do the will of him who sent me and to complete his work' (Jn 4:34) and of the attitude of the one who said 'the one who sent me is with me; he has not left me alone, for I always do what is pleasing to him' (Jn 8:29). Out of that attitude of being fully in tune with the Father's will, he could assure his disciples that 'I will do whatever you ask in my name … and I will ask the Father, and he will give you another advocate, to be with you forever' (Jn 14:13-16). This being in tune with the will of the Father provides a vision for the whole Church of what it is called to be: a community in tune; in tune with the continual 'intercession' of Jesus in heaven; in tune with all the movements of knowing and loving and sending that are taking place at the heart of the mystery of the Trinity. The call of God to the Church is to be a community of believers in tune with the deepest desires of the divine persons, of the whole communion of saints, of the whole human family. The call to Christian unity on every level is a call to be in tune.

In tune with Christ's own prayer

It is in the Liturgy of the Sacraments and in the Liturgy of the Hours that the Church most characteristically celebrates its vocation to be in prayerful tune. The liturgy celebrated with faith and devotion orchestrates all the Church's links with heaven and earth. From an early stage of Christian history, the Liturgy of the Hours was seen to be a necessary complement to the Liturgy of the Sacraments. In celebrating the Liturgy of the Hours, the Church felt herself to be in tune with the prayer of Christ in the course of his earthly life and with its continuation in heaven at his Father's right hand. On earth, Jesus both shared in and transformed the characteristic Jewish ways of praying. He recited the 'Hear, O Israel' prayer twice daily. Thrice daily he prayed a well recognised hymn of benediction and praise. He was known to 'rise early' to pray (Mk 1:35) and to 'spend the night in prayer to God' (Lk 6:12). He prayed at great moments of decision and crisis. In the way he preached and embodied the kingdom of his Father, he transformed the accepted ways of praying. This transformation involved giving centrality to the place of the Abba, Father, and the continual seeking and asking for the attitudes and relationships that are desired by the Father. Since the kingdom of God has come (Mt 12:28) and is 'among you' (Lk 17:21), the disciples of Jesus are invited to 'pray always and not to lose heart' (Lk 18:1).

The Hours

The Christian Liturgy of the Hours is a special tuning in to this transformed way of praying, so characteristic of Jesus' prayer on earth and continued in a new form in heaven. Over the centuries, many efforts have been made to articulate the meaning of this Prayer of the Church. Nowhere has the effort been more successful than in Pope Paul VI's Apostolic Constitution promulgating the revised Divine Office (1970). With the authors of the *General Instruction on the Liturgy of the Hours,* he was aware of the continual need to shape the kind of office suited to parish church and cathedral, as distinct from the office uniquely suited to a monastic community. For both, he clearly envisaged a prayer and a worship in perfect harmony with the 'Canticle of Praise, unceasingly hymned in heaven and brought into this world of ours by our High Priest Jesus Christ' (*Introduction*). In this context, he reflected on the liturgy which 'arose within the local churches under the leadership of the priest as a kind of necessary complement to the sacrifice of the eucharist, the highest act of worship of God, extending this worship into the different hours of daily life'. Since the Liturgy of the Hours is the prayer of the whole people of God, various forms of celebration are encouraged. The important consideration is that the Liturgy of the Hours should sanctify and consecrate the different times of the day. The language of sanctifying and consecrating is strongly reminiscent of the 'priestly prayer' of Jesus Christ (Jn 17) in which priesthood, sacrifice and intercession become one. Pope Paul clearly envisaged a harmony between the readings in the Hours and the readings at Mass, a praying people in harmony with all people who have prayed the psalms throughout the ages and who still pray them, a deepening harmony between voice and mind, a praying Church in harmony with the entire community of mankind which is in various ways joined to the interceding Christ. The 'beloved spouse of Christ' thus puts into words 'the wishes and desires of the whole Christian people' which makes intercession for the necessities common to all mankind (par 8). The prayer of the Church, the body of Christ, becomes the very prayer which Christ addresses to the Father. In the Divine Office, 'our voices re-echo in Christ and his in us' (par 8). In the fully harmonised prayer of Body and Head is the source of personal prayer for the individual and the power of the intercession of a Church inseparably united to the interceding Christ.

Pope Paul saw the personal prayer of the individual as being 'nourished' by the Liturgy of the Hours. When the method and form of celebration is chosen which most helps the persons taking part, 'one's personal, living prayer must of necessity be helped' (par 8). In the process, the Liturgy of the Hours finds continual links with the 'liturgy' of life. Both keep resonating with the whole history of salvation, the stages of which are being continually highlighted in the course of the liturgical year. Out of this interlinking of the prayer of the individual, the prayer of the Church, and the prayer of Christ, comes the power of Christian intercession. The intercession of Christ and of his Church are far more than a series of petitions. They are the continual insertion of individuals and groups into the unbroken, living communication between Father and Son, immersed in the movement and love of the Holy Spirit. It is for this reason that the Church of Christ has always seen herself to be an interceding Church. The same biblical word expresses the intercessions called for in 1 Tim 2:1ff and the intercession of Jesus in heaven (Heb 7:25; Rom 8:34). Pope Paul sees the intercessions at Lauds as helping to 'consecrate the day'; he sees the 'supplications' at Vespers as following the pattern of the prayer of the faithful at Mass. He sees all three as linked with the Lord's Prayer recited, according to an ancient custom, three times during the day (par 8). He sees all expressions of prayer as part of the 'magnificent hymn of praise to God', resounding throughout the Church and united to the 'hymn of praise sung in the courts of heaven' (par 8).

In dialogue with God

Many of the themes outlined in Pope Paul's Apostolic Constitution are taken up and developed in the Instruction which it introduces. The various forms of the prayer of Christ on earth are highlighted; prominence is given to the fact that the unity of the prayer of the Church is brought about by the Holy Spirit (par 8); the praise of God in the hours is seen as a foretaste of the heavenly praise sung unceasingly before the throne of God and the Lamb (par 16; Rev 7:10); the Liturgy of the Hours is seen as a source of apostolic fruitfulness and of strength to preach Christ (par 18); the essential structure of the liturgy is seen as a dialogue between God and us (par 33). In both Constitution and Instruction, the role of the ordained person in the Liturgy of the Hours is set in context. Pope Paul emphasised the fact that Christian prayer is primarily the prayer of the entire community of mankind joined to Christ himself. In this context, he speaks of those who have 'received from the Church the mandate to celebrate the Liturgy of the Hours'. He invites those who have received sacred orders and thereby in a special way bear in themselves the sign of Christ the priest 'and those who by the vows of religious profession have been specially consecrated to the sacrifice of God and the Church' to recite the office not as a duty but as people moved to it 'because of its inherent excellence and because of its spiritual and pastoral assistance' (par 8).

The Instruction gives much attention to listing those who 'by special mandate are deputed to celebrate the Liturgy of the Hours' (par 17). Those who are in sacred orders or who have a special canonical mission are seen as called 'to direct and preside over the prayer of the community' (par 23). The many references in the Instruction to the role of priest and bishop centre on the fact that the bishop 'represents the person of Christ in an eminent and visible way and is the high priest of his flock' and that priests, united to the bishop and the whole presbyterium, 'also represent the person of Christ the priest in a special way'. Both priest and bishop pray the Hours in the name of and on behalf of the Church. For both, the Liturgy of the Hours is an expression of priestly shepherding, a source of devotion and nourishment for personal prayer, the continual source of 'a wealth of contemplation to feed and foster their pastoral and missionary activities' (par 28).

The Prayer of the Church

The close connection between eucharist, pastoral care and the leading of the faithful at the Liturgy of the Hours has a long history in the Western Church. The tendency to privatise the Divine Office and see it as the prayer not of the Church but of those in major orders, and of some categories of religious, arose out of a variety of developments in the course of history. The movements to restore its original public character have met with varying degrees of success. It will take a long time before the Prayer of the Church is fully reclaimed by the whole Church. It will take a long time before the existing format of the Prayer of the Church is fully adapted for the varying situations of the different kinds of Christian communities. There is still need for much patience and room for much experiment.

The ordained person has the overall presidency of the interceding and worshipping Church. He has a special responsibility to facilitate this work of adaptation and to encourage the formation of leaders of praying communities. It was fitting that in his Apostolic Exhortation on the formation of priest-shepherds (1992), Pope John Paul II should emphasise the need for visible witness to the links between pastoral ministry, the Liturgy of the Sacraments and the Liturgy of the Hours (pars 26, 48, 72). Pastoral ministry, especially ordained ministry, involves many relationships with the word of God and with the many expressions of his word. In the interaction between the Liturgy of the Eucharist and the Liturgy of the Hours, is a very rich expression of the wide range of meanings of the 'word of God'. The psalms of the Divine Office continually celebrate the great word-deeds of God in his creative, supportive and redemptive initiatives. The becoming flesh of the Word of God is celebrated as the Liturgy of the Hours merges with the Liturgy of the Eucharist, in which the word is celebrated at its highest sacramental intensity. The Eucharist and the Prayer of the Church that surrounds it advance 'the peace and salvation of all the world'. The person who presides at all of this in the name and person of Christ the Head is encouraged to keep creating an atmosphere in which he himself is in tune with the Church, local and universal. The Church thus becomes in tune with the rest of the human family and with the living, interceding Christ. In this great harmony, the disharmony of sin is continually repaired by the Lamb who keeps taking away all the sin of all the world. The interceding Church is one in voice with the interceding and sacrificing Christ. Petition and intercession are transformed into the intercession of Christ. His intercession is identical with his sacrifice and with his perfect praise of his Father.

George Guiver, C.R., *Company of Voices*, (Pueblo, 1988).

Robert Taft, *The Liturgy of the Hours in East and West*, (Liturgical Press, 1985).

CHAPTER 19

Hand-made

A very small child was once asked 'Why does the Catholic Church honour Mary so much?' 'Because she was hand-made by the Lord,' was her reply. Here, indeed, was the praise of God coming 'out of the mouths of infants and suckling babes' (Mt 21:16). All the feasts of Mary are celebrations of the hands of God at work in fashioning the mother of his Son, before, during and after her earthly existence, from Immaculate Conception to Assumption. In many places, the bible praises the hands of God. In a sense, the hands of God are God himself. It was the hands of God that created the universe, guided every movement of history, redeemed his people, authorised and empowered people for great tasks. In short, it was by his hands that his will came to be done and that his plans reached their destination. The same hands were at work in Mary in preparing her to be a new temple, in making her into a new temple (Lk 1:35) and helping her to give the world 'something greater than the temple' (Mt 12:6). It was the action of his Spirit in her that inspired her to say 'Here I am, the handmaid of the Lord.'(Lk 1: 38). From that moment, the hands of the 'slave-girl' of the Lord have been praying hands and helpful hands. Some of the earliest representations of Mary are scarcely distinguishable from the image of the praying person, the *orante*. One likes to think that the inspiration for two of the parables of Jesus came as he watched the busy working hands of his mother: the parable of the yeast that a woman took and mixed with three measures of flour until all of it was leavened (Mt 13:33); and the parable of the woman who loses one of her ten silver coins and keeps searching until she finds it (Lk 15:8-10). It is the same active hands that are portrayed as she tests the baby's bathwater in the Duc du Berry's Book of Hours and makes baby-clothes for the child she is expecting, as portrayed at one of the pillars in Chartres cathedral.

For the sake of his body
The 'glories' which the hands of God achieved in Mary were not

for Mary's own sake. They were for the sake of her Son and for the sake of all the members of her Son's body. In turn, all the movements of the hands of Mary, in prayer and in other forms of action, were for the sake of that body. All her journeyings, as recorded in the gospels, were to be for the benefit of others. Her journey to Elizabeth was a sharing of joy. Her first recorded action after her child's birth was a hand action. 'She wrapped him in bands of cloth and laid him in a manger' (Lk 2:7). The Presentation of the Lord in the temple led to the revelation of the thoughts of Simeon and Anna, and, later, of many other great hearts. The journey to Egypt was the expression of a willingness to go to endless pains to preserve the life of the One who came to give life. The search for her lost son in the temple precincts led to a revelation of his real identity. His first sign, at her request, in Cana of Galilee, was a foretaste of his great 'hour'. Her appearance in the crowd elicited Jesus' teaching on real brotherhood, real sisterhood, real motherhood (Mk 3:21-34). Her presence at his execution evoked his statement that indicated the breadth and depth and height of her motherhood (Jn 19:26-27). Her praying hands were powerfully active in the midst of those who 'were constantly devoting themselves to prayer' (Acts 1:14) before the great coming of the Spirit. The death and final glorification of Mary in her Assumption into heaven were the crowning of the life of a woman who was always willing to be the hand-maid of one greater than herself. Is it any wonder that we have now come to see her as the 'type' of the whole Church along every stage of life's journey? Is it any wonder, either, that in her assumption glory, which is her intimate sharing in the resurrection glory of her son, she keeps giving the Church continual signs that she is 'accompanying' all believers throughout history. From time to time, the Church has given official approval to devotional practices related to some Marian appearances. These are occasional special reminders of the continual action of the woman of the praying, caring hands, for all the members of the Church, at all times, everywhere.

The husband of Mary
The husband of Mary was a man of skilled hands. The gospel presents him as a builder (Mt 13:55). It is likely that as Jesus was growing up, Joseph was engaged in the reconstruction of the capital

town of Sepphoris. It is not fanciful to think that Jesus was deeply influenced by the skilled work of the hands of Joseph. The words in which he described his relationship with his Father in heaven must have been strongly coloured by the example of the one whom he must have addressed as 'Abba' in his childhood days: 'The Son can do nothing on his own, but only what he sees the Father doing: for whatever the Father does, the Son does likewise' (Jn 5:19). His analogies from the building world are many and impressive: the speck in your neighbour's eye and the log in your own (Mt 7:3-5); the importance of good foundations for a building (Mt 7:26-27); the story of the man who built a fence around his vineyard (Mt 21:33); the Church that he himself will build on a rock (Mt 16:18). The strong, skilled and loving hands of Joseph must have been a continual source of protection and reassurance to Jesus and his mother. This confidence in Joseph's protective hands has for many centuries been a feature of the Church's life. It has been the inspiration for the various feasts and devotions which express his patronage and protection, and the conviction that his hands, like those of the handmaid of the Lord, are always active in the Church's life.

The work of God's hands
Very basic to the Christian faith is the belief that each human person is uniquely fashioned by the hands of God and that the life and death of each of us is in the hands of God. The conviction receives many expressions in the pages of the bible. A psalmist praised God because 'it was you who formed my inward parts; you knit me together in my mother's womb. I praise you for I am fearfully and wonderfully made' (Ps 139:13-14). In the gospel, Jesus uses the image of the little bird that does not fall to the ground without the providence of the Father, to illustrate the special care that the same Father has for each of us (Mt 10:29-31). Perhaps the most powerful image of St Paul for expressing the same message is the one of the potter and the clay. 'But who are you,' he asks, 'to argue with God? Will what is molded say to the one who molds it, "why have you made me like this?" Has the potter no right over the clay, to make out of the same lump one object for special use and another for ordinary use?' (Rom 9:20-21; cf Jer 18:5-6). These are just a few of the many scriptural images to

express the work of God's hands in the shaping of the life of each one of us. The doctrine itself is a very beautiful one but it is a difficult one to believe and to accept in a fully personalised way. With our contemporary understanding of human genetics, the doctrine receives new challenges. And still, the conviction that each of our lives, at every stage, is in the hands of God is at the heart of all prayer, all spiritual direction, all spirituality, all faith, all hope. It must also be at the heart of all effective preaching of the good news. It is the unfolding of the great revelation of God as Abba, Father. It was into God's fatherly hands that Jesus commended his own spirit (Lk 23:46). Any understanding of the role of divine providence in our lives, of the interaction of God's sovereignty and our freedom, of the extent to which we are co-creators of the world with God, must begin and end with the conviction that without the continual touch of his hand, the works of human hands can become mere idols (Ps 115:4).

Imposition of hands
It is in all this context of the hands of God, and of human hands as agents of his hands, that the place of the imposition of hands in the Church's sacramental life receives its fullest meaning. The 'imposition of hands' or 'laying on of hands' is a ritualised extension of the normal gestures that we associate with the human hands. We touch with our hands, and we keep in touch with our hands. We show affection in the ways we use our hands. We give and take with our hands. We make and break with our hands. We reach out our hands in welcomes and goodbyes. We use our hands to emphasise and to give warning. We assure and reassure with our hands. We make strong assertions of approval and disapproval in the way we use our hands. Add to these the various figures of speech that have the hands as their starting point, and one can get some glimpse of what might be behind the more ritualised action of the laying on of hands.

It is not surprising that, in the Judaeo-Christian tradition, the ritual laying on of hands has had a prominent place. In Leviticus, Exodus and Numbers, the action of laying on of hands was associated with the offering of sacrifice; the offerer somehow identified with what was being offered. The meaning of the laying on of hands, in this context, became clearest on the original Day of

Atonement (Lev 16). Aaron laid both hands on the head of the scapegoat and confessed over it all the iniquities of the people of Israel (v 21). The act was an act of transference, the symbolic transferring of the guilt of the people. The variety of forms of laying on of hands in the Hebrew bible expresses a variety of ways of transferring: the transfer of blessing, the transfer of wisdom; the transfer of authority. In Gen 48:14, we have the account of Jacob blessing the two sons of Joseph. He laid his right hand on Ephraim and his left hand on Manasseh, crossing his hands. The result of the blessing would be a fruitfulness whereby his own name would be perpetuated and the two boys would grow into a multitude on the earth (v 16). Because Moses had laid hands on him, Joshua was full of the spirit of wisdom (Deut 34:9). On the instruction of the Lord, Moses laid his hands on Joshua and commissioned him for his special task (Num 27:18-23). Laying on of hands was recognised as a way of inducting Levites into office and of commissioning people for special tasks (Num 8:10; Deut 34:9). The practice of imposition of hands for commissioning people for office seems to have continued in Judaism, especially as a sign by which rabbis and official teachers were initiated into office. In the gospels, the laying on of hands is presented as one of the patterns of action characteristic of the ministry of Jesus and of his disciples: Mk 16:15-18; Lk 4:40; cf Acts 9:17. Sometimes he healed by 'laying on hands' (Mk 6:5; Lk 4:40; 13:13); sometimes by touch (Mt 8:3-15; 20:34); sometimes by a combination of both (Mk 8:22ff); sometimes by word alone (Mt 8:5-13). He blessed children by laying hands on them (Mt 19:15). The laying on of hands had a variety of meanings in the early apostolic Church. The Holy Spirit was received through the laying on of hands of the apostles (Acts 8:17; 19:6). Paul is recorded as having healed the father of Publius when he visited him and cured him by praying and putting his hands on him (Acts 28:8). When he led the disciples in Ephesus to baptism in the name of the Lord Jesus, he laid his hands on them; the result was that the Holy Spirit came upon them, and they spoke in tongues and prophesied (Acts 19:1-7).

Ordination
Against this biblical background, we come to understand something of the meaning of the Church's practice of the laying on of

hands. In some of the pages of the New Testament, the laying on of hands provides a basis for the special understanding and meaning which this ritual action was later to receive in the Christian Church. The foundation was being laid for the kind of commissioning and installation that we now understand by the word 'ordination'. Each contributed something to how we now see the sacrament of holy orders. Four of the texts are in the Acts of the Apostles; three in the Letters to Timothy. The installation of the seven 'deacons' in Acts 6:5-6, is done in the context of a laying on of hands, an election process, a commissioning, and prayer. When Paul and Barnabas were being 'set apart' for missionary work, the prophets and teachers, after fasting and prayer, laid their hands on them and 'sent them off' (Acts 13:2-3). The word used to describe the appointment by Paul and Barnabas of elders in Acts 14:23 is literally translated 'to elect by raising of hands'. The 'appointing' was accompanied by prayers and fasting and a form of profession of faith. The coming of the Holy Spirit and the speaking in tongues and prophesying in Acts 19:6 came after a laying on of hands by Paul. The First Letter to Timothy speaks of the gift that was given him 'through prophecy with the laying on of hands by the council of elders' (4:14). The context highlights Timothy's role in relation to the 'ministry of the word' (v 13). Later in the letter, there is a caution against laying hands too quickly on any man (5:22). The Second Letter to Timothy envisaged the gift given by the laying on of hands as a spark that must be fanned into a flame (1:6).

By the beginning of the third century AD, the ritual laying on of hands combined with prayer had become the universal, or almost universal, way of 'ordaining' bishops, presbyters and deacons. The practice has continued over the centuries. The action was performed, with variations in the details of both practice and interpretation, in different churches. Some variations in the understanding of the centrality of the imposition of hands in the sacrament of holy orders led to the authoritative declaration by Pope Pius XII, in 1948, that the essential ritual action in the sacrament of holy orders is the imposition of hands by the ordaining bishop. In the reforms of the Second Vatican Council, the imposition of hands by a priest was emphasised in the new rites of reconciliation and anointing of the sick. The imposition of hands had already been prominent in the sacrament of confirmation as the sacrament of the post-baptismal giving of the Holy Spirit.

Sacrament of hands

It could be said that the sacrament of holy orders is the sacrament of hands. It is conferred by the imposition of hands. It is conferred on those whose ministry is largely one of the use of hands. In the celebration of the eucharist, this involves a special taking, blessing, breaking and giving. The anointing of hands in priestly ordination is related to the same actions. The imposition of hands at ordination is clearly a mandate, an authorisation and empowering, to act 'in the name and person of Christ the Head'. It also gathers into one sacramental action all the symbolism of the action of God's hands and the many forms of the laying on of human hands that have become part of the rich heritage of the Judaeo-Christian tradition. To receive and to give blessing, healing, and reconciliation is part of the call of every Christian at baptism. To help promote this baptismal call, the hands of God give a further energy to those on whom hands are laid at ordination, for a mission of blessing, healing, reconciling and of fashioning a new creation, in communion with the Son of the handmaid of the Lord.

Kenan B. Osborne, OFM, *Priesthood*, pp 70-75.

'Imposition of Hands', *New Jerome Biblical Commentary*, Index, p 1450.

CHAPTER 20

Anointed and anointing

Christians are an anointed people. The name that stayed with them was not the name of Jesus but a name that interpreted his mission, the name of Christ, the anointed one. In announcing his mission, in his first great synagogue appearance, Jesus identified with the anointed, prophetic figure upon whom the Spirit of the Lord would come, in the last days, anointing him to bring good news to the poor, to proclaim release to captives and recovery of sight to the blind, to let the oppressed go free, to proclaim the year of the Lord's favour (Lk 4:18-19). This coming on him of the anointing Spirit had already been signalled at his baptism, when the heavens were torn open and the Spirit descended on him like a dove (Mk 1:10). By the power of the same Spirit, the group of twelve were to be involved in his own mission, proclaiming that all should repent, as well as anointing with oil and curing many who were sick (Mk 6:13). Towards the end of his public ministry, his kingly, messianic status was somehow recognised by the woman who insisted on anointing him on the head with a very precious unguent (Mk 14:3-9). By the same action, she was preparing him for his burial. Far from disapproving of such prodigality, he assured the questioning onlookers that what the woman had done would be told in remembrance of her, wherever the good news is proclaimed in the whole world (Mt 26:13). In his post-resurrection preaching, Peter highlighted the main aspects of the public ministry of Jesus: how God had anointed this Jesus of Nazareth with the Holy Spirit and with power, and how he went about doing good and healing all who were oppressed by the devil, 'for God was with him' (Acts 10:38). Peter saw the raising of Jesus from the dead as the full authentication of the anointing which he had received at his baptism and at the beginning of his public ministry.

Basic symbols
The ritual of anointing is one expression of the basic human action of pouring out in a way that affects or transforms a person or an

object. Anointing with oil had a particular prominence in the ancient Near East. In the Hebrew world, anointing with oil could have both religious and secular connotations. The meaning of anointing in religious contexts was closely linked with its meaning in secular usage. Oil expressed strengthening and energising (Ps 109:18). Oil suggested healing and the restoration of health, as is indicated in the sending out of the twelve (Mk 6:13). Oil sometimes suggested joy and wellbeing; when Jesus insisted that his disciples should not be demonstrative about their fasting, he told them to anoint their heads as for a banquet (Mt 6:17). Oil also suggested the beautifying of the human features, as when Judith is described as anointing herself with precious ointment (Jud 10:3). Oil suggested respect, welcome and hospitality, in a variety of forms (cf Lk 7:46). At first sight, all this might seem to evoke the practices of bygone cultures, but closer reflection on our contemporary uses of, and almost dependence on, oil, would indicate that little has changed since the days of our biblical origins.

Kings, priests, prophets
In the era of the monarchy, anointing had a particularly prominent place in the installation of kings (1 Sam 16:12). The king was both civil ruler and religious leader. He was 'the Lord's anointed' (1 Sam 10:1) in a way that made him responsible to the Lord himself. After the exile, the anointing of priests, a practice already known at an earlier stage of history, became common. It would appear that what happened at the formal anointing of the king was transferred to the installation of the high priest. The anointing was extended to altars and to other objects associated with worship. There is also evidence that some prophets were anointed, in a way that was some way related to the anointing of kings (1 Kgs 19:16). The prophetic 'anointing' described in Is 61:1-3, which was the setting in which Jesus placed his own mission (Lk 4:16-19), suggests a special action of God's Spirit empowering both the prophet and those who heard him to be transformed by the action of the word of God.

The royal anointing, the priestly anointing, and the prophetic anointing converged in the person and ministry of Jesus. He was both the anointed one and the anointing one. In turn, his disciples were to be the nucleus of the messianic community who themselves would be the anointed ones and the anointing ones. Over the centuries, the various secular and religious meanings of anointing were drawn on, as the full meaning of the mission of the Church was unfolded. The Church has come to see herself as having a mission of strengthening, of healing, of joy-giving, of beautifying, of showing respect and esteem. The symbolism and the reality of anointing have been drawn on in a great variety of ways. Sometimes the emphasis has been on the figurative meaning of 'anointing', the various outpourings of God's Spirit on the Christian people. More often, the emphasis has been on the actual use of oil, in its being poured out at various key moments in the Church's sacramental life.

Three oils
We have become used to three kinds of sacramental oil, corresponding to the different emphases in the symbolic action: the oil of catechumens, the oil of the sick, and the oil of chrism.

The oil of catechumens, for both infant and adult, is used in a context which evokes the anointing of athletes and the providing of strength and energy for life's combat. Ideally, at least in the initiation of adults, there is envisaged an anointing which affects the whole body and is localised at least in breast and hands (*RCIA* par 194). There is a recognition of the need of God's exorcising action and of his helping and strengthening action along life's journey.

The oil of the sick is used for announcing and celebrating the good news for the sick, as expressed in the Letter of St James (5:14-15). The message there is not about the therapeutic qualities of oil, which were well-known in the ancient world. The emphasis is rather on the anointing done in the context of faith, in the name of the Lord. There is an inseparable connection between the Lord's name, faith in him, anointing, prayer, the forgiving of sins, and the multiple saving action of the Lord who has the power to raise people up. The possibility of physical healing is to be seen within that context. The celebration of the sacrament of the anointing of the sick is a strong point of contact between the mission of the whole Church and the particular mission of ministerial priesthood.

The oil of chrism is used in the sacraments of baptism, confirmation, and holy orders. In each of these three sacraments, there is a symbolic sealing action of the Holy Spirit, related to the conferring of what came to be called the sacramental character. Baptism is conferred in the name of Father, Son, and Holy Spirit. In confirmation, the essential words are 'be sealed with the gift of the Holy Spirit'. The gift of the Spirit in holy orders is for the upbuilding of the community initiated by baptism and confirmation.

All the sacramental anointings are for the well-being and growth of all the members of the kingly, priestly, and prophetic people. This is the significance of one of the changes in Church practice since the Second Vatican Council. To emphasise that the sacramental oils should be easily obtainable, it is no longer necessary that the oil should be from the olive, or that the chrism should contain balsam; the oil can now be that which derives from various plants, and, instead of balsam, it is sufficient to use perfume additives with a pleasing fragrance. In the same spirit, there is a growing use of plant oils and various perfumes in the context of some prayer services and the celebration of sacramentals. It is one way of expressing that, for the worship of God, we should continually draw on what the earth gives abundantly and what human hands make.

Anointing and ordination

For many centuries, anointing with chrism has been part of the ordination rite in the Catholic Christian tradition. Bishops are anointed on the head; priests are anointed on the palms of the hands that will be so much part of their ministry. In the presbyteral ordination, the anointing is accompanied by a prayer that the priest be preserved to sanctify the people and to offer sacrifice; in the anointing of the bishop, God is asked to pour out on him the oil of mystical anointing. The anointing is less emphasised now than in the ordinations in some previous ages. What is less well recognised is that anointing did not become a regular part of presbyteral ordination until the seventh or eighth century. It would appear that it was introduced in the Franco-Germanic churches along with the clothing and the handing over of the instruments that expressed authority. In the Roman Church, this practice merged with an understanding of priesthood that saw strong connections with the priesthood of Aaron, which, in turn, gave prominence to the clothing with vestments and to anointing. All of this led to a way of anointing in the sacrament of orders that shifted emphasis from the outpouring of God's Spirit to the performance of a rather elaborate ritual.

It is understandable that in the recent simplification and renewal of the rites of ordination, there should have been a diversity of views about the place of anointing. The decision eventually arrived at was to continue with the practice of anointing, but in a way that is clearly secondary to the imposition of hands and the accompanying prayer. Whatever about its Aaronic or medieval political overtones, it is good that anointing should still have a clear place in the sacrament of ordination. It links priestly ministry very directly to the whole mission and ministry of Christ, the anointed one. It is a highlighting of the fact that priestly ministry exists to bring further strength, healing, joy, beauty and dignity into the life of all the members of the Body who were themselves anointed in the messianic community at baptism and confirmation, and who all have a saving mission to the whole human family.

The Ministry of anointing

Priestly ministry is for the anointing of the whole body of Christ. Over the centuries, Christians have expressed a diversity of attitudes towards the human body. In some of their ascetical practices and in some of their ways of treating the body, there have been suggestions of a certain hostility to and suspicion of the body. On the other hand, Christians have often taken unpopular stands in emphasising the dignity and beauty of the human body, at conception and at all the stages leading up to and including death; and, after death, there is a very strong epxression of respect for the visible remains of the human person. The apparent contradictions in the Christian approaches to the human body arise out of the realisation, on the one hand, of its fragility and weakness, and, on the other hand, of its glorious destiny as expressed in the doctrine of the resurrection of the body. This variety of facets of the mystery of the human body are captured in the first letter of St Paul to the Corinthians. The implications of the letter are that in the continual reality of both its fragility and its seeds of glory, the body needs the ongoing anointing that links it with the full mystery of Christ, the anointed one.

Priestly ministry provides a continual anointing for the kingly people. Jesus came proclaiming the kingdom, the reign of God. This reign of God is a continual call to a new set of attitudes, a new set of relationships. These attitudes and relationships are epitomised in the beatitudes, both in the more 'social' colouring of Luke's version, and the more 'spiritual' setting of Matthew's version. For Christians today, the living of the beatitudes often makes demands that lead in a direction opposite to that of the prevailing values and culture. To live in this tension, every believer needs a continual anointing, figurative and ritualised, that draws its strength and meaning from the Lord who is the source of all anointing.

Priestly ministry provides a continual anointing to enable Christians to exercise their baptismal priesthood. The whole priestly people is called to offer a daily sacrifice of praise to God, in their bodies, in their lives. The anointing of those in ordained ministry is not done for the private good of the ordained persons, but for the well-being of the whole body of Christ and for building it up. The ordained person is empowered and authorised for a ministry which enables all the baptised to keep their eyes fixed on the one high priest who continually looked towards his Father and became the source of all effective priesthood.

Priestly ministry provides a continual anointing for prophecy. Each of the baptised is called to be a prophetic person. The prophet voices the will of God. The prophet experiences God in his or her own life and communicates that experience to others in a way that calls for a change in their way of living. In this, the prophet's message becomes a source of new life and energy, inviting people to a gospel lifestyle. When the gospel is proclaimed in a way that bears the marks of the one who was anointed to preach the good news (Lk 4:18), the hearers are anointed with a new strength, new healing, new joy, new beauty, new dignity.

Priestly ministry provides a continual anointing by the Holy One, who is the source of truth and of knowledge (1 Jn 2:20). It gives people the assurance that they are 'anointed with the truth'. This is due to the work of the Paraclete who guides people into all the truth (Jn 16:13); what the Paraclete teaches is what Jesus taught (Jn

14:26). The truth into which Jesus and his Spirit lead us is not a set of abstract propositions but rather the personal revelation of the Father in Jesus who is 'true' God and 'true' man. It is the truth that expresses the qualities of the God of the covenant who revealed himself in his loving kindness and in his being fully true to what he had promised.

The Church of Christ has, over the centuries, built up a impressive corpus of true doctrine. This must be continually taught and preached. But perhaps the more urgent call of truth today is to the truth that is embodied in persons, the truth that manifests and authenticates itself in the beauty of a life well and fully lived. For this, there is need of much anointing. For the Christian, who is christened in the name of the anointed one, there is only one authentic source and fountain of this anointing. That source can never dry up.

James L. Empereur, SJ, 'Anointing', in *The New Dictionary of Sacramental Worship*, ed. P.E. Fink (Gill and Macmillan, 1990).

'Anointing' in *The New Jerome Biblical Commentary*, Index, p 1435.

CHAPTER 21

In partnership with God

We have only one priest. He has offered his sacrifice once-for-all (Heb 9:26). This sacrifice is perfect and it makes people perfect (10:14). And still we speak of a priestly people. We describe their ordained leaders as priests. We continue to speak of offering the sacrifice of the Mass. This tension of language is only one expression of the apparent contradictions that arise when we try to describe the partnership between human beings and God in all that concerns the shaping and perfecting of the universe. The partnership could be said to have begun when God took counsel within God's self and decided to make human beings 'in our image, according to our likeness' (Gen 1:26). This decision by God has been interpreted in various ways over the centuries. An interpretation which has received much acceptance sees it as an aspect of God's command to the human beings to 'fill the earth and subdue it' (v 28). The ensuing partnership has been expressed in such daring words as 'pro-creation' and 'co-creation'. These underline the inseparable interplay between God's activity and human activity at every stage of the development of human beings and of the the universe, and in the re-creation of the universe that was set in motion by the coming of Jesus Christ. In the course of the centuries, there have been many attempts to formulate the nature of the divine-human partnership. Any reflection on what has been the human contribution to the working out of the divine plan makes it clear that God has left much scope for the inventiveness of human minds and human hands. Indeed, it would appear that God has allowed himself to be powerless unless he receives some forms of human cooperation. Only when we find ourselves thinking in terms of human beings improving on, adding to, completing, the work of God, do we know that we are beginning to see ourselves as somehow competing with God rather than as being his fellow-workers.

Controversies
Over the centuries, two sets of controversies tested the ability of Christians to image the God-human partnership. One arose within the Catholic schools of theology. Its main focus was on reconciling the total sovereignty of God and the autonomy of human beings in their freedom. In this controversy, one approach emphasised human autonomy in the making of decisions. The other stressed that God is the principal cause of everything that happens, even the most free aspects of human decisions. The debate still continues, under new forms and with new names. The second set of controversies highlighted other aspects of the divine-human relationship. A major issue at the time of the Reformation was how a human being could take any credit before God for anything affecting human salvation. A vigorous resistance was expressed by some reformers to any suggestion that the human being could take any initiative in anything that concerned salvation. This was at the back of many of the stands taken on 'faith alone', 'grace alone', 'scripture alone'. It was very central to the many disputes about salvation, atonement, justification, sanctification. It very much coloured the Reformation controversies on priesthood and sacrifice. Any suggestion that the priesthood of Christ could in any way be amplified by ordained priests or that his sacrifice could in any real sense be repeated in any form of human ritual was strongly resisted.

The many questions that arose and arise about the divine-human partnership can be approached from several perspectives. The mystery of the Incarnation is, of course, the great divine-human partnership that sheds continual light on all points of contact between what is divine and what is human. The God who alone saved us and saves us has always fully involved and still fully involves humanity in the very process of its own salvation. In human flesh and through human flesh, God saved and saves human flesh. In the Catholic tradition, three concepts have been used to throw light on divine-human interaction in the working out of salvation. These are: 1) analogy; 2) participation; 3) instrumental causality.

1. Analogy
When we apply a common term to describe the action of God and

the action of a human being we are always talking analogously. We are using the term in meanings partly the same and partly different. This use of analogy at the same time respects both the mystery and infinity of God and the fact that the creature, especially the creature made in God's own image and likeness, shares somehow in the riches of the being and activity of God. A term that is applied to both God and to the creature is always used in meanings that are dissimilar; but it is at the very same time used in meanings that have real similarity.

2. Participation

Reflecting on the meaning of analogy gives us some understanding of what it means to say that creatures, in a great variety of ways, participate in the perfection and activities of God. In the Christian vision of things, all that is in the heavens and on the earth is continually disclosing the glory of God. Whatever is one and good, and true, and beautiful, in the whole of creation, participates in the unity, goodness, truth, and beauty of the triune God. Whenever a human being thinks and wills in a truly human way, he or she participates somehow in God's own way of thinking and willing. By baptism into Christ, the Christian is initiated into a whole process of participating in the mystery of Christ's life, death, resurrection and sending of the Holy Spirit. This is the great divinisation that is the state of grace. The Christian life is a continual participation in, sharing in, the covenant relationship which was sealed in the life-blood of Christ (Heb 10:16-25). This covenant relationship is the basis for the continual communion and fellowship of human beings with each other and with God. This fellowship and communion is at the centre of the whole mystery of the Church. It arises out of God's gracious decision to be humanised in the Incarnation and his continuing gracious invitation to us to be divinised. It is an open invitation to us to keep participating in the life and activity of God.

It is in this context that we must see the teaching of the Second Vatican Council that the priesthood of the baptised and the ministerial priesthood, though differing essentially, are ordered to one another, because each, in its own proper way, participates in the one priesthood of Christ (LG 10). The language of participation is further developed in the Decree on the Ministry and Life of Priests. In that Decree, the sequence of thought is as follows: there is no such thing as a member of the mystical body who does not participate in the mission of the whole body; through the apostles, Christ has made their successors, the bishops, participants in his own consecration and mission; the office of presbyters participates in the authority by which Christ himself builds up and sanctifies and rules his body; since they participate in the function of the apostles, in their own degree, presbyters are given the grace of God to be the ministers of Jesus Christ among the nations (*PO* 2).

3. *Instruments*

When we speak of human beings participating in the being, the life, and the activity of God and of Jesus Christ, we must always remember that we are speaking the language of analogy. We must also remember that every human agent is totally dependent on and subordinated to the activity of God who is the first cause of all that is. In this sense, we speak of human beings as instruments of the Father, of the Son, and of the Holy Spirit. In the very refined thinking, worked out by people like St Thomas Aquinas, persons and things are seen as instruments of the activity of God in God's promoting of the good order of the universe. God is continually elevating persons and things to produce effects that reflect God's own infinite power and glory. This is particularly evident in the world of signs and sacraments – in the sacramentality of Christ's humanity, in the sacramental nature of the Church, in all the activity that is involved in the seven sacraments. In the whole range of sacramental action, persons and things are moved and elevated beyond their own power to produce effects proportionate to the design and intention of God. Like the instrument in the hand of the great musician or sculptor, the human instrument makes his or her own distinctive contribution to the effect that is wished by God. God has freely willed to keep working through limited and imperfect human instruments. As the human instrument makes its own contribution to the effect, he or she is elevated by God, the principal agent, to action that is beyond his or her own power. In the working out of his providence, we can never separate his action from the action of his created instruments. This is a reason why, as we await the Second Coming of Christ, we live in a Church that is both moving to perfection and limited by imperfection. In the meantime, the Church must keep praying that, as good instruments, all her members will be fully attuned to the continual creative action of the hands of God.

A Christian conviction

The conviction that human beings truly participate in the saving action of the one Saviour and thereby become partners with him, has been strong in the Church from the beginning. There is evidence for it at every stage of the Church's history. It received further expression in the teaching of the Second Vatican Council about the priestly, prophetic, and pastoral mission of Christ. The Council clearly presented the Church as participating in, and being a partner in, this triple mission. It presented ministerial priesthood in the context of the same triple mission. This expressed a conviction that was in the Church from the beginning. In the two letters to the Corinthians, St Paul saw his own apostolic ministry as both a work of service and an intimate sharing in the work of Christ. He is both God's servant and God's fellow worker in the Church-community which is God's field, God's building (1 Cor 3:9). He is both a slave (9:19), and a steward (4:1); he is God's envoy (2 Cor 2:17) and ambassador (5:20). He is a servant of justification (3:9), entrusted with the message of reconciliation (5:18-19). He has received the authority to build people up (10:8) and he hopes that, as their faith increases, his sphere of action among them would be greatly enlarged (v 15). Elsewhere again, he does not hesitate to 'command by the Lord' (1 Thess 5:27). The Pastoral Epistles pick up a similar imagery of stewardship (Tit 1:3) and responsibility (1 Tim 3:5).

Collaboration

Participation in the triple mission of Christ by the whole Church, and more specifically by those in ordained ministry, is not an adding to or an improvement on the triple mission of Christ himself. It is the disclosing, manifesting and application of the boundless riches of Christ (Eph 3:8) by those who continue the mission of those whom Jesus insisted on calling friends, not servants, because he had disclosed his intimate plans to them (Jn 13:15). It is a friendly service and a friendly 'slavery' to the action of the Spirit who keeps the Church in living touch with the sacrifice and intercession of Christ which continue without interruption in the presence of the Father (Heb 7:25; 9:24). In this setting, we see the source of all collaborative ministry. Jesus described his Father as still working; he presented his own saving activity in the same imagery (Jn 5:17; cf 4:34; 5:36). The call for labourers into the Lord's harvest (Mt 9:38) is a call to participate in the work and labour of the Lord himself. This is collaboration at its greatest.

Every effort to express our human collaboration with the divine persons must be done with eyes fixed on the one who alone deserves the name priest by right (cf Heb 12:2). Any time we call a human being a mediator, we must keep our eyes fixed on the one mediator between God and humankind, the man Christ Jesus (1 Tim 2:5). Because Jesus is fully at one with his Father and because he has fully identified with our human condition (Heb 4:15), any priestly mediation, any going between God and humankind must be done in relation to his priestly mediation. Jesus is continually in the presence of the Father as mediator, advocate (1 Jn 2:2) and intercessor (Heb 7:25; Rom 8:34). There he continues the works of priesthood, mediation, advocacy, and intercession, which he performed continually on earth. In a sense, his work is finished (Jn 19:30). In another sense, it continues forever, and is summed up in his work of intercession. Any intercession done by the Church on earth and by the saints in heaven is done in tune with and in the power of the continual interceding of Christ and the interceding of the Spirit (Rom 8:26).

Ministerial partnership

The priesthood of the ordained is happily called by the name of 'ministerial' priesthood. It is a ministry, a service to the priesthood of Christ and to the priesthood of all those baptised into Christ. It exists in order to promote and activate the priesthood of the entire people of God. It provides a unifying focus for the entire priestly activity of the entire priestly people. It exists in order to call forth, encourage and co-ordinate the exercise of the many charisms which the Spirit keeps giving to the Church. It is a priesthood of motivating, enabling, facilitating, and animating. It must forever have in mind the unifying and building up of the whole Christian community, the body of Christ. In this, it is an instrument and sacrament of Christ's priesthood in a Church which is itself both instrument and sacrament. The person who proclaims the gospel has the responsibilities and obligations of a person commissioned (1 Cor 9:16-18). Whatever images we use to express the meaning of ministerial priesthood, it is good and salutary to remember both the riches and the limitations of the analogous language of priesthood. It is good for the human instrument to keep recognising the source of its energy. It is good for the priest to remember that all initiatives in priesthood, mediation, and intercession are taken by Jesus Christ, the great priest, mediator, intercessor. All priestly ministry is carried out on his invitation and by his encouragement. In this it becomes a participation in the empowering and authorisation which he himself received from his Father.

To this setting of partnership between God and humankind, all priestly ministry must keep continually returning for new light, new hope, new energy.

St Thomas Aquinas, *Summa Theologiae*, l q. 105, a.5; 1/ll q.111, a.2 ad 2; 111 q. 64, a.1.

James F. Anderson, *The Bond of Being*, (B. Herder, 1954).

PART IV

Body, Blood, Covenant

CHAPTER 22

Unifying the body

We have inherited a variety of ways of thinking and speaking about the human person, about our living bodies. We use one set of words to describe our immediate contacts with the rest of the physical, material world, by sight, taste, touch, hearing, smell. We use somewhat different words to describe our thoughts, our innermost secrets, our aspirations, our hopes. In every culture there has grown up a variety of words expressing the different aspects of body, spirit, mind, heart. The early pages of the bible put it all in good perspective. In the second account of creation, the emergence of the first human being is presented as a key stage in the unfolding of God's work of creation. God is portrayed as forming the human being from the dust of the ground and breathing into him the breath of life: 'and the man became a living being' (Gen 2:7). This special 'living being' combining earth's dust and God's breath is described in various ways throughout the Hebrew bible, sometimes, for example, in terms of 'flesh', sometimes in terms of 'soul', always in terms of a mysterious unity. About two centuries BC, under the influence of Greek philosophy, more refined distinctions were made between 'body' and 'soul', but, even then, the emphasis was on the essential unity of the whole human person.

The Incarnation

The Incarnation, as the word suggests, was the entering of God into a unique and personal intimacy with human flesh: 'The Word became flesh' (Jn 1:14). The preaching of Jesus was aimed at the salvation of the whole person. He came to give not his soul but his whole life as a ransom for many (Mt 20:28). He warned against the attitude by which one could gain the whole world and forfeit one's life (Mk 8:36). He alerted his hearers to the action of the evil one who can destroy the whole person in hell (Mt 10:28). St Paul too was to be concerned about the salvation of the whole person: spirit (*pneuma*), soul (*psyche*) and body (*soma*) (1 Thess 5:23). For Paul, the body was the whole person as seen and experienced in daily existence and daily relationships. The soul was the inner principle of life in the animated body. The spirit was the human person as open to what we would today call transcendence, and capable of intimate communication with God's Spirit. The meeting place of body, soul and spirit was the 'heart' (Rom 5:5). Elsewhere, again, Paul speaks of the thinking person as 'mind' (*nous*) (1 Cor 14:14). He recognises the limited and defective human condition as a condition in the 'flesh' (*sarx*), a condition into which the Son of God has entered (Rom 1:3). In practice, our 'fleshly' existence is involved in a struggle with the 'spiritual' way of living: what the flesh desires and what the Spirit desires are opposed to each other (Gal 5:17). The ideal, for Paul, is body, mind and spirit fully integrated by the guidance of the Spirit (Gal 5:25).

Unity of the person
While it has been influenced throughout history by various schools of philosophy, including those with dualistic tendencies, orthodox Christian teaching has always managed to emphasise the unity of the human person. Sometimes this unity has been expressed in terms of 'body' and 'soul', sometimes in terms of 'body, soul and spirit', sometimes in terms of 'spirit and body'. In Christian thinking today, the emphasis is coming to be placed more and more on the unity of the whole person. In stressing this unity, there is a continual search for a language to express what happens at death and between death and the final resurrection. There is also a search for words that will do justice to the convergence of both God's creative act and the pro-creative acts of human beings in the coming into existence of each new human person. For the same reasons, Church teaching continues to give great prominence to the preciousness of every human body, at conception, before birth, at all stages through life, and at death. This concern of the Church can sometimes be a wearisome struggle. It has brought its share of opposition, of ridicule, and of downright rejection. In the struggle, we cannot for one moment afford to forget that our lofty teaching on the human body can never be divorced from our understanding of the mystery of the eucharist, of the whole Church as the body of Christ, and of the doctrine of the resurrection of every human body. It would appear that, very often, the four teachings have, in fact, become de-

tached from each other. There is an urgent need to join them together again.

The body letter

In the task of re-assembling the body, we can have no better men-
tor than St Paul. His first letter to the Corinthians is a powerful
linking of the four teachings. The letter could be described as the
body-letter, the great charter for the human body.

In the early chapters of the letter, Paul sets the scene for his teachings on the body. He invites his readers to a way of living that will
prepare them for the Lord's coming (chap. 1). He laments the existence of factions (1). He calls for a following of divine, not worldly,
wisdom, a 'spiritual' rather than an 'unspiritual' perspective (1, 2,
3). Christians, he insists, are God's temple; the building up of this
temple must be done with great care (3). He spells out the implications of his own apostolic call to be a servant and a steward (4).

The body a temple

The first great body-topic is introduced in chapter five. The community at Corinth were tolerating in their midst an incestuous
man. Paul's decision was that this man must be excommunicated
from the community for a time, to help change his 'fleshly' attitudes into 'spiritual' ones. These gross fleshly attitudes are
unacceptable in a people who believe that Christ has been sacrificed as our paschal lamb; our living and feasting must be 'with
the unleavened bread of sincerity and truth' (vv 7, 8). So there is a
kind of behaviour, especially in the area of sexuality, that is simply incompatible with the Christian calling. One should not eat
with a person who so misbehaves (v 11). The same message is
given even more forcibly in chapter six (vv 12-20). In their depre-
ciation of the human body, some Corinthians had persuaded
themselves that sins involving the body did not count before God;
sin was only in the realm of motive and intention. Paul tells them
that they have totally misunderstood the nature and destiny of
the human body. The human body is inextricably linked with the
Lord's body. Our human bodies which together form the
Christian community are members of Christ. The Christian must
make a choice as to whether he will give his body over to the Lord
or give it to a prostitute. He cannot have it both ways. The union

with the Lord is not only bodily but 'spiritual'. The fornicator sins against his own body which is not really his own because it is a temple of the Holy Spirit, bought by the ransom price of Christ's body. Out of the one new temple in which the bodies of all Christians form a unity, glory must continually go up to God. The same exalted understanding of the body lies behind the teaching in the seventh chapter on marriage and on virginity whereby one desires to 'be holy in body and spirit' (v 34). The strong teaching on sexual immorality in chapter six is transposed into the context of the worship of idols in chapter ten. This time the setting is explicitly eucharistic. Once again the Christian must make up his or her mind whether to take part in the pagan temple banquet or in the eucharistic banquet. One cannot do both. The communion and participation in the Christian eucharistic meal is a communion, an intimate sharing, in the very body and blood of Christ. The communion is a union with Christ and of Christians with each other. What began in baptism is deepened and further enriched by the sharing in the one loaf by which believers are united to Christ in an intimacy that merits the name of being made into 'one body' (vv 16, 17). Any compromise with idol worship would work against that intimacy, that communion, that common union. The clear implication is that the Christian must 'flee from the worship of idols' (v 14).

The eucharistic body

This leads Paul into the second great body-topic in chapter eleven. There were serious abuses in the liturgical assemblies in Corinth. Things had become so bad that Paul was able to say that when the Christians gathered together it is not the Lord's Supper they were eating (v 20). The abuse was not about unsuitable eucharistic presidents, nor about a wrong choice of readings and prayers, nor unsuitable venues. Rather it was an abuse that was the very negation of the essence of the sacrament of love and unity. The abuse was the divisiveness by which the slaves and the poor were humiliated. The result was that some of the rich were eating and drinking judgment on themselves; they were not 'discerning the body' (v 29). In the very celebration of the sign of the unity of 'the body', they were promoting dis-unity. By the time the slaves and the working poor arrived at the celebration of the

Lord's Supper, the wealthy had already over-indulged. This contributed to the humiliation and hunger of the poor with whom Christ himself had so much identified. The whole situation called for the kind of re-evaluation whereby people would 'examine' themselves before 'eating of the bread and drinking of the cup' (v 28). Only this way can the eucharistic eating and drinking be an expression of love rather than an act of eating and drinking judgment (v 29). Only this way can the agapé be a love-feast, in reality as well as in name. Only this way can the whole Christian community be seen to be 'the body'.

A gifted body

The third great body-topic is in chapter twelve. It is introduced by Paul with a further reminder that the various forms of idolatry are incompatible with the Christian way of life. The sure test of one's abandonment of pagan ways is the ability to say 'Jesus is Lord'. Only the Spirit makes this possible (v 3). The Spirit, in turn, gives a variety of gifts. The one Lord gives a variety of services for the good of the whole community. The one God provides a variety of activities (vv 4-6). Each person receives some manifestation of the Spirit for the good of all (v 7). Having listed some of the gifts given by the Spirit, Paul introduces his famous extended analogy of the human body (vv 12-30). The message is both simple and profound. It is simple in the sense that it arises out of the obvious unity of the human body and the interdependence of all the members, and is a call for continual collaboration and co-ordination towards a common purpose. It is profound in its endless implications for the Christian community which Paul simply calls 'Christ' (v 12). As well as drawing on the well known analogy of the 'body politic', Paul is elaborating further what he said about Christians being 'one body' with Christ, especially in the eucharist. We are dealing here with more than analogy. There is a unique organic identification between Christians and Christ who in Eph 4:15 is described as the head into whom we must 'grow up in every way', and who in Col 1:18 is called 'the head of the body, the Church'. Over the centuries, the implications of that identification have been worked out in an endless variety of ways. It is significant that St Paul's teaching on the body in 1 Cor 12 is followed immediately by the great hymn in praise of the primacy of the charity and the directives on the right use of all the spiritual gifts (chaps. 13, 14).

The resurrection body

The fourth great body-topic is Paul's teaching on the ultimate destiny of the human body in Christ (chap. 15). The basic argument is simple: Christ died, and he was raised (vv 3, 4); he is the first fruits of those who have 'fallen asleep' (v 20); in him all of us will be made alive (v 22). Paul's position is not based on human arguments for survival after death or on the immortality of the soul. It is really the continuation of what he said earlier about the body of Christ. It is a variation on the theme that what God has joined together human beings cannot separate. Our bodies have become one body with Christ; nobody can bring about a separation. The risen Christ is a 'life-giving spirit' (v 45), bringing to full ripening all the seeds of glory which he had sown in his members, and perfecting his image in them (vv 42-49). The language of sowing/harvesting and of imaging had a great biblical precedent. Paul made good use of it in his resurrection teaching. The real sower is God himself (v 38). The image that will be fully reproduced in us at resurrection time is the image of the 'man of heaven' (v 49), the 'last Adam' (v 45), Christ himself. Here we get the full disclosure of the possibilities in the words 'body', 'soul', 'mind', 'spirit' which Paul uses in such a variety of ways in his letters. Paul envisages a total transformation of 'flesh and blood' (v 50) into a body in full glory. The 'change' (v 51) will be brought about by the One who is a 'life-giving spirit' (v 45), the One who is himself filled with the Spirit, and giving full life to all the members of his body. Only he can make imperishable what is perishable; only he can make God's power work in what is weak; only he can make 'spiritual' what is 'physical'; only he can make immortal what is a mortal body (vv 42, 43, 44, 53, 54). This is how death is 'swallowed up in victory' (v 54). The swallowing up is done by the one through whom God has given us the victory (v 57).

The body is one

Christian life is one. The human person is one. Life on this earth is one with what is going on 'in heaven' and what will be brought to completion in the resurrection. Christian moral teaching, including teaching on every area of sexuality, is one with the full range of the rest of Christian belief. When this vision of one-ness breaks down, and becomes fragmented, many of our Christian positions become unconvincing. A regular journey through the first letter to the Corinthians can help unify the many aspects of the mystery of the one body. It can provide a continual incentive for ministry. Paul wrote the letter convinced of his own call to be an apostle (1:1), a servant and steward of the mysteries of God (4:1). This did not lead him to belittle any of the other ministries which, like his, were gifts of the Spirit (chaps. 12, 13, 14). Ordained ministry today is seen more and more as a gift of unifying. One expression of this ministry must be the promoting of the holistic vision of the human person as inseparably body, soul, mind and spirit. This must be done in the context of Paul's four great body-topics. Ordained ministry is a ministry of headship, in a special relationship with Christ the Head and shepherd. This headship is a sharing in the authority of Christ. More important, it is a sharing in the work of Christ as 'life-giving spirit' (1 Cor 15:45) to every member of his body. This sharing provides endless challenges for all ministry, all priesthood, because the Christian priest is the one who keeps offering up sacrifice out of the living body.

Jerome Murphy-O'Connor, OP, *1 Corinthians*, (Veritas Publications, 1979).

W.F. Orr & J.A. Walther, *1 Corinthians*, (Anchor Bible, Doubleday, 1976).

CHAPTER 23

Remembering the covenant

Preachers and teachers of the gospel are sometimes at a loss to find a starting point for their preaching or catechesis of the mystery of the eucharist. At a time when we need more than ever to remember our origins in the life, death and resurrection of Christ, it would be difficult to find a better starting point than the simple command of the Lord: 'Do this in remembrance of me' (Lk 22:19). The eucharist is the great sacrament of memory. It is true that, for some centuries, many Catholics have had misgivings about describing the Mass as an act of remembrance. There are still shades of the 'mere remembrance', for so long associated with some of the early reformers. Yet it is becoming more and more clear that in the biblical context, and indeed in every truly human context, religious and secular, no genuine remembering is a mere recollection of what took place in the past. All good remembering is a remembering with a purpose; remembering often involves a re-shaping of our attitudes; it often leads to a new programme of doing. Many great movements in history had their origin in a celebration of remembrance.

There is a growing agreement among Christians that sacrifice, memorial and sacred banquet are essential and inseparable ingredients in the understanding of every eucharist. The exploring of the riches of the biblical background of remembrance and 'memorial' was one of the most significant elements in the preparation of the joint Anglican-Catholic statement on the eucharist in 1971. A similar emphasis is seen in the Catholic/Lutheran agreement, 1979, and the Lima ecumenical statement, 1982. The eucharistic memorial is no mere calling to mind of a past event; it must be understood rather as the making effective here and now of what happened in the past. It is the Church's effectual proclamation of God's mighty acts; Christ instituted the eucharist as a memorial (*anamnesis*) of the totality of God's reconciling action in him. In the eucharistic prayer, the Church continues to make memorial of Christ's death, and, in making this memorial, the members of

173

Christ, united with God and one another, give thanks for all Christ's acts of mercy, entreat the benefits of his passion on behalf of the whole Church, participate in these here and now, and enter into the movement of his self-offering.

God remembering

In recent years, one of the most significant contributions towards an understanding of the words of institution was Joachim Jeremias' study of the meaning of 'remembering' in *The Eucharistic Words of Jesus* (London: SCM, 1966). One of his basic contentions was that, in the religious and cultic language of the time of Jesus, the formula *eis anamnesin*, 'in remembrance', was for the most part used in connection not with human remembering but with God's remembering. When God is asked to remember, the prayers and needs of his people are presented before him, with the intention of inducing him to act. His remembering consists of a display of mercy or an act of divine punishment. The important consideration is that God's remembering is never a simple remembering but, always and without exception, an effective and creating event. When the bow was in the clouds, he would remember his covenant (Gen 9:9-17). He remembers those in need by showing them his mercy; he remembers our sins by pardoning them or punishing them. Thus when God no longer remembers sin, he forgives and forgets it (Jer 31:34; Heb 8:12; 10:17). When God remembered King David and the hardships he endured, his remembering had some immediate and striking effects: he blessed the virtuous with riches; he provided the poor with food; he vested the priests in salvation, and Zion's devout ones shouted for joy (Ps 132). When God remembered the iniquities of Babylon (Rev 18:5) he performed an act of judgment on Babylon. Zechariah's realisation that God had remembered his covenant (Lk 1:72) was his joyful acknowledgement that God is here and now fulfilling his great covenant promise. When Mary praised the Lord for remembering his mercy (Lk 1:54), she was really thanking him for doing a new and mighty act of mercy. The reply of Jesus to the repentant criminal's request for remembrance was an assurance that, on that very day, they would be united together in paradise (Lk 23:42-43).

In the eucharistic context, the implications of God's remembering

are clear. The person and work of Jesus must be continually remembered and celebrated. His command that the eucharist be
celebrated in remembrance of him yields its deepest meaning if
we understand it primarily as meaning 'so that the Father may
remember me'. Since the Father's remembering is always an expression of God's creative power, the eucharistic action makes
present the once-for-all sacrifice of Christ. This is presented anew
to the Father and its fruits are applied to 'the many' (Mt 26:28).
When the death of the Lord is proclaimed, and his coming is announced and anticipated, God is reminded of his Son's work of
salvation 'until he comes' (1 Cor 11:26). God's promises have not
all been fulfilled, but our Christian faith and hope give us assurance that they will be fulfilled. The eucharist is a prayerful and
worshipful reminder to him to remember all his promises. His
creative remembering will reach its completion in the parousia, in
the final triumph of the Messiah.

Remembering actively

From the point of view of strict exegesis, few scholars would now
accept the position of Joachim Jeremias regarding the 'memorial'
words of Jesus. All would agree with his understanding of God's
remembering, but most see the words of Jesus as an invitation
directly to his disciples to remember actively the saving events of
his life and death. Yet it cannot be denied that, in the celebration of
the eucharist, God is, in fact, the principal rememberer. And our
remembering has value only insofar as God is remembering. To a
Christian searching for the meaning of the eucharistic words, it is
interesting to note that, at the feast day liturgy of meals, the head
of the Jewish family prayed 'may the memorial of ourselves and
of our fathers, the memorial of Jerusalem ... the memorial of the
Messiah ... the memorial of your people ... arrive, be seen, accepted,
heard, recalled and mentioned before you ... remember us, Lord,
our God, to do us good and visit us because of it and save us ... renewing us ... spare us.' The Passover itself was annually celebrated
'in remembrance'. Every detail of the meal was designed to make
the participants remember God's saving activity in the past, his
saving activity here and now, and the fact that, in the future, he
will fulfil all that he has up to now promised. What the people remembered was seen to be ineffective unless God was at the same

time remembering, and making his people the beneficiaries of the covenant. As the story was retold, the original experience of the Exodus was relived. The Passover was a reminder to God and to the people. Both reminded each other (cf Ex 12:13-14). As the past was remembered and made present, God was asked to bring to completion the saving work he had begun.

Making present

Though only one part of the eucharistic action is technically called the anamnesis, the whole celebration is an act of remembrance, just as it is an act of thanksgiving and an act of communion. The work of our salvation is re-presented to the Father. He remembers every stage of his own mighty works and of his saving presence to his people from the beginning: his saving presence in the smoke and the fire and the waters of the exodus; in the passover event; in the Sinai theophanies; in the Shekinah, localising his presence; in the entry to the Promised Land; in the temple where his name had a dwelling place on earth; and finally in the incarnation of his Son which is the fulfilment and culmination of all these events. In the eucharist he remembers his saving presence to his people in the new temple which was the body of his Son. He remembers all the saving actions of his Son; he remembers his passion, death and resurrection. He remembers his Son's promise to be present to his people all days until the end of the world, and his promise to return in glory. In the course of the eucharistic celebration, he is asked to remember those who are alive and to remember mercifully those who have died in the peace of Christ. In effect, he is asked to perform a new creative and saving act by which the living will benefit by his gracious power, and the dead will receive solace and joy by approaching nearer to the face of the living God.

We all remember actively

If God is the principal rememberer in the celebration of the eucharist, he is not the only rememberer. The assembled faithful are also invited to remember. This would, in fact, seem to have been the emphasis of Jesus in his 'memorial' words. It is in the eucharist, above all, that disciples obey the Lord's command to understand, to be perceptive, to have open minds, to have eyes that see and ears that hear, to remember (Mk 8:18). The worshipping community must remember all the work of Christ. And, just as

God's remembering is always an active and saving event, so the remembering of believers must bear fruit in the kind of lives they live. There is much in common between the Jewish notion of memorial and the Christian idea of sacrament. Both are concerned with making present now the saving activity of the past. By celebrating the eucharist, believers are to re-enact sacramentally the events of the Last Supper which inaugurated the new covenant. Their remembering must involve action, achieving, a keeping of promises. They must allow the saving events of the past to flow into the present. In remembering all the saving work of Christ, they must remember to do. The worship and thanksgiving which they offer to the Father at Mass must be the first fruits of their remembering, and these, in turn, must so influence their daily living that it truly becomes a living sacrifice to God. Their offering of themselves to God and their entering into the movement of Christ's self-offering to the Father must overflow into their lives.

Every man and woman involved in any form of eucharistic ministry is called to help the eucharistic community to be a remembering community. Priestly ordination is a call to be a remembering person and to lead a remembering community. A key part of priestly ministry is the alerting of people to the possibilities for remembering at every stage of every eucharist.

A programme for remembering
The eucharistic prayer, in particular, provides a rich programme for remembering.

The strong sense of the communion of saints, the sense of continuity with the Church of the apostles, and the emphasis on intercession, are part of the remembering programme in the first eucharistic prayer.

The second eucharistic prayer underlines the freedom of Jesus' choice in accepting death; it prays to the sanctifying Spirit for the gift of unity; the Father is asked to make us grow in love by the influence of the same Holy Spirit; we are reminded that the gifts we offer to God become life-giving and saving; we are reminded that even our very standing in the presence of God and serving him are a gift from God.

The third eucharistic prayer draws our attention to the fact that the victim whose sacrifice has made our peace with the Father is the victim who reconciles us with each other and with God; it is in him that we become one body in the Spirit who makes our lives an everlasting gift to the Father.

The fourth eucharistic prayer presents our memories with a panorama of the whole story of creation and redemption, and the various covenants which the wise and loving God has made with his wayward people.

The eucharistic prayers for Masses with children remind us of the continual call to all of us to become like the children.

The eucharistic prayers of reconciliation alert us to what is a crying need in every human community, daily.

Forgetting
If the eucharist is a time of remembering, it must also be a time of forgetting. Our remembering can be treacherous. Very often, what we remember we should forget; what we forget we should remember. Many Christians today are in danger of a spiritual amnesia, a forgetting of many aspects of their heritage. A well celebrated eucharist, as well as being a time for jogging the Christian memory, should be a time for true forgetting and true forgiving. Like remembering, forgetting should lead to action. Active remembering often demands active forgetting. As God remembers the sacrifice of his Son, he forgives the trespasses of his wayward family. All the members of this family, gathered to offer their gifts at the altar, should help each other to be reconciled before they offer the gifts (cf Mt 5:23). The people of God must be continually taught to have a 'grand memory for forgetting' (R.L. Stevenson, *Kidnapped*).

About two hundred years before the time of Jesus Christ, Jesus the son of Sirach wrote:

> Remember the end of your life, and set enmity aside;
> remember corruption and death, and be true to the commandments.
> Remember the commandments and do not be angry with your neighbour;

remember the covenant of the Most High, and overlook faults (Ecclus 28:6-7).

Since these words were written, the end of human life has new meaning in the death and resurrection of Jesus Christ. By the unique expression of love by which Jesus laid down his life for his friends, we have been given a new motive to set enmity aside. The death of Jesus has removed the sting from the enemy, death. The thought of dissolution can be the very makings of our hope to be 'with Christ' (Phil 1:23). The commandments have been summed up anew in the love of God and the banishing of ill-will towards the neighbour. The Most High has made a new and eternal covenant with his people and he has promised us that he will no longer remember our offences. He has given us the supreme expression of remembering and forgetting, and he has taught us how we, in turn, can best remember and best forget.

Luis M. Bermejo, SJ, *Body Broken and Blood Shed*, chap. 2.

Thomas Lane, CM, 'Remembering the Covenant', in *The Furrow*, Vol 23, (1972) No 12.

CHAPTER 24

Inviting to his supper

In the early years of the recent liturgical renewal, many Catholic Christians were uneasy when they heard the eucharist described as a meal or as a banquet. There were many reasons for this. Having been used to the very formal setting in which the eucharist had for so long been celebrated, many found that the invitation to gather round a table to eat and drink was a threat to the kind of reverence and mystery which had always surrounded their approach to the altar of God. This was closely related to what had been the characteristic Catholic attitude to the eucharist since Reformation times. The stress had been on the sacrifice which continued through all generations the sacrifice which Christ offered when his blood was shed on the cross at Calvary.

Sacrifice, memorial, banquet
In the great statements which were the landmarks of the liturgical renewal, it was made very clear that the eucharist is at the same time and inseparably a sacrifice, a memorial, and a sacred banquet. The *General Introduction to the Roman Missal* (1970) stated that the Mass is both the Lord's Supper and the sacrifice of his body and blood. This was simply drawing attention to what had always been an elementary but sometimes forgotten part of Christian belief. For long, the official name of Holy Thursday in the Catholic missal had been Thursday of the Lord's Supper; and the 'sacred banquet' had never been without a place in Catholic doctrine and devotion. In a sense there is nothing more obvious than that the eucharist is a meal. The first eucharist, in which the disciples were told to keep on 'doing this', was celebrated in a meal context, in the sign of breaking and eating a loaf, and of sharing a cup. It took place at a table, probably in the home-setting of guests reclining on cushions (cf Lk 22:12). It was in the upper room of a family home, not in a formal public building, secular or sacred. The basic meanings of eating and drinking must have easily suggested themselves: hunger, thirst, nourishment on many levels. The symbolism of sharing, communion, fellowship, was

interwoven with these basic and obvious meanings. There was an explicit invitation to take, eat, drink, with an order to keep on doing all that had been experienced in that special meal. The atmosphere of the meal was one of communion and community. All ate from the loaf that was broken and they drank from the cup that was passed round. Jesus both presided and served (Lk 22:27). The bread had all the signification which it has in human nourishment and table-fellowship. Bread is the product of the work of many hands, from the hands of those who planted the grains to the hands of reaper, baker and server. The wine of the supper was a festive drink – water being the normal drink of most Palestinians. Like bread, wine is the product of the work and the touch of many hands, from planting to fermenting, from aging to serving. When it is drunk, especially in an atmosphere of fellowship, it gladdens the heart (Ps 104:15). It is in the setting of these basic meanings of eating, drinking, sharing, that we must begin to understand the celebration of the Christian eucharist.

No ordinary meal
But this is only a beginning for our understanding of the eucharist. The eucharist is no ordinary meal. It is not just an expression of human sharing and fellowship. It is a symbolic and sacramental meal. The taking of a wafer and the sipping from a cup suggest that we are beyond normal allaying of biological hunger and thirst, and beyond normal fellowship. At the Last Supper, the Lord gave a totally new meaning, a totally new purpose, to a familiar ritual. Because it took place in a setting that we would now call sacramental, the basic sign of eating and drinking contained all that the Lord wished it to contain. What it signified was the self-giving of the Lord in the whole process of his living, dying, rising and sending of the Spirit. The Messiah was at table with his friends and declaring them blessed in their call to the supper of the Lamb (Rev 19:9). The basic pattern followed in the Last Supper was the pattern of a Jewish religious meal. Jewish family meals began with a 'blessing'. The one who presided blessed God and performed a simple ritual action over the bread; later, at least on special occasions, there were prayers and ritual action over the wine. It is in this kind of setting that the Last Supper took place. The setting evoked the whole religious story of a people. The

bread evoked memories of the Exodus 'bread of affliction'. In the light of what was soon to happen, the red wine spoke for itself. Jesus was, at the same time, host, server and food. The command to 'do this' was the ensuring of the continuation until the end of time of his very special thanksgiving and blessing that were so pleasing to God that the bread and wine became his body given and his blood poured out, as food to be eaten and as drink that would be life-giving. No wonder that the basic form of the Mass has always been that of a great prayer of thanksgiving over bread and wine which become food and drink for our nourishment now, and leading to life everlasting.

In early Christian times, this took place in the context of a larger meal, the agapé. Practical difficulties and abuses led to the separation of eucharist and larger meal. The community meal was replaced by a liturgy of the word. In the meantime, the body and blood of the Lord were coming to be understood more and more in sacrificial terms. Here was the body and blood of the one who had offered the perfect sacrifice, once-for-all. By the fourth century, the churches being built by Christians included a stone altar in the centre. An altar suggests sacrifice; a table suggests a meal; a table-altar suggests both. As we reflect on the implications of this development, it is good to keep remembering that the first eucharist took place at a table in the sign of a meal. This must always be our starting point for an understanding of the eucharist. From this starting point, we go on to appreciate that the food and drink offered at the table are the body and blood given in sacrifice. The appeal of St Paul in his rejection of idol-worship is so rich in meaning that it envelops all the meanings that Christians were in time to find in the mystery of the table-altar: 'The cup of blessing which we bless, is it not a communion in the blood of Christ? The bread which we break, is it not a communion in the body of Christ? Because there is one bread, we who are many are one body, for we all partake of the one bread' (1 Cor 10:16-17).

The Jewish setting

In our continual search into the meaning of this communion in body and blood, in this unique meal, we can get much help from recalling the religious meals with which Jewish people were familiar at the time of Jesus and in exploring the significance of some of the meals in which he himself participated. In the Jewish world, every meal had a religious character. The meal celebrated both communion with God and the many ties that link human beings with each other; both of these forms of communion were given new meanings by the Exodus events. There were two related traditions about the covenant of Sinai; one emphasised that this agreement, this contract, was concluded in blood, in a kind of rite of consanguinity; the other emphasised the covenant meal. In the desert journey, the experience of the manna from the heavens and the water from the rock left a profound impression, both as a sign of God's presence and as a testing of faith. The gospel accounts of the beginnings of the Christian eucharist pick up the message of both the manna and the water. The extent to which the Last Supper followed the ritual of the Passover meals remains a debated question. The three synoptic gospels, especially Luke, follow the Passover framework. John locates the Last Supper on the day before the Passover meal. Paul simply says 'on the night when he was betrayed' (1 Cor 11:23). In all the accounts, the great Passover themes and motifs come alive. In the original Exodus, the Passover meal helped to interpret what God was doing for his people. As the Passover continued to be celebrated over the centuries, it unfolded new meanings in all its stages of eating, drinking, blessing. The Last Supper was the celebration of the new Exodus. Every stage, every action of the meal was given a new meaning by the one who was at the same time, host, servant and food. As with the Passover, what God did in the past, he was doing again, and more. Everybody at the supper was going forth from a new Egypt. With the various blessings and takings of food and drink, Jesus was establishing the new covenant. Instead of the 'bread of affliction' and the cup of the covenant, he gave the bread of his own body, and the cup of his blood, and he invited all present to a full communion, a fully shared life, in both.

Gospel meals
Each of the meals of Jesus recorded in the gospels discloses something of the meaning and significance of the great eucharistic meal. In the multiplication of the loaves, Jesus was already preparing his disciples for food that is greater and more lasting. In John, this takes the form of a direct appeal not to labour for 'the

food which perishes, but for the food which endures to eternal life' (Jn 6:27). In Mark, it is part of the instruction to the disciples who were slow in perceiving and understanding (8:14-21). In both, the disciples were being prepared more and more for a eucharistic interpretation of the multiplication event. The miracle at the Cana meal was the first of the 'signs' of Jesus (Jn 2:11). For John it was inseparably linked with the blood and water from the side of Jesus when his hour eventually came on Calvary and with the fulfilling of the promise to give 'food which endures to eternal life' (Jn 2:4; 6:27; 19:34). The meal in the house of Matthew (Mt 9:10-13), turned inside out the meaning of words like 'friends', and people of 'good reputation'. It was a good anticipation of the giving to drink of the blood 'poured out for many for the forgiveness of sins' (Mt 26:28). The meal in the house of Simon the pharisee (Lk 7:36-50) becomes a time of love that leads to repentance and forgiveness, in an atmosphere of deep questioning. At the meal in the house of Martha and Mary (Lk 10:38-42), the ability to listen and make space for the Lord is shown to be the key to true brotherhood, sisterhood, service. The meal in the house of the pharisee on the Sabbath Day (Lk 14:1-6) becomes a lesson in the primacy of human need over law. In the Bethany meal in the house of Simon the leper (Mt 26:6-13; Mk 14:3-9; Jn 12:1-11), there is a meeting of the themes of anointing, serving, betrayal, dying, rising. Other events which reveal a deep meaning in the very human context of eating and drinking were the raising of the daughter of Jairus (Mk 5:43), the healing of Simon's mother-in-law (Mk 1:29-31) and the reception in the home of Zachaeus (Lk 19:1-10). The meals at which the disciples 'ate and drank with him after his resurrection from the dead' (Acts 10:40-41) were at the same time celebrations of deep fellowship and a further 'revealing' of Jesus to his disciples (Jn 21:14).

He took, he blessed, he broke, he gave

With such a wealth of meaning in the eucharistic meal which contains what it signifies, namely the sacrifice of Christ our Passover, there is need for a continual search for ways of gathering together the implications of all that is signified. There is no better starting point than the pattern which Jesus followed 'while they were at supper' – he took, he blessed, he broke, he gave. These remain the programme for every liturgy of the eucharist. In the four actions, all the faithful are involved in various ways. To unify and integrate them is a special responsibility of the priest-president, in his role as maker of sacramental unity. After the completion of the 'liturgy of the word', he continues to proclaim the word in sacramental form. He completes the 'taking', which is the preparation of the gifts, with some presidential rites and prayers. In the eucharistic prayer which is the great 'blessing', he exercises his special presidential role. In addressing the Father, in the name of the whole gathering, he prays the prayer of praise and thanksgiving in which the people's gifts from the earth become the heavenly food and drink. Beginning with the Our Father, he leads up to, and personally does, the symbolic 'breaking'. In the 'giving' rite, he 'gives' to the ministers the consecrated bread and wine which they 'give' to the faithful. These presidential actions unify the sacramental expression, in a way that involves all the faithful, of the four familiar actions which Jesus did and which he commanded to be done as his memorial:

He took: At the Passover, the action of 'taking' was a distinctive part of the ritual. The head of the house took the bread and cup and raised them somewhat as he said the words of praise that interpreted the age-old ritual. The preparation of the gifts today and the act of raising them up is not strictly an act of offering but rather an act of appreciation and gratitude for all of creation as God's gift in the stewardship and development of which we are all involved. It is largely in a right set of relationships with the whole universe that the continual sacrifice of praise goes up to the God who took flesh and keeps taking away the sin of the world.

He blessed: Jewish prayers of blessing and praise were expressions of marvelling and joy for the wonderful deeds of God. There was a special quality about the informal 'blessings' of Jesus in the gospels, as when he blessed his Father for disclosing his secrets to little ones (Mt 11:25-26) and for raising a dear friend from the dead (Jn 11:41-43). All his blessings were gathered together in the Last Supper in which he saw the new Exodus at work and the great work of reconciliation celebrated. All the motives for praise, marvelling, and joy, were embodied in his prayer of blessing. These, in turn, are to be captured in every eucharistic prayer. It is in continuing Jesus' style of blessing God, which he expressed most characteristically in the 'breaking of bread' (Lk 24:35), that the Church is most distinctively herself. It is here that the Risen Lord keeps 'appearing' anew.

He broke: In apostolic times, the eucharist was associated with, and perhaps called, the 'breaking of bread'. The symbolism is obvious. The breaking of bread was a Jewish ritual at ordinary meals. At the Last Supper, Jesus broke and distributed the one loaf which he had made into his body. The sacramental continuation of this action is an ongoing sign of unity and charity in the assembled Christian family. The whole family is fed with one bread from one table-altar. The ideal is that the priest-president himself breaks the bread for the communion of the entire assembly. The practical problems which this can present must be seen in the light of the ideal. The secondary symbolism in the breaking opens up a vision of the Lord's action in taking to himself all the broken members of a broken humanity.

He gave: The basic meaning of sacrifice is the giving of a gift to God, as a sign that we belong to him and want to continue belonging to him. Gift-giving is a basic experience between friends. It is a necessary basis for all 'holy order'. Our gift to God must always be set in the context of God's continual initiative in gifting each of us, reaching out to us, and inviting us to respond. In the eucharist, Christ keeps giving us his whole self, body and blood, soul and divinity. The motivation is solely one of love. At his death, Jesus gave himself to the Father. In the eucharist, he gives himself, sacramentally, to us. He has 'ascended on high'; he has 'made captivity itself a captive'; he keeps 'giving gifts to his people' (Eph 4:8). In this continual giving, is the meeting point of all sacrifice, all memorial, all holy banqueting.

The Church is the community of those being continually invited to the Lord's Supper, the sacrament of taking, blessing, breaking, giving. The Lord himself is the one who invites. By being faithful agents of the Lord in this work of inviting, all those in Christian ministry find their truest identity.

Gregory Dix, *The Shape of the Liturgy*, (London: A & C Black, 1945).

Kevin Seasoltz, *Living Bread, Saving Cup*, (Liturgical Press, 1982).

CHAPTER 25

An approach to sacrifice

For many people, the word 'sacrifice' conjures up disturbing pictures of renunciation and deprivation. There are good grounds for this understanding of sacrifice. A genuine spirit of sacrifice will often call for a variety of forms of 'giving up'. But these express the side-effects and implications of the call to sacrifice rather than the essence of sacrifice itself. True sacrifice is an expression of praise of God, of appreciation of who he is, of a desire to live one's life in communion with him and in harmony with what he desires.

There is no one definition which captures all the nuances of sacrifice in different religions, in different cultures, throughout the different ages. But most of the words which try to capture the mood of sacrifice are very positive words. These include gift, homage, fidelity, communion, life. Even in sacrifices that involved radical destruction and whole-burnt offerings in holocaust form, what was most sought after was a harmonious relationship with the deity. In the Judaeo-Christian tradition, this search for harmonious relationships has always involved an admission of the sins that disrupt right relationships. This is why, in the same tradition, the element of expiation for sin was always a key factor in the understanding of the language of sacrifice. It is why communion with God and the repairing of the damage caused by sin have always been, and still are, at the heart of the work of a sacrificing priesthood. It is in the context of expiation and of the removal of the damage that is continually caused by sin that renunciation and the other more negative aspects of sacrifice must find their place. Every time we say 'yes' to God we have to say 'no' to whatever is ungodly in our lives. The person seeking a genuine communion with the all-holy God soon finds in his or her life attitudes and forms of behaviour that are incompatible with divine communion and intimacy and that need to be purified. It is in the desire to remove these that the more negative demands of sacrifice manifest themselves. Hence the costly and painful aspects of sacrifice.

The covenant

For those who are part of the faith tradition of Abraham and his descendants, sacrifice has always been seen as part of the covenant relationship. The covenants that led up to the Sinai covenant were all in some way sealed by sacrifice. In the covenant sacrifices there was a special emphasis on blood which so obviously symbolises life and life-sharing. The Sinai covenant, in turn, was sealed and ratified in the kind of solemn ritual that became its annual memorial at Passover time. The promised new covenant was eventually ratified in a context that had many links with the Exodus and with the Passover. In the accounts of the Last Supper, prominence is given to the sacrificial blood poured out, the blood of the one who inaugurates the new and everlasting covenant, and that is 'poured out for many for the forgiveness of sins' (Mt 26:28). It is in the light of the sacrifice of Christ inaugurating the new covenant that we must keep re-assessing every attempt to see the Christian life in terms of sacrifice.

A gift to God

At the heart of all authentic sacrifice in the covenant tradition was the desire to offer a gift to God and the desire that God would accept the gift. Behind this desire to give and to be accepted was the desire of the human heart to be purified from sin and to be at one with one's fellow offerers and with God. From the earliest days of the covenant, this spirit of true sacrifice was in danger of being overlaid by an excessive emphasis on external ritual. This continual tendency occasioned many signs of disapproval from the God whose sole concern was to ensure the right dispositions of the heart. Time and again, the prophets indicated God's displeasure with sacrifices that were ritually perfect but that did not express the right ordering of the human heart. Perhaps the strongest rejection of this mere externalism in sacrifice is in the book of the prophet Amos. He portrays God as 'hating' and 'despising' the sacrificial offerings at festivals and solemn assemblies. God is resolutely rejecting and refusing to look on what is offered. Instead he wants justice to 'roll down like waters' and 'righteousness like an ever-flowing stream' (5:21-24). It is out of strong prophetic words such as these that the call grew for 'spiritual sacrifice'. Spiritual sacrifice was never seen as a substitute for ritual sacrifice; but the prophets emphasised that it was the dispositions and motivations of the heart and spirit that gave meaning and value to the ritual and cultic actions; it was in the heart and spirit that true sacrifice took place. The only gift acceptable to God is the gift of a pure heart and a spirit in tune with God's Spirit.

The sacrifice of God's servant

The stipulations for sacrifice in the book of Leviticus (chap. 16) provided some inklings of the possibility of vicarious sacrificial offering. On the great annual Day of Atonement, the priest laid his hands on the scapegoat and confessed the sins of Israel; the scapegoat, laden symbolically with Israel's sins, was driven into the desert. But the scapegoat was not seen as vicariously atoning for Israel. However, this yearly experience was to throw some light on the figure in the four songs of the Suffering Servant in Second Isaiah (42:1-4; 49:1-6; 50:4-9; 52:13-53: 12). The identity of this suffering servant has always been a matter for debate. The composite picture of the servant, emerging from the four songs, came to find a striking expression in the person and mission of Jesus Christ. The accounts of his suffering and dying have many echoes of the servant songs (e.g. Mt 26:28; Mk 10:45; 14:24; Lk 22:20-27; 1 Cor 11:23-25). His offering of himself had all the requirements of spiritual sacrifices as desired by the prophets, as did the complete letting go of his own body that allowed all his life-blood to be 'poured out for many' (Mt 26:28). When the death of Jesus is seen at the same time as the offering of the Suffering Servant (Is 53:10 ff) and the sacrificing of the Paschal Lamb (1 Cor 5:7; 1 Pet 1:19) we have the fulfilling of all the prophetic promises of a new covenant, to be written in the heart and, literally, coming out of the heart. In the apostolic writings this provides a framework for the meaning of the death of Jesus. His sacrificial death achieves atonement for sins (Rom 3:24ff) and reconciliation between us and God (2 Cor 5:19ff; Col 2:14). Of the many references to the sacrificial blood of Jesus, perhaps the key text is St Paul's description of the sharing of the eucharistic cup as a sharing in the living and life-giving blood of Christ (1 Cor 10:16). In the letter to the Hebrews, all the sacrificial themes are gathered together in the use of the extended typology of the Day of Atonement. The high priest of 'the good things that have come' (9:11) has entered, once for all, into the holy place. He has brought his own blood. He has obtained eternal redemption. He has offered himself through the eternal Spirit. He is the mediator of a new covenant. He has removed sin by the sacrifice of himself (v 14).

In body and spirit

The sacrifice of Jesus was the perfect spiritual sacrifice. It was also the perfect bodily sacrifice, costing all his body and all his blood. In his body and in his Spirit, Jesus kept offering a perfect gift, a perfect sacrifice to his Father. His teaching on sacrifice was totally in line with the teaching and aspirations of prophets like Hosea (6:6). He desired 'mercy, not sacrifice' (Mt 9:13; 12:7). From his teaching and example, his disciples were to distil an attitude to sacrifice that would do justice to both its 'spiritual' and the 'bodily' aspects. St Paul appealed to his readers to present their bodies 'as a living sacrifice, holy and acceptable to God, which is your spiritual worship' (Rom 12:1). It is in the same perspective that the letter to the Hebrews calls for the continual offering of 'a sacrifice of praise to God' (13:15) and recognises as pleasing sacrifices the various fruits of human lips and the actions of human hands (v 16). According to the letter to the Ephesians, the source of and inspiration for all Christian loving is the death of Christ who 'loved us and gave himself up for us, a fragrant offering and sacrifice to God' (Eph 5:2).

The eucharistic sacrifice

In the early Christian centuries, the idea of the Christian life as a 'spiritual sacrifice' and a 'sacrifice of praise' was further developed. All true witnessing to Christ was recognised as in some way an expression of sacrifice, but this was uniquely true of the witnessing which was called martyrdom and which drew on all the resources of body as well as spirit. The source of all Christian sacrificing was seen to be the saving death of Christ, but it was not till the third century that the eucharist came to be described in explicitly and consistently sacrificial terms. In the ordination ritual of Hippolytus, there are clear indications that the bishop, and already to a certain extent the presbyter, is seen as a person ordained to offer sacrifice. At about the same time, St Irenaeus was describing the eucharist in sacrificial language. This language was taken up by many of the fathers of the Church. Some of these emphasised the language of spiritual sacrifice. Others were more explicit in applying to the eucharist the sacrificial categories of the Hebrew scriptures. Throughout the Middle Ages, the eucharist came to be more and more described in sacrificial categories. In the Reformation controversies, the sacrificial nature of the Mass became a central issue. The Council of Trent defined that the Mass is a propitiatory sacrifice, not a mere commemoration of the sacrifice of Calvary; it is a true sacrifice in its own right; it is offered for the living and the dead; it is a true representation of the sacrifice of Calvary; the victim and priest are the same as at Calvary, the mode of offering being different; it is not a new sacrifice; it is not a repetition of Calvary; it is a true memorial.

The description of the Mass as a propitiatory sacrifice touches on all the debated questions about the nature of redemption and justificiation. Much of the Reformation controversies took as their starting point the teaching of St Paul that as sinners we are justified by God's grace as a gift, 'through the redemption that is in Christ Jesus, whom God put forward as a sacrifice of atonement by his blood' (Rom 3:25; cf 4:25; Heb 10:12-14). In all of St Paul's teaching about redemption and justification, he was clear that, in God's designs, the only effective way of dealing with sin and the network of evils and broken relationships that are the result of sin, is in the redemptive blood of God's Son. In the Reformation controversies and in the related ones that continue till the present day, there has been a growing dissatisfaction with any understanding of propitiation as human beings attempting to placate and appease an angry God. There has been a growing acceptance of the idea of the process of expiation being the action of a loving God reaching out to purify and re-orientate a people who had become defiled and disorientated. Every aspect of this expiation is seen as done on the initiative not of human beings but of God. By this initiative, he turned into a saving act the decision of humans to crucify his Son. The result is the great at-one-ment. The sacrifice of atonement which God put forward in the blood of Jesus (Rom 3:5) took place on the very mercy-seat on which Jesus the high-priest presented his perfect offering to his Father in the heavenly Holy of Holies (cf Hebr 2:17; 9:12; 1 Jn 2:2; 4:10). God's initiative in atonement is essentially the same as is his initiative in all the process of human justification and sanctification.

A memorial sacrifice
The sacrificial nature of the eucharist has been a topic on the agenda of most of the ecumenical discussions of the past few decades.

Contrary to many expectations, there has been general agreement on seeing the eucharist as the sacrifice of the Church to the Father. Discussion on the precise ways in which the eucharist is a sacrifice has helped to refine the emerging theological language. Any suggestion of a repetition of, an adding to or a completion of the once-for-all sacrifice of Calvary has been eliminated. Equally strong is the emphasis that the eucharist is far more than an act of human remembering. Two words provide a key to the growing ecumenical consensus. These are 'memorial' and 'sacrament'. The continual exploring of the biblical anamnesis-memorial has opened up ways of seeing how a past religious event can be made present now. Connections are being seen between this kind of remembering and the rich implications of the Christian understanding of mystery and sacrament. Already in the first half of this century, Dom Odo Casel was exploring the Church's understanding of the eucharist in terms of presence-in-mystery. In the meantime, much has been done to re-instate aspects of sacramentality that had been hidden in the Church's tradition. We are beginning to be at home with the idea that Jesus Christ in his humanity is the primordial sacrament and source of all sacramentality. In this context, it is interesting to look at the sacrificial language of the Lima document of the World Council of Churches, on *Baptism, Eucharist and Ministry*. Having described the eucharist as 'the great sacrifice of praise' (par 4), it goes on to say that 'the eucharist is the sacrament of the unique sacrifice of Christ, who ever lives to make intercession for us' (par 4). There is a strong theological precedent, in people like Aquinas and Abbot Vonier, for seeing the eucharist as a sacrament containing, effecting and communicating all the reality it signifies, namely the sacrifice of Christ. One can confidently hope that with an even more enriched understanding of sacrament today we have here a word that eventually will do justice both to Catholic orthodoxy and Reformation concerns. The Lima statement sees close connections between the sacrifice of Christ and the intercession of Christ. It envisages Christ as continually uniting the prayers of the faithful into his own intercession, so that the faithful are transfigured and their prayers accepted (par 4). It sees the eucharist in terms of 'representation' and 'anticipation' expressed in thanksgiving and intercession, in both of which the Church is united with the Son, its great High

Priest and Intercessor (par 8). This is in line with much contemporary study of sacrifice; there is good support today for understanding the intercession of Christ (Heb 7:25; Rom 8:34) not as a postscript to his sacrifice but as the continuation in heaven of the sacrifice itself. The Lima emphasis on sacrament, thanksgiving and intercession is a fine backdrop for understanding what Christians do when they gather for the eucharist. They become a people in full tune with the one sacrifice of Christ, their Head.

Who offers the sacrifice?

Who offers the sacrament-sacrifice of the eucharist? Whatever about past controversies, Christians today are agreed that the primary offerer in every eucharist is Jesus Christ offering himself to his Father. By the same action, he offers himself to his people for whom he died. As head of the body which is the Church, he draws all his members into communion with his offering. All other offering by the members of the body must be seen as a participation in this one offering. In every eucharist, the whole Christ is offering the whole Christ, for the life of the whole world. The whole Christ is offering a spiritual sacrifice, a sacrifice of praise. This sacrifice of praise has the full riches of a sacrament. In the eucharist, all the members of Christ's body are in full sacramental contact with the once-for-all propitiatory sacrifice of Christ in which his body was broken and his blood poured out. All are invited to full and active participation in this sacrifice.

It is the task of the president of the eucharist to proclaim the word of God at its highest level of sacramentality. Acting in the name and person of Christ the Head of the priestly and sacrificing body, he must proclaim the word in such a way that all the worshippers will be finely tuned to the sacrifice, the thanksgiving, and the sacrificial intercession of Christ. It is in this setting that he most fully becomes a sacrament of the one High-Priest. It is in this setting that he can best see his vocation to be a teacher of sacrifice and a teacher of prayer.

Robert J. Daly, SJ, *The Origins of the Christian Doctrine of Sacrifice*, (Darton, Longman & Todd, 1978).

Luis M. Bermejo, SJ, *Body Broken and Blood Shed*, pp 51-110.

CHAPTER 26

Character and covenant

It is part of defined Catholic teaching that in baptism, confirmation, and holy orders a character, 'a certain spiritual and indelible mark' is imprinted on the human soul. In recent years, there has been much searching into the biblical and other sources of this teaching and there have been many investigations into what the teaching is about and into the historical circumstances in which it was formulated. The word 'character' is found only once in the New Testament. It is in the description of God's Son as the 'reflection of God's glory' and the 'character' of God's very being (Heb 1:3). The text has not been much used to justify a doctrine of sacramental character, but it, in fact, can throw much light on how the baptised, the confirmed, and the ordained are related to Jesus Christ and to his Church. The word 'character' literally means a mark made by a seal, a die, or similar instrument, normally in a way that identifies or that expresses ownership and belonging. Before ever a theology of sacramental 'character' emerged, some Church fathers liked to explore the possibilities in another word for seal, *sphragis*, to help express the way the sacraments, especially baptism, affect the human soul and leave on it the imprint of God's being. They explored the meaning of the 'seal of the living God' (Rev 7:2-8), the anointing that God has given us 'by putting his seal on us and giving us his Spirit in our hearts as a first instalment' (2 Cor 1:21-22), our being 'marked with the seal of the promised Holy Spirit' (Eph 4:30).

The emergence of a doctrine

It is in the third century conflicts with the Donatists that the beginnings of a doctrine of sacramental 'character' appear. The question at issue was whether heretical baptisms should be repeated. Later, Augustine taught clearly that since it is Christ himself who baptises, the effect of the sacrament is permanent; it is not to be repeated. Significantly, he saw the invocation of the Trinity in baptism as a kind of sealing, a character. This linking of baptism, the action of the Holy Spirit, and the sealing by which Christians become the 'property' and 'possession' of Christ were to be the basis of all later understanding of sacramental character. The Donatist objections, and variations on them, concerning unworthy ministers and unworthy recipients of baptism, confirmation and holy orders, surfaced again in the twelfth and thirteenth centuries. These were to exercise the minds of various theologians and of popes. There was a growing conviction about the importance of the unrepeatability of the three sacraments. Adequate theological justification for this conviction was sought in the scriptures and in the Church's tradition. By 1439, the time was ripe for a statement by the magisterium in the Council of Florence. The statement was confirmed in the Council of Trent in 1563. In neither Council is there a developed teaching as to the exact nature of the character. The emphasis is on the fact of the sacramental 'marking' and its finality.

Many ingredients
The emergence of the teaching on sacramental character is an interesting example of what we would today call the historical conditioning that affects the expression of revelation. Practical issues in the Church's history occasioned the formulation of a doctrine that drew out of Church sources new things and old. As the doctrine came to be formulated, valuable contributions were made by the Church's most prominent philosopher-theologians. Alexander of Hales saw the character of each of the three sacraments as an ontological reality adhering logically to the soul; a 'habit' that marks the soul, disposing it to receive further grace. St Thomas saw the character more in terms of a potency, and a power by which the recipient is deputed to be active in Church worship. In the context of ordination, this was principally the power to consecrate and absolve. Duns Scotus saw the character more in terms of a relation linking the recipient with God and the Church.

Ontological reality, potency, habit, power, relation. In a sense, this is very much the language of another age and culture. It is a language that seems cold and remote. But the message that is behind each of the words has emerged in new forms in our own day. The relationship between being and doing has a lot of contemporary interest. Potency and act have been coming up in various forms in 'process' theology. The word 'habit' continues to suggest a quality that perdures through every change. Power is not a popular Church word today, but there is a great desire to distinguish the power which is the creative energy of God at work in Church from the power which is an expression of worldly domination. Relation seems to be an indispensable word for expressing the immanent life of the Trinity and the many ways in which human beings are disposed towards each other, towards creation, towards the divine persons. A new search into each of these words can disclose many riches for an understanding of character in general and for the character of the sacrament of orders in particular. A look at the dictionary list of the uses of the word 'character' shows both the nuances contained in the word and the ways in which its various uses can throw a little light on what is meant by sacramental character. These uses include: distinctive mark; distinctive handwriting or lettering; moral strength, backbone; the 'creation' of a novelist or artist; a person 'whose distinctive qualities and characteristics survive any attempts at levelling out'.

Human character, sacramental character

An interesting contemporary attempt (by John Macquarrie) at linking many of the existing approaches to the sacramental character given in ordination is the exploring of the use of the word 'character' in ethical theory. The line of argument could be summarised as follows:

Priestly 'character' must be seen not in the static sense of a mark once made but in the dynamic sense of a process set in motion at ordination and inviting to a continual growth throughout a whole lifetime. It must be seen not primarily in terms of function and role but in terms of the priestly heart, the priestly spirit. It must focus on what the ordained minister is rather than on what he does.

It is here that we can be helped by contemporary ethical theory about moral character. We have inherited two approaches to ethical theory. The first approach stresses commands, actions, overt behaviour. In priestly terms, this would tally with a functional approach to ministry. The second approach stresses virtue and the formation of moral persons and communities. This fits in well with the Catholic emphasis on the ethics of virtue, on formation on the way to priesthood, on the 'ontological' approach by which ordination is seen as affecting the inner being of the one ordained. Ideally the functional approach and the ontological should complement one another. Both approaches can be helped by the way modern ethicists see character. Character is seen by them not as a thing but as a pattern that can be traced in a person's behaviour. We recognise a person's behaviour as being 'in character'.

Character shows elements of directionality, of consistency. It is most strikingly expressed in the behaviour of a person whose life is dominated by one all-consuming purpose or direction. It is character that gives order and unity to a diversity of purposes and interests. Immediate concerns are subordinated to ultimate concern. Character is shaped and constituted by the value-judgements and priorities of the person.

Character is a process; it needs formation; it needs time to grow. It needs to be continually exercised, developed, deepened. As it develops and deepens, it expresses itself in recognisable patterns. It is never closed to new approaches, new possibilities. It recognises all the sources from which it comes. First in these is the genetic inheritance of each individual. This is inseparably bound up with one's propensities, capacities, strengths and weaknesses. This was partly what was behind the Church's instincts from early times 'not to be hasty in the laying on of hands' (1 Tim 5:22). It is also related to the contemporary emphasis on drawing on psychology and related disciplines in the selection and formation of candidates for ministry. In the shaping of character, we are further influenced by whatever happens to us from outside: the accidents of our history and upbringing, the impact of culture and the assumptions of contemporary society, and education on various levels. Then there are the active elements in the making of character, the choices we make and keep making, and then living with their consequences.

In the Christian perspective, all these ingredients of the making of character are suffused by a conviction that the workings of divine grace, in prayer, in the sacraments, in every area of human living, are a source of continual conversion and of endless possibilities in the development of human character. It is in this setting that we must see what is special about priestly character which is something fully human but also fully divine. What is specific about the priestly character is that it has its source in vocation, in the special gift of God, in the initiative taken not by the human being but by God. The call to ordained ministry is an extension of our divine election into the Church of Christ, celebrated in baptism. It is a call to a new set of relationships with Christ and with all the members of his body. In this context, the requirements for presbyteral ministry as outlined in the Pastoral Epistles could be summed up as a call for 'men of character', in whom the gift once given through the laying on of hands must be continually fanned into a flame (2 Tim 1:6).

The call of God once given continually invites the response and co-operation of the one called. The character given at ordination follows a process corresponding to all the stages of growth that apply to character in the ethical and moral context. In the person ordained, the all-consuming direction and purpose is the reign of God which lays hold of one's life and becomes the draw and motivation for everything one does 'because of the kingdom of heaven' (Mt 19:12). The response to the reign of God in the life of the person who has received the character of ordination is subject to the same rhythms of setback and growth that characterise the history of one's character in the ethical usage. In the priestly context, the growth of the character requires much of the kind of renunciation that keeps one's 'eyes fixed on Jesus' (Heb 12:2), to the exclusion of the draws of other lifestyles. The character of ordination must be continually exercised and deepened. As it is lived out in new situations, it unfolds meanings that may have been hidden when one first responded to one's call. The sacramental character involves the ordained person, the community one is called to serve, the great High Priest to whom one is configured. The living out of this network of relationships is subject to all the light and shade that are part of every human journey. But the Christian hope of both the ordained and the non-ordained is based not on human resources but on the faithful God whose Spirit is the source of all sealing, all character, and who gives a variety of gifts for the building up of the body.

Living the covenant

This contemporary attempt to keep exploring the meaning of character contains many elements that were not envisaged when the doctrine of sacramental character first emerged. But it manages to gather together many precious insights about the kind of 'sealing' that is received at ordination. It leads easily to what is the richest context for an understanding of priestly character, God's covenant relationship with his people. In this context we can best see the ordained person's permanent relationship to God the Father, to the Holy Spirit, to Jesus Christ and to the members of his body which is the Church. Again and again, God offered a covenant to his people. In each offering of a covenant, God showed the great qualities of loving-kindness, and fidelity. In his covenants with Abraham, he promised a posterity of faithful people whose numbers would be countless. The covenant of Sinai was sealed by a meal and by blood (Ex 24:1-11). The covenant was made and renewed in the intimate terms of fatherhood and sonship (Ex 4:22), motherhood and childcare (Is 49:14-15), the details of parenting (Hos 11:1-11), the husband-wife relationship (Jer 2:2).

Covenant and marriage

The basic covenant formula is inspired by the marriage formula. It is no wonder that God kept calling for new ways of drawing his people to fidelity in their covenant relationship with him. The covenant of the future would be written into the human heart (Jer 31:31-34; Ezek 36:23-38). Eventually that covenant was introduced by the one who was himself the anointed one who was the fulfilment of a personal covenant with King David, and whose mission was to introduce the new messianic age. At his messianic banquet he sealed the new covenant in his blood and in a meal, and he promised a more perfect banquet 'new with you in my Father's kingdom' (Mt 26:29). This new covenant gives a whole new meaning to the basic relationships suggested in the first covenant. The teaching and preaching of Jesus had given a whole new meaning to all the familial language of father, mother, brother, sister. It had made becoming like little children a requirement for admission into the kingdom of heaven. It had led to the revelation of the fact that God's Spirit invites us to cry 'Abba, Father'. The source and resource for all Christian marriage came to be the mystery of the relationship between Christ and his bride (Eph 5:25-33). The full flowering of all relationships would come in the celebration of the wedding of the Lamb and his bride (Rev 19:7-9). That celebration will disclose the full meaning of God's original choice of a marriage formula as the best one to express his own covenant relationship with his people (Rev 21:3).

The three sacraments of 'character' are best understood in the context of all these riches of the new covenant. Baptism establishes a permanent relationship with the Father who is lovingly kind and faithful; with the Son who gave himself for the Church and cleansed her (Eph 5:25-26); to the Spirit who does not withdraw his gifts; to the world to which Christ keeps giving life through the Church. Baptism is the first and greatest sealing, charactering, of the Christian. This baptismal sealing is the beginning and source of all further sacramental sealings. The baptismal sealing by God's Spirit is completed and further celebrated in the sacrament of confirmation. The sealing at ordination is not an extra spiritual bonus and prize for the ordained. Rather, it exists for the purpose of enabling. It exists in order to help all the baptised and confirmed to live to the full their relationships with the divine persons, with the whole communion of saints, and with the whole of creation.

Ordained ministry is carried out in the name and person of the one priest who has offered his one sacrifice, once-for-all. For this the ordained is sacramentally configured to Christ, head, and shepherd. The ordained person is sacramentally sealed for this. This sealing is the beginning of what has been variously described in terms of an ontological reality, a potency, an empowering, a set of relationships, a call to be a man of character. The God of the covenant invites the ordained to be a continual sacrament of his own loving-kindness and fidelity. The local Church which had so much to do with his formation and with his final approval for ordination, rightly looks on him as being very much their own possession and they feel right in claiming his life-long-service.

The ordained person, in turn, is confident that he is not on his own. He knows that he has been specially sealed and charactered to express the riches of the covenant that is always both new and eternal. This sealing, in turn, enables him to keep on preaching the word, celebrating the sacraments, and shepherding God's people. The awareness of his sacramental union with the Head will be a continual source of new life and an ensuring that the authority he exercises will be in the name and person of the one who introduced a whole new style of headship. The 'justice' which colours his own life and which he preaches to others will be an expression of the justice of God himself, the righteous one (Rom 3:25), whose righteousness consists of being totally faithful to the covenant. In the living out of this God-like faithfulness lies the programme for a life of being sealed and stamped by God, a life of character, a life of being God's instrument in forming and fashioning the image of Christ in all those sealed in baptism and confirmation.

John Macquarrie, 'Ministerial Character', in *The Expository Times*, Vol 87, No 5 (1976), pp 147-151.

Paul Bernier, SSS, *Ministry in the Church*, pp 135-141, 189-192, 232-236.

PART V

A Way of Life

CHAPTER 27

Living by the word

Spirituality is a search. It is a search for a harmony between the body, the mind, and the resources of the human spirit. It is a search for ways in which the movements of the human spirit can be in tune with the continual promptings and invitations of the Spirit of God. Since pastoral ministry is about face, presence, and voice, it follows that the spirituality for the man or woman in ministry must be a continual search for a face-to-face relationship with God and with God's people, a search for a more real presence on all levels of one's being, a search for a daily hearing and communicating of the voice of the Lord. If the ordained person's role is to proclaim the word of God at its highest level of sacramental intensity and to feed God's people by bringing the word into every area of human existence, then in the living out of the holiness to which he is called, in the midst of the community of the baptised, the special characteristic of his spirituality must be living by the word.

It is possible to have a one-dimensional understanding of the word of God, to regard it, in practice, as a collection of written texts to be explained and preached. The reality is that the word of God is God's continual disclosing and revealing of his innermost designs by the many deeds in which he manifests his power and the many words he has spoken to the world through such people as the prophets. God's word, in fact, is always a deed and each of God's deeds is always a word. In the economy of salvation, the creation of the world was God's original word-deed. It became the paradigm of all his later word-deeds: 'For he spoke, and it came to be; he commanded and it stood firm '(Ps 33:9). The same creative word continually conserves and directs the movements of creation: 'He sends out his command to the earth; his word runs swiftly ... He sends out his word '(Ps 147:15-18). His redeeming word came to the patriarchs and the prophets, encouraging them to shape with him a covenant people. This self-communication reached a high point with Moses when God invited him to 'hear his voice' (Sir 45:5) and when he spoke to him 'face to face – clearly, not in riddles' (Num 12:8). It was by his ongoing communication with the prophets and by his teaching them that they, in turn, were enabled to communicate God's message effectively. Thus empowered and assured by the word of the Lord, the prophets preached in a way that invited God's people to lift up their voice with strength (Is 40:9). In the words of the prophets, especially, the word of God was powerfully at work, going forth from his mouth, not returning empty, accomplishing his purposes, succeeding in the thing for which it was sent (Is 55:10-11). In the Book of Wisdom, the creative word of God is personified in the way that wisdom itself is personified (18:15). In proclaiming the kingdom of God, and embodying its coming in his own ministry, Jesus gathered in his person and ministry all that was greatest in the prophetic tradition and the wisdom tradition. He was the high point of all the word-deeds of God. In John's gospel he is presented as God's Word become human flesh (1:14). The result is that all the words he spoke were word-deeds, full of God's power. They were 'spirit and life' (6:63). No wonder that the words written down by those who were the special witnesses of his life, death, and resurrection, and by those who had close links with them, came to receive special reverence in the Church, especially whenever the liturgy came to be celebrated and the word of God proclaimed. Reformation and post-Reformation controversies about the relationship between word and sacrament are, in our own day, giving way to an appreciation of the inseparable links between the written word, the preached word, the sacramental word, the pastoral word, the prayed word. The *Constitution on Revelation* from the Second Vatican Council has helped us to revise our understanding of the 'sources of revelation'. We are seeing more clearly that Jesus Christ, 'in whom the entire revelation of the Most High God is summed up' (par 7) is the source of revelation and that the scriptures and the various expressions of the Church's authentic tradition are privileged points of contact with that one source. But even scripture and tradition taken together are not to be equated with the word of God which is always 'living and active', and 'sharper than any two-edged sword' (Heb 4:12-13).

A spirituality of the word

The spirituality of the ordained person is a spirituality of that ever-living and ever-active word. It is a spirituality of one who hears the word, studies the word, ponders the word, prays the word, teaches the word, proclaims the word at its highest level of sacramental intensity, brings the word into every area of human living, and lives the word. It is the spirituality of one who is in continual living touch with the ways in which God's word has been communicated over the centuries and is still communicated: the creation and conserving of the world, God's directing of human history, his redemptive designs, his speaking through the prophets, his wise providence, all leading to his Word becoming flesh and still dwelling among us in the many ways in which he manifests his real presence, especially in word and sacrament. The ordained person is called to live, work, and pray in the ambit of all these manifestations of God's word. His spirituality is wherever his ministry is. His ministry is a ministry of the word and to the word. Each of God's words is a present reality as well as a past event.

The task of the person in ordained ministry is the continual making of connections. He must seek to make connections between the word of God and the daily lives of people. He must seek to make connections between word, sacrament, and pastoral ministry. This must be done in continual partnership with Jesus Christ and with all those who exercise baptismal priesthood. The universe had its origins 'from harmony, from heav'nly harmony' (Dryden, *A Song for St Cecilia's Day*). The dream of God for the universe is a world in harmony, in tune. But the world fell out of harmony, in the mess we have come to call original sin. Into a world out of harmony and out of tune, the Son of God came, saying 'I am coming ... to do your will, O God' (Heb 10:7). The letter to the Hebrews gives us his programme for the only true priesthood, the only true sacrifice, the only true at-one-ment, the only true in-tune-ment:

* He walked every step of life's journey in a way that fully pleased God;

* For us, he has broken through every barrier that separates us from God, and made living contact with every level of human ex-

istence, and has led us in the journey into the innermost recesses
of the mystery of the living God;
* His sacrifice consisted in pleasing God in every level of his own
body, and by giving us all the life-blood that flows from that body;
* He has shown us the way and repaired every stage of the way, to
God;
* He has brought to completion all the partial and piecemeal ways
that lead to God;
* With our eyes fixed on him, and continually inserted into his one
sacrifice, we can in our own bodies offer a sacrifice of praise by
our lips, our hearts, and our active hands;
* Obeying our 'leaders' and right participation in the assemblies
of Christians will help keep us in tune with the one sacrifice of the
one priest.

The vocation of all those who share in the priesthood of the one
High Priest is to keep re-making, in him, the broken connections
between earth and heaven where our High Priest is. The one who
is to proclaim the word at its highest level of sacramental intensity
is in a unique position to keep searching for ways to make the connections, in word, sacrament, and pastoral ministry.

He is called to make connections between the word of God and
the complexities of the surrounding culture. The details of these
connections differ in the 'old' Christian world, in the newly freed
Christian world, in the world emerging from paganism. In all of
them, there seems at present to be something of an 'exilic' situation; Christians generally are finding that there is a thinning out of
the reserves of the inherited spiritual patrimony. In an age of spiritual amnesia, people in pastoral ministry are often finding that
they themselves have to be the Christian memory. With the in-
roads of many new forms of secularism, it would seem that we are
involved in a call for a kind of Copernican revolution in the work,
lifestyle, and prayer-style of those in ordained ministry, and in
the re-shaping of their relationships with men and women in
other forms of full-time or part-time Church ministry. And still it
is in this very exilic and secularised situation that the ordained
person must keep reading the signs of the times, that he must
learn to recognise the presence and saving action of God, that he
must see the face of the Christ who is as much the alpha, the

omega, and the focal point of this stage of human history, as he was at any other stage. Awareness of this tension between the presence of the Lord and his apparent absence will keep him ever alert to new opportunities of planting the seed of the word. This alertness will help him to keep recognising the sacred points of contact with the holiness of God in the midst of every secular experience. It will teach him that the secular world too is God's creation, and that it continually reveals God's glory.

He is called to make connections between the priesthood of all the baptised, the priesthood of the ordained, and the priesthood of our one High Priest. All these, in turn, are to find connections with the prophetic and pastoral ministry of all who share in the mission of the One who is the Great Prophet and Good Shepherd. In promoting the prophetic ministry of the whole people of God, he seeks for new ways to encourage all the baptised to speak and teach the word of God, both in the Church assembly and outside it. In the proclaiming of the word of God and the celebration of the sacraments, he comes to realise that his special responsibility for the word does not give him a monopoly of the word. He encourages all the baptised to communicate to each other the ways in which they experience the word of God.

He is called to make connections between his own direct ministry of the word and his ministry in such areas as education, politics, and cultural pursuits. In doing this, he may discover that the phenomenon of worker-priests is more than a historical curiosity.

He is called to make continual connections between the various senses in which the Church of Christ is the Church of the body; above all, to show how the mystery of every aspect of every human body, from conception to resurrection, is inseparably connected with the eucharistic body of Christ and with Christ the head who keeps giving gifts to all the members of his body, the Church. He must show, further, how the Church as body of Christ has many connections with all other people of goodwill.

He is called to make continual connections between time and eternity, between the manifestations of judgment, purgatory, hell and heaven that take place in daily events and the 'last things' that will be the definitive unfolding of God's designs.

He is called to make connections between what God had in mind 'in the beginning' when he 'created them male and female' (Gen 1) and the many ways in which the male-female complementarity is being re-imaged today in Church and society. This will demand a continual openness to possibilities of re-structuring of some forms of ministry in the Church and the kind of male-female collaboration which it will require.

He is called to make connections between fidelity to the traditional forms of private prayer, the well-tried forms of eucharistic and Marian devotion, and the kind of scriptural spirituality that leads immediately to the celebration of word and sacrament. This will be part of his making of connections between the tradition of spirituality in which he himself was formed and the new approaches to spirituality and spiritual direction that are unfolding in the Church today.

He is called to keep re-inserting all his ministry into the mystery of Father, Son and Spirit. Every light on the relationships between the three divine persons becomes a light on the mission of all who are baptised in the name of Father, Son and Spirit. Ordained ministry, in turn, seeks to advance the network of relationships that constitute the Church of the Son which is kept alive by the Spirit who is continually being sent by Father and Son.

All this spirituality of connections is unified by the ministry of reconciliation and the making and building up of eucharistic communities. In a sense, the ministry of reconciliation is the full-time work of the Church and of her ministers. It is worth noting that one single instance of reconciliation in which St Paul was involved, and which provided the context for his expression 'in the person of Christ', required the making of a number of delicate connections, involving him, the offender, the whole community, and Christ himself (2 Cor 2:5-10). This provides the pattern for all the ministry of reconciliation. Reconciliation, in turn, is inseparable from the eucharist which is the summit and source of all preaching of the word (PO 5) and indeed of all pastoral action. Here is the high-point of the many manifestations of the real presence of Christ to his Church. Every moment of a eucharist well celebrated will resonate with people's lives in Church and world.

The one presiding over it will be much more than one who recites sacramental words in a multiplicity of sacramental actions. He will be alive with the word.

A habit of mind

Ordination is a call to be a 'man of mystery' and an encourager of those willing to live and be immersed in the mystery of Christ and his Church. This demands a habit of mind and heart that enables the ordained person to 'delight in the law of the Lord' and 'on his law ... meditate day and night' (Ps 1:2); to 'pray always in the Spirit' (Eph 6:18); to join himself and those in his pastoral care to Jesus Christ whose priestly work in heaven consists in always interceding for us, an interceding that is the continual presence of his priesthood before the Father (Heb 7:24-25). The man ordained in his name and in his person must develop a way of 'centring' on that interceding which becomes the habit of mind and heart of the man of mystery, the 'mystic'. That habit of mind and heart regards what one is as more important than what one does; it allows the mustard seed grow into all one's being before it grows out to the world. Concern for the word thus becomes the all-absorbing existence of the man of mystery. In the spirit of the prophets, he will 'devour' the word; it will become the joy and the delight of his heart (Jer 15:16); he will 'feed on' the word and 'be fed' by it (Ezek 3:1-3). This will require much prayerful absorption in the scriptures, those privileged points of contact with the word of God, and in whatever helps to illumine their message. He will be at all times ruminating, always pondering, always musing, always praying, always wondering how the word can become flesh now. He will at all times try to live and act in the person of Christ, with heart, lips and hands in Christ-filled harmony with every man and woman who is called to be Christ's face, Christ's presence, Christ's voice. Every act of his ministry will be the act of one who lives by the word.

Robert M. Schwartz, *Servant Leaders of the People of God*.

Kenan B. Osborne, OFM, *Priesthood*, pp 333-337.

CHAPTER 28

Celibacy and the kingdom

The founder of Christianity was fully God, fully man. In the words of the Creed of Nicaea, he was 'eternally begotten of the Father ... begotten not made'. The same Creed affirms that 'by the power of the Holy Spirit he became incarnate of the Virgin Mary, and was made man'. His unique relationship with Mary and Joseph seems to have been lived out in a setting that was basically loving and supportive. At the time of his disappearance, the question asked by his mother was an expression of love and concern on her part and on the part of the man she called 'your father': 'Child, why have you treated us like this? Look, your father and I have been searching for you in great anxiety' (Lk 2:48). The love and support he received in the family setting in Nazareth were at the heart of the compliment paid him by the puzzled neighbours when they asked a question which needs some explanation in terms of accepted Catholic teaching: 'Where did this man get this wisdom and these deeds of power? Is not this the carpenter's son? Is not his mother called Mary? And are not his brothers James and Joseph and Simon and Judas? And are not all his sisters with us?' (Mt 13:54-55).

Changing family language

Though, theoretically, there is no incompatibility between the mystery of the Incarnation and the possibility that Jesus could have been a married person, all the evidence we have sustains the conviction that he, in fact, lived a totally celibate life. This was fitting in one who took flesh in a way that would touch and transform the flesh of every man, woman and child in the human family. But there is every evidence that he had a great respect and esteem for married life. According to the gospel of John, his first sign was performed in a marriage-feast setting. Much of his teaching is situated in the context of normal family living. On the occasion of a question about the possibility of divorce, he directed the attention of his hearers back to God's plan for man and woman 'at the beginning' (Mt 19:4) and he warned that 'what God has joined to-

211

gether, let no one separate' (v 6). And still he was convinced that
his own person and message would provide a ferment which
would change the meaning of all the basic words in every family
setting. That ferment seems to have been already at work in his
life when he was only twelve years old. Later, when he was told
that his mother and brothers were outside asking for him, he
replied 'Who are my mother and my brothers?' And, looking
around, he said, 'Here are my mother and my brothers! Whoever
does the will of God is my brother and sister and mother' (Mk
3:32-35). He promised eternal life to all those whom he praised for
having left house or wife or brothers or parents or children for the
sake of the kingdom of God (Lk 18:29-30). To emphasise the radical nature of all discipleship, he said to the large crowds who were
travelling with him 'whoever comes to me and does not hate father
and mother, wife and children, brothers and sisters, yes, and even
life itself, cannot be my disciple' (Lk 14:25-26). In the same radical
spirit, he stated that he had come to bring fire to the earth (Lk
12:49). The result was that families would be divided 'father
against son and son against father, mother against daughter and
daughter against mother, mother-in-law against daughter-in-law
and daughter-in-law against mother-in-law' (v 53).

For the sake of the kingdom
It is in this overturning of accepted values and the radical changing of all familial language and relationships on account of the
kingdom of heaven that Christian celibacy had its origins and
must continually look for its meaning. To his disciples who were
stunned by his very high ideal for marriage and who asked
whether, perhaps, it were better not to marry, he gave his reply
about the 'eunuchs who have made themselves eunuchs for the
sake of the kingdom of heaven' (Mt 19:12). He was not really re-
plying to their question but, as was his wont, he was setting their
question in a wider, deeper context. But, at least, in its literary
context in the gospel, the eunuch ideal is set side by side with the
marriage ideal. And the most satisfying interpretation of the
eunuch words is that they express an ideal on its own right rather
than a situation in which the victim of a broken marriage decides
not to enter a new one. The words are crude, even shocking. It is
likely that they are a direct rebuttal by Jesus of an insult hurled at

him and his disciples by people who were disturbed by their very challenging lifestyle. They are words that evoke violence, the violence which God's enemies try to inflict on the kingdom and the violence which those who accept his kingdom are willing to endure (Mt 11:12).

The position of the apostles

There is a variety of conflicting traditions about the marital status of the twelve special apostles of Jesus. All we can say with any certainty is that Peter was, at some stage, married. We get little help here from St Paul's rhetorical question: 'Have we not ... the right to take a believing woman (wife) around with us like all the other apostles and the brothers of the Lord and Cephas?' (1 Cor 9:5). Paul is not articulating a Church discipline either for his own time or for the future. It is almost certain that, in speaking about the 'other apostles', he was not referring to the original group of the twelve. It is even less likely that the man who earlier in the same letter held up his own unmarried state as an ideal (7:25-29) should now be giving a contradictory message. Paul's statement in the seventh chapter is perhaps the best known expression of the Christian ideal of celibacy. He made it clear that on the topic of virginity he had no command from the Lord, only his own conviction (v 25). The benefits which Paul saw as accruing from the life of virginity were as follows: a keener realisation that 'the present form of this world is passing away' (v 31); a freeing from anxiety (v 32); an undivided attention to the affairs of the Lord (v 32); and a consequent holiness in body and spirit (v 34); the promotion of 'good order and unhindered devotion to the Lord' (v 35). The framework in which Paul sets these values is historically conditioned, for example by the expectation of an imminent return of the Lord. Later Christian writing has given much attention to this conditioning. People have also asked whether Paul is downgrading and giving second place to Christian marriage. Any answer to that question must pay attention to the teaching in Ephesians 5 about the 'great mystery" (v 32) in which the relationship of husband and wife is expressed in terms of the relationship of Christ and the Church. In general, one can say that the values which Paul saw in virginity remain forever valid; the thought-patterns in which they are expressed are coloured by history.

A way of life

With the teaching and example of Christ, and the encouragement of St Paul, it is not surprising that, from earliest Christian times, many disciples were drawn to the ideal of virginity/celibacy. Celibacy as a way of life was not unknown before the time of Christ. It is, and was, to be found in a number of world religions. Some rabbis are on record as having lived in a celibate way. It would also appear that at least long-term, not necessarily perpetual, celibacy was accepted in some Essene groups. Among the early Christians, the life of virginity after the example of Christ had particular appeal for those drawn to the austere and ascetical lifestyle of hermits. Virgins, like the martyrs whose attitudes they shared, soon got a privileged place in the lists of saints. In the early centuries, there are no indications that celibacy was a requirement for those approved for Church ministry. In the Pastoral Epistles, it seems to be assumed that the presbyter/bishops were, on the pattern of Jewish religious leadership, good models of married domestic life.

An emerging discipline

With the passing of the centuries, a discipline of celibacy emerged. A history which would set the details of that developing discipline in right perspective has yet to be written but the landmarks of the history are well-known. The local Spanish Synod of Elvira, (306 AD), did not forbid marriage for the ordained, but it decreed that those ordained must live in permanent continence, as an expression of their consecration. After some discussion and a strong diversity of views, the ecumenical Council of Nicaea, 325 AD, prohibited the marriage of those in major orders. At the Council of Carthage, 390 AD, it was proposed that bishops should observe absolute continence 'as the apostles taught and antiquity observed'. Various local councils and synods continued to make local legislation. At the Byzantine Council in Trullo, 691-2 AD, it was agreed that married presbyters should abstain sexually during their times of sacramental duty. Different disciplines concerning celibacy emerged in the Western Church and in the Eastern Church. In the first Lateran Council, 1123 AD, celibacy was declared obligatory for all in major orders. This ruling was confirmed by the Council of Trent. The pattern that emerged in the Eastern Church was of celibacy for bishops and non-marriage for all clerics after their reception of diaconate. The Second Vatican Council reiterated the requirement of celibacy for those in major orders in the Western Church. Priestly celibacy was the subject of an encyclical of Pope Paul VI in 1967. The Roman Synod of 1971 reiterated the emphases of the Council and of Pope Paul. It declined to approve, as a matter of general policy, the ordination of married men. *The Code of Canon Law*, 1983 gave expression to the existing discipline. It has been further emphasised by Pope John Paul II, notably in *I Will Give You Shepherds* (1992).

A chequered history

The story of celibacy in Christian ministry is a story of success and failure, light and shade. Alongside the high motivation of a radical following of Christ, there appear to have been, on the part of legislators and those legislated for, a variety of less noble reasons. Even in the fathers of the Church and in other great Christian writers, it is not always easy to extricate the more questionable reasons from the more directly christological and ecclesial ones. One recurring concern was the importance of ritual purity, a concern inherited from Old Testament prescriptions, and, to some extent, from pagan religions. This concern is not to be confused with abstention as a form of devotional penance, a sexual fast, of the kind recommended by St Paul to married lay Christians (1 Cor 7:5). Both approaches presented problems when the daily celebration of the eucharist became a common practice.

A variety of motives

Other influences which must be recognised in the shaping of attitudes towards ministerial celibacy were some neo-platonic, stoic and gnostic attitudes to the body and to sexuality, with the consequent fears of genital activity as defiling. There were also the very practical questions which kept recurring about the ownership and passing on of Church property. This was one of the areas in which it was felt that a celibate cleric could be more easily 'uprooted' than could a married one. It was not until the Second Vatican Council and the contributions of Pope Paul VI that the Church was finally able to distil fully the evangelical foundations of priestly celibacy and to separate them from the secondary and sometimes questionable approaches to the topic that had considerable influence over the centuries. In his 1967 encyclical, Pope Paul VI managed to combine a profound appreciation of Christian marriage, a sensitive regard for Eastern traditions and practices, an understanding of priestly celibacy in the Western tradition, based on the centrality of the kingdom of God, an identification with the total mystery, person, mission and ministry of the risen Christ whose second coming Christians await in hope, and a search for the kind of celibate priestly ministry which is an incentive to and expression of pastoral charity.

Many questions
The topic of priestly celibacy has been under critical scrutiny, both among believers and unbelievers, at every stage of its history. In the Churches and ecclesial communities that emerged from the sixteenth century Reformation, the discipline of obligatory celibacy was modified or removed. From many directions, a whole new questioning took place around the time of the Second Vatican Council, and the discussion has not abated. In his 1967 encyclical, Pope Paul VI summarised well the main sources of the questioning. At the heart of it is the concern as to how what is essentially a free gift given to some can be made mandatory for all. This question encourages us to search deeper for the meaning of the different kinds of God's gifts and to realise that here is a gift in the form of an invitation, a gift not ready made, a gift always in the making, a gift in process, a gift for which, as with the 'better' gifts, one must keep 'striving' (1 Cor 12:31). Lived celibacy is a decision, a daily decision. It helps us to keep asking what are the elements that are truly mandatory in the teaching of the Lord of the Church. There is much in the sacramental and disciplinary life of the Church, even in very crucial areas, that he left to be decided over the centuries in the light of the Church's lived experience. All his 'mandates' and the Church's mandates must be continually examined in the light of his new 'mandatum' of love, in the form of the washing of feet of his disciples and the sign which he gave us in bread and wine on the night before he suffered. Indeed in the light of Pope Paul's eloquent presentation of priestly celibacy as a total identification with the total mystery and mission of Christ, one might wonder whether the ideal of celibacy for those acting in the person of Christ the head is so compelling that it can no longer

be contained in the words used by even Pope Paul himself: 'obligation', 'law', 'discipline'. The relationship between charisms and the great Christian mandate may also help throw light on the objection that what is a free choice on the part of monk and religious should not be made a requirement for all in diocesan priesthood. Monastery, religious life and diocesan priesthood are three modalities of one radical discipleship. The monastic vocation highlights a value that is a requirement for all disciples. It is worth remembering that, at root, the words 'solitude', 'celibate' and 'monastic' are different expressions of the word 'alone', and that being alone with the teacher is a requirement for all who take Christian discipleship seriously.

Today's concerns

With a growing positive appreciation of the human body and of marriage, is the celibacy requirement an anachronism? In an age of much breakdown in marriage, is there need for strong witness to married fidelity by those in Church leadership? Have human prescriptions about requirements for ministry been placed before people's right to the eucharist? Is the insistence on celibacy a subtle form of Church control and Church power, in ways that negate rather than promote the good news? Should the Church modify her discipline in cultures where there is no tradition of celibate values? With the many failures of celibates, has celibacy ceased to be an effective sign of the kingdom? These are some of the searching questions that will continue to be asked, and asked persistently. However we approach them, it is certain that only a fascination and inebriation with the person and mystery of Christ can keep transforming both Christian marriage and Christian celibacy. Even with that fascination, both the married person and the celibate must live with the continual failure and breakdown that are part of the sinful human conditon, in daily need of redemption. It is worth noting that at the very time when celibacy is being under so much scrutiny in the Western Catholic tradition, it is being rediscovered as an expression of the pearl of great price in some other Christian Churches. Every rediscovery of the treasures of the gospel has its repercussions in the exercise of authority and in every aspect of the Church's eucharistic life, including the providing of suitable ministers.

Even in the most exalted teaching on priestly celibacy in recent years, emphasis has been placed on the fact that celibacy is not required by the very nature of Christian priesthood. But, for many centuries now, the Catholic Church in the West has continued in its decision to limit ordination to ministerial priesthood to those who are willing to live a celibate life. Christians exercise their priesthood by offering their bodies as a sacrifice to God. The Church sees it fitting that the man who is sacrament of the Head of the body should donate all the energies of his own body in pastoral charity towards all the members of the body.

There have been a small number of exceptions to the Church's practice over the centuries. It is possible that the years ahead will see some modifications of the existing discipline, for example by some further ordaining of married men. Whatever the details about what the future holds, celibacy will be effective to the extent that celibate people will keep their eyes continually 'fixed on Jesus, the pioneer and perfecter of faith' (Heb 12:2), and on his new mandate. This concentration on the Lord will require the rediscovery and the owning again of ways of renunciation and ascetical practices which were proved to be precious, indeed essential, throughout the ages. It will require the seeking of a more evangelical lifestyle, a seeking of some form of wholesome community living that will be a protection against the unhealthy forms of aloneness. It will require a cordial relationship between bishop, priests and deacons. It will require a form of collaborative ministry with men and women, married and celibate, in a way that will preserve the values of both 'intimacy' and 'distancing'. It will be realistic about all human needs, including what psychology and other disciplines reveal about our affective lives. With the support and understanding of the whole Christian community, and tuned to and contributing to the *sensus fidelium*, those in celibate ministry to the body of Christ will keep 'making themselves that way' for the sake of the kingdom. Each of them will be able to say 'the gift I have received is not so much what I am doing for the kingdom of God but what the ever-dawning kingdom of God keeps doing to me'.

Pope Paul VI, *Priestly Celibacy*, 1967.
Raymond J. Gunzel, *Celibacy*, (Sheed and Ward, 1988).

CHAPTER 29

Intimacy and distancing

The best of human communication is a blend of intimacy and distancing. Living the Christian life involves a continual combination of intimacy and distancing. Success and failure in pastoral effectiveness can be partly gauged by the ways in which intimacy is combined with distancing. In being in touch with the depths of one's own being, in touching the depths of another person, in touching the depths of God, we are somehow in the world of intimacy. In the very search for all of these depths, we learn that we are out of our depth, that we are always somehow distant from ourselves, from other persons, from God.

Distant God, intimate God

The God in whom Christians believe is both infinitely distant from us and, in St Augustine's words, more intimate to us than our innermost selves. On the one hand, he has been revealed as the transcendent God, beyond all human understanding and comprehension. According to the assurance of Jesus, no one has ever seen him (Jn 1:18). Nobody has known his mind; nobody has been his counsellor (Rom 11:34). And still he is the immanent God. Even without referring directly to the Christian revelation, St Paul was able to assure the Athenians that 'in him we live and move and have our being' (Acts 17:28). Jesus invites us right into the intimacy of the mystery of the life of God by revealing God in the personal language of 'Father' and 'Abba' and in all the implications of such language for our attitudes and relationships. The programme he presents for living is one in which 'those who love me will keep my word, and my Father will love them, and we will come to them and make our home with them' (Jn 14:23). He keeps standing at the door and knocking, assuring us that, if we hear his voice and open the door, he will come in to us and eat with us and we with him (Rev 3:20). Here we have a programme for the closest intimacy, for the kind of praying and living that brings us truly in touch with our own centre and with the centre of the mystery of God.

Descending and ascending

The immanent secret life of Father, Son, and Spirit overflows into creation, and the great economy, the great design of God, is disclosed. This 'coming down' and 'coming in' to us of God was his answer to the yearnings of any human heart that had ever prayed 'O that you would tear open the heavens and come down' (Is 64:1). The incarnation of the Son of God was the tearing open of the heavens and the coming down of God. Since then our communication with God has been a continual descending and ascending, on God's part and on our part. The one who has ascended is the one who has descended (Rom 10:6-7). In this ascending and descending of the Son of Man, the heavens are continually opened and a communication is made possible between God and human beings (cf Jn 1:51; Acts 7:56). It is in this setting of intimacy with God that the Christian life is lived, in the Church that sees herself as a sacrament of intimacy (*LG* 1). And still, this intimacy involves a continual distancing. The God we worship in our hearts transcends all our experiences. Though Jesus has assured us that he is with us always, 'to the end of the age' (Mt 28:20), and though he is always present to his Church, there is a sense too in which he is always absent from his Church. The bridegroom has been taken away from us (Mt 9:15). He must 'remain in heaven until the time of universal restoration' (Acts 3:21). The saying of Jesus to the apostle Thomas highlighted the ambivalent situation of those who have not seen and yet come to believe (Jn 20:29). While we are 'at home in the body', we are 'away from the Lord' (2 Cor 5:6). In this condition, we need the words of encouragement addressed to those who love the Lord though they have not seen him (1 Pet 1:8). Here indeed we have the combination of true intimacy and real, even tantalising, distancing.

The example of Jesus

During the time that Jesus lived on our earth, it would appear that he both experienced moments of deep intimacy with his Father and moments of distancing that clearly indicated his will to identify fully with the various tensions in the normal human life. He was both able to rejoice because he alone knew the Father and was known by the Father (Mt 11:27) and to show the kind of distress and agitation (Mk 14:33) that culminated in his asking 'My God,

my God, why have you forsaken me?' (15:35). He experienced the
kind of human tension that at the same time drew him to mourn
for his dead cousin, in a deserted place by himself (Mt 14:13), to
have a practical compassion for hungry multitudes (vv 15-21),
and to give reassurance to his disciples when they had to cope
with a wind that was against them (vv 22-33). He experienced intimate friendship with men and with women, but there was a
strange aloneness about his moments of special closeness to his
Father (Mt 14:13) as when he withdrew from his disciples to wres-
tle with the implications of his imminent death (Lk 22:41). The
same blend of intimacy and distancing should characterise both
the fasting and the prayer of his disciples. Their fasting was to be
done with head anointed and face washed, so that it would 'be
seen not by others but by your Father who is in secret' and who
would reward them accordingly (Mt 6:18). Their praying was to
be done in the kind of space that they can make for themselves by
going into their room, shutting the door and praying to 'the Father
who is in secret' (v 6).

The 'room' and the 'centre'

It is this need for the blend of Christian intimacy and distancing
that is being re-discovered today in the second thoughts of many
who had been critical of the 'monastic' influences in their early
formation for secular priesthood or for membership of societies of
apostolic life. In the course of history, it is true that many practices
concerning priestly prayer and work were taken uncritically from
the monastery setting. But the monastic ideal stands for values
that are indispensable, not merely for every priestly life but for
every Christian life. The monk, as the word connotes, is called to
give witness to the essential Christian call to being alone, the
aloneness that makes one search for and find God in the room in
secret, and in the continual flight from the world, not the world
which God loved and for which Jesus died (Jn 3:16), but the world
for which Jesus refused to pray (Jn 17:9). This great monastic insight must be continually translated into the circumstances in
which each disciple of Christ finds himself or herself today. More
and more it is becoming clear that the 'room' in which this search
for God must take place is space in the depths of the human heart.
The search for this room is behind the growing popularity of dif-

ferent forms of centring prayer. The 'centre' is not a place; rather it
is the meeting point of body, mind and spirit which is the human
heart. This is the real centre of the universe, where God loves to
dwell. To find that centre, we are obtaining much help from various forms of divine and human wisdom that have accumulated
over the centuries. Our search is helped by the realisation that,
while God can be co-known and co-loved in every human experience, he remains a hidden God who will always be found if we
keep seeking him with and in a sincere heart. It is also helped by
the realisation that the call to be 'contemplatives' and 'mystics' is
addressed not to the chosen few but to all who are called to believe.

A generation of intimacy?

More, perhaps, than any generation in the past, our generation
has been speaking and writing a lot about intimacy. There has
been a new search for the human depths, for how we can be in
touch with our own depths, and out of them communicate with
the depths of another person and with the depths of God. There
has been an explosion of interest in human affectivity, in the place
of the feelings and emotions, and in the search for the holistic development of the human person. There has been a widespread
interest in identifying personality types and in finding the source
and direction of one's various drives and compulsions. All this, in
turn, has generated in many people a deep yearning to find new
ways of sharing their innermost selves with other persons, to be
able to talk, with understanding and trust, to another person,
about one's whole range of human feelings and experiences. It is
soon found that this kind of intimate sharing must be in some way
mutual, that there must be some reciprocity.

Intimacy and ministry

This has obvious implications for all those involved in various
forms of pastoral ministry. It can be said that in the attitudes to
pastoral ministry which we have inherited, the emphasis was on
preserving suitable distance between the minister and the person
ministered to. Contemporary emphasis on intimacy has had its
repercussions here. Even allowing for the distinction between
sympathy and empathy, the exercise of ministry sometimes
makes it difficult to draw suitable lines between intimacy and dis-

tancing. This is being experienced in a special way by those who exercise celibate ministry. There has been an ongoing re-evaluation of the relationship between celibacy and priesthood. However one assesses the situation, it must be agreed that there is a real problem here. One aspect of the problem is the diminishing numbers of candidates presenting themselves for celibate priesthood; another is the number of celibacy-related failures in and resignations from priestly ministry. One way in which the problem is being faced is by the emphasis on a developmental approach to the formation of seminarians and the ongoing formation of priests. Another is in the growing recognition of the urgency of providing for every priest an atmosphere of real friendship, real community living, real collaborative ministry with men and women. Related to this is the providing for priests the kind of programmes in which they will be realistic about the implications of their affective needs, their need for genuine friendship and intimacy. The celibacy that is in every sense 'true' will lead to a realism about one's own needs as well as a healthy sensitivity to the needs and rights of every other person and a recognition of the moment when there is a crossing of the lines and some entanglements between all these needs and rights.

Intimacy and celibacy

One hopes that today's searching questioning about priestly celibacy will lead to a discovery of what is its real meaning. In essence, the celibate ideal is not based on any of the partial reasons that may have led up to the existing discipline. It is not even about being available for more people, more time, more work. It is primarily about intimacy, a personal, loving intimacy with the Lord in his spousal relationship with his Church. It is a witness to the resurrection way of living that will be in the future but has begun in the present. It is motivated and sustained by the intimate prayer-relationship with the Lord, a relationship that must daily become more alive, more real. But it remains true that the Lord is always distant from us as well as intimately near to us. For the present, heaven must contain him. Though the Word became flesh, and though he still dwells among us, we are at the same time 'at home in the body' and 'away from the Lord' (2 Cor 5:6). In this dual citizenship is both the cross and the glory of celibate ministry. It gives meaning to the fact that, while celibacy is not incompatible with friendship and affection, there are forms of intimacy which the celibate person must forego for the sake of the kingdom of heaven.

Heart and mind

The emphasis on the affective, intimate aspects of human living in some Church circles today has led to a reaction against what is cerebral and intellectual. This tension is not new in Christianity. In its extreme forms it has led to various movements of illuminism and gnosticism, a bypassing of the normal workings of the human mind in one's acquiring of true knowledge and wisdom. Sometimes the tension has been expressed in terms of the reasons of the heart that the mind can never know. Our ability to help people be realistic about both heart and mind depends very much on our feel for the word of God and on the quality of our preaching of that word. The word has ways of entering into areas of the human depths that cannot be easily described in any of our familiar categories. The letter to the Hebrews describes the word of God as 'living and active, sharper than any two-edged sword, piercing until it divides soul from spirit, joints from marrow; it is able to judge the thoughts and intentions of the heart' (Heb 4:12). Far more than the modern-day scanning devices in the medical world, the word of God touches and reaches into human depths hitherto unnamed and unknown. Here we have a very helpful programme for the effective preaching of the word of God. Only the word of God can penetrate into the innermost and most intimate areas of the heart of the preacher of the word, into the heart of every hearer of the word, into the heart-to-heart relationship between preacher and hearer, and between hearer and hearer. There is a continual and growing need for the kind of preaching that characterised the first post-Pentecost spread of the gospel. When Peter had proclaimed that the very Jesus whom the people had crucified had now been made into Lord and Messiah, they were cut right into the heart (the 'quick') and they asked 'What should we do?' (Acts 2:37). Peter's reply was simple: 'Repent' (v 38). Here we have the classic description of what for many Christian centuries was called 'compunction'. Compunction is literally a compound puncturing, a puncturing of human pride, conceit and all the resistances that the human heart sets up against the word of God. It includes that blend of confidence and fear of the Lord that accompany true conversion. It is significant that it should have been so well generated by the man whose consciousness of sin made him ask the Lord to depart from him (Lk 5:8), who wept bitterly as he repented of his betraying (Lk 22:61-62), who with much feeling said 'Lord, you know that I love you' (Jn 21:17).

Compunction and devotion
All authentic preaching of the gospel should divide soul and spirit, joints from marrow. It should generate compunction and conversion. It should touch and actuate the loving devotion that rises out of the heart. In many ways, the word 'devotion' has become peripheral to the life of the Church. It is sometimes wrongly confused with forms of devotion that come and go. All worship of God must, in fact, rise up out of the devotion of the heart. God alone is the one who sees the quality and depth of that devotion and of the faith that accompanies it. To be devout is not an optional extra for a Christian. The preacher today has a crucial role to play in the rediscovery of the realities behind the words 'devotion' and 'compunction'. These realities lead us into the intimate and innermost areas of our own hearts. They teach us to reverence the mystery of other human hearts, to know intuitively the time for intimacy and the time for distancing. The foundation is thus laid for communication with the intimate and distant God, the God who is always at home with us and always transcendent, the God who teaches us how to be truly intimate and truly distant. We are in this way assured of some glimpses of the mystery behind all intimacy and all distancing, in the loving kindness of the heart of our God.

Readings: As for chapters 8, 28

CHAPTER 30

Poverty that enriches

Jesus Christ proclaimed the good news of the reign of God. As a sure sign of the coming of God's kingdom, he announced that he himself had come to bring good news to the poor. The good news for the poor was that he would declare them rich. Influenced by later ways of thinking, we might wonder whether Jesus offered riches for the body or riches for the human spirit. The truth is that the message of Jesus was good news for people who were in any form of human need, whether it be need of food and drink or need of God. He showed that all human needs are linked with each other: attending to one should alert us to the reality of the others. Jesus did not wish to distract people's attention from their day to day needs. He placed all human needs in perspective by telling his hearers about his Father, about his Spirit and about himself in relation to both. He brought the good news that he would make people sharers in the riches of his Father, in his own riches, in the riches of the Holy Spirit by whom he had been anointed (Lk 4:18). In doing so, he set his Church a programme for all time. In his own person, mission, and miracles, he embodied the whole range of the riches that God has to give. As a result of his dying, rising, and sending of the Holy Spirit, his disciples were able to articulate further the implications of these riches.

The God who enriches

Even before the coming of his Son, God had revealed himself as the source of all true riches, all glory, all greatness, all strength (1 Chron 29:11-13). He is the one who 'makes poor and makes rich' (1 Sam 2:7). With him alone are 'riches and honour, enduring wealth and prosperity' (Prov 8:18). In the mystery of his Son, these riches were to be disclosed and dispensed in ways that surpassed all hope and expectation. Through his incarnate Son, he lavished the riches of his grace upon human beings, in a way that brought redemption and forgiveness (Eph 1:7). These riches cannot be measured (2:7). They contain depths that no human mind can plumb (Rom 11:33). Every expression of the riches that God gives is a glimpse of God's own glory (Rom 9:23). Above all, it is a glimpse of his mercy which was at the heart of all of his covenant initiatives. All the riches of God are communicated to human beings as a result of that mercy. Acting out the love which is the source of these riches, he 'made us alive together with Christ' (Eph 2:5). The news of the 'boundless riches of Christ' is at the heart of the Church's preaching. This news must be brought to the Gentiles as well as to those whom God had originally chosen (3:8). The reason is the unique generosity of our Lord Jesus Christ who 'though he was rich, yet for your sakes he became poor, so that by his poverty you might become rich' (2 Cor 8:9). The enriching that resulted directly from this divine poverty is a reason for continual thanks to God because it keeps manifesting itself 'in speech and knowledge of every kind' (1 Cor 1:4-5). In the midst of human weakness, the disciples of Christ are strong. While being in one sense the rubbish of the world, they have all that they really want. In their riches, they have become kings (1 Cor 4:8-13). These riches poured into the hearts of believers achieve more than filling them with heavenly thoughts. They enable believers 'to do good, to be rich in good works, generous and ready to share, thus storing up for themselves the treasure of a good foundation for the future, so that they make take hold of the life that really is life' (1 Tim 6:17-19). Believers thus become makers of the kind of society in which the poor can live a richly human life.

Riches and poverty

The riches of believers are compatible with various kinds of poverty. Indeed God has 'chosen the poor in the world to be rich in faith and to be heirs of the kingdom that he has promised to those who love him' (Jas 2:5). Similarly, 'those who store up treasures' can fail to be 'rich toward God' (Lk 12:21). The fact that the Christian can be at the same time both poor and rich is made possible by the strengthening and empowering by which God's Spirit can transform the inner being of believers. The action of the Spirit draws the Christian into the life of the Father from whom every family in heaven and on earth takes its name. Out of the riches of the Father's glory, the Spirit does his work of transforming human lives. The result is that Christ dwells in the heart of the believer, through faith. All this provides a continual grounding and rooting in love and a filling with all the fulness of God (Eph 3:14-19). The community of human beings on earth have a share in the community living of the divine persons. The result is that the poor come to be treated with respect, justice, and love.

God of riches

According as the Church succeeded in formulating a clearer doctrine about the mystery of the triune God, believers came to have a deeper understanding of the riches of the Christian vocation. It is true that there were times in Christian history when belief in the triune God came across as a remote and bewildering truth. But the real mystery of the three divine persons is about the loving intimacy of a Father who alone knows the Son, of the Son who alone knows the Father (Mt 11:27), in an atmosphere that is pervaded by the presence of the Spirit who alone comprehends what is truly happening in the depths of God (1 Cor 2:10-11). The best attempts over the centuries to express the immanent life of the triune God keep harping back to the conviction that the inner life of God is the unlimited expression of communitarian ways of knowing and loving – knowing and loving that express the full riches of the divine way of being. As the Church came to ponder her own call to share in the riches of God, she glimpsed 'what no eye has seen, nor ear heard, nor the human heart conceived' namely 'what God has prepared for those who love him'. This is what God revealed to the Church through the Spirit (vv 9-10). What God was preparing for the Church through the Spirit was an intimate sharing in God's own communitarian life. The call to the Church is nothing less than to 'become participants of the divine nature' (2 Pet 1:4). This is the full implication of the invitation of Jesus to 'be perfect as your heavenly Father is perfect' (Mt 5:48).

The call to share in the communitarian life of God is the highest call that was ever given or could be given to human beings. It is the call continually addressed to the Church. It is the call and the invitation which the Church must keep addressing to the whole human family. In this call lie the real riches of the Church. In distributing these riches lies the great mission of the Church. Because God has been humanised, human beings are divinised. The life of grace to which the Church invites human beings is a life of personal sharing in the way in which the divine persons share. This sharing, this communion, defines the mission of the Church. In promoting it, the Church truly becomes the universal sacrament of salvation. The Church's message of sharing must not remain a set of beautiful, abstract concepts. It must be embodied daily in the way Christians share and the way they help others to share.

Covenants and riches

The plan of God to enrich human beings was the reason for all his initiatives in making covenants. It was the reason for his promise to Abraham that in him all the families of the earth would be blessed (Gen 12:3). It was the reason for his special concern for those who in human terms would never be thought of as rich. In the Exodus, his choice of a people and his wish to make a covenant with them was based not on their human attractiveness but on the fact that he found them impoverished and the victims of oppression. It is for this reason that 'he sustained them in a desert land, in a howling wilderness waste' (Deut 32:10). The covenant was the great expression of both his justice and his compassion. He had found a people who were in the condition like that of strangers, widows and orphans. His desire to keep enriching them in their poverty would be at the core of his side of the covenant. The people of the covenant, in turn, were to show their fidelity by a sensitive care for those who were literally strangers, widows, and orphans. The later religious reforms, and the warnings of the prophets, were to highlight this aspect of the covenant. The ideal of God for his people was that of a just and familial kind of society, in which human avarice and injustice would be recognised and denounced for what they were. The records of the Exodus events, and of what followed on them in the centuries of settlement, provide many expressions of the kind of human greed and injustice that were the negation of the covenant. This situation was further complicated by the various movements of foreign domination.

Riches for the marginalised

The Palestine into which Jesus was born had inherited all the complexities of a society badly damaged by human greed and by various movements of domination. Those most damaged were the very people who, in God's plan, should have been the first beneficiaries of the covenant. Everywhere, there were poor people in situations which we would today call marginalised. In both the rural and urban sections of society, there were many victims of unjust taxation, of unjust distribution of land, of ways of living that were anything but egalitarian and communitarian. This state of affairs was not helped by a religious leadership that often concentrated on minutiae and by-passed those 'weightier things of the law' (Mt 23:23) which were at the very heart of the covenant. Into such a society, Jesus came proclaiming the good news of the reign of God. That good news had special implications for those who should have been the first beneficiaries of the covenant, but were not. These were the various categories of marginalised people who comprised the main following of Jesus. To them, he simply said 'blessed are you who are poor' (Lk 6:20). Jesus, sent by the Father, at whose initiative all the great covenants had been made, was introducing the kind of community in which the poor, the marginalised, and the sinners, far from being left on the margins, would be seen to be at the centre of the plan of a compassionate and just God. These were the people who soon came to be involved with Jesus in the various table fellowships that were foretastes of the final messianic banquet in which all worldly ways of placing people will be reversed. Those who had hitherto felt excluded will now occupy the real places of honour.

It is not surprising that, from an early stage, the 'beatitudes' of Jesus should have been 'spiritualised' in ways that stressed the personal spiritual dispositions necessary for entry into the kingdom. But, in the initial good news of the kingdom, the emphasis of Jesus was on the limitless compassion of the God who, in calling people into a wholly new kind of human community, wishes first to enrich those poor and despised who counted for so little in socio-economic conditions that had been so damaged by human injustice and greed. This enriching would be their sharing in a community which would be shot through with God's own love, compassion and justice. Only the imminent intervention of God himself, whose reign Jesus announced, could make that community possible. With the sending of the Spirit of the risen Christ, his disciples were empowered to be agents for the making of such a community. Its blueprint is already recognisable in the picture of the ideal Christian community as shaped by the early believers:

They 'were together and had all things in common; they would sell their possessions and goods and distribute the proceeds to all, as any had need' (Acts 2:44-45). The motivation for this kind of sharing, in which rich could not be distinguished from poor, came from the fact that 'they devoted themselves to the apostles' teaching and fellowship, to the breaking of bread and the prayers' (v 42). Daily sharing in the riches of heaven drove the disciples to radical ways of sharing the goods of the earth.

A Church that enriches
The mission of the Church has always remained such a mission of enriching. Her understanding of this mission has been coloured throughout the ages by different ways of understanding such topics as the relationship between material poverty and spiritual poverty, the relationship between the secular and the sacred, the body-soul relationship, the relationship between the temporal and the eternal. Contemporary approaches to topics like these tend to favour attitudes that are holistic and that look on the whole human family as one, in a universe that is one and that awaits its final transformation and re-creation at the second coming of Jesus Christ. As Christians look on the realities of poverty in today's society and as they re-read the original message of Jesus, they see an equal urgency in the need to eradicate the material poverty that dehumanises and the need to eradicate spiritual poverty. In searching for effective ways of doing this, we are getting more keenly aware of the social, political, economic and cultural setting in which the good news must take flesh and contribute to the enrichment of human living. The emergence of various theologies of liberation in recent decades expresses a yearning for a true enriching of various categories of people who are victims of different forms of human oppression and of unjust structures. This yearning is in strong continuity with the spirit of the Sinai covenant, with the charter for the reign of God as expressed in the beatitudes, and with the early Christian ideals of human community. As such, it deserves the support of all Christians. It is not an option. It is not a programme for one section of the world only. Disagreements about ways of enriching the poor arise out of different understandings of what really enriches and what might have the makings of further impoverishment.

Two urgent calls

Two areas of Church life reflect in a special way the Church's understanding of poverty and riches. One is what is technically called 'religious life'. The other is ordained ministry. Commitment to a life of poverty has always been part of the life that draws its inspiration from the evangelical counsels. In some recent perspectives, the counsels are seen not as an option for the few but as somehow part of the programme for all disciples. In this perspective, those called to religious life should provide a clear headline for the true detachment from material goods and for the total dependence on God that should be a characteristic of all Christians. If it is true that avarice is the greatest temptation for Christians today, then the most urgent challenge to religious life is to bear effective witness to gospel poverty. In the same perspective, religious life is a call to identify with the lot of the poor and of all those who remain victims of any oppressive systems. For religious, the option for the poor is not optional. This is indeed a demanding programme and one that may call for many radical changes in the ways in which religious poverty will be lived in the future.

In the meantime, official Church teaching on the ministerial priesthood is putting more and more emphasis on radical discipleship as the basis of that way of life. Evangelical poverty is seen not as an optional part of that discipleship but as being at its centre. In the priestly ideal, evangelical poverty seems to be following the same historical trajectory as did clerical celibacy. It took a number of centuries before celibacy became a requirement for all candidates for ordination in the Western Church. The implications of recent official teaching on priestly ministry would seem to be that, in the future, failures in priestly poverty will be seen to be as reprehensible as failures in priestly celibacy. Some would see this as a strange blurring of the lines of demarcation between two distinct ways of Christian discipleship, the monastic way and the way of the secular priest. But it would be sad if this kind of questioning led to hasty conclusions. It should lead all concerned to keep searching the scriptures for the foundations of being a disciple of the teacher who himself made a clear decision to have nowhere to lay his head (Mt 8:20). It should help all disciples to keep finding new meaning in the good news that Jesus brought to the poor. It should help them to appreciate the many self-emptying decisions he made as he entered into the poverties of the human condition. It should help all disciples, especially those who are so by vow or by ordination or by both, to be attuned, in mind and feelings, and in simplicity of lifestyle, to those who are victims of any poverty that dehumanises rather than enriches. It should be an urgent reminder to all Christ's disciples to keep hearing the cry of the poor. It should help the Church to lead all those made in the image and likeness of God to a richer relationship with the Father who is rich in mercy, with his Son who taught what constitutes riches and poverty, with the Spirit who keeps helping all of us in our poverty and weakness. These richer relationships will contribute to the enriching of the quality of life in every area of human society, as we all move, in hope, towards a new heaven and a new earth.

John O'Brien, CSSp, *Theology and the Option for the Poor*, (The Liturgical Press, 1992).

John P. Meier, *A Marginal Jew*, (Doubleday, 1991).

CHAPTER 31

Last things, first things

In a moment of insight and surprise, the poet Oscar Wilde mar-
velled at the possibilities of the human mind. This led him to wonder
why he

> had not been told
> that the brain can hold
> in a small ivory cell
> God's high heaven and hell.

Different people have different ways of understanding God's
high heaven and hell. All would agree that the words touch on
ultimate questions about God, about human beings, about the
universe. For Christians, the life, death, and resurrection of Jesus
Christ are the context for all ultimate questions. His paschal mystery has brought God's ultimate plan to 'perfection' and fulfilment (Heb 9:9). He has achieved for us a liberation that is eternal
(v 12). In his resurrection, he has entered not an earthly tent but
heaven itself, once-for-all, at the climax of history (vv 24-26). He is
the pioneer of our salvation, and God 'for whom and through
whom all things exist' has made him 'perfect' (Heb 2:10).

Since priestly ministry in the name of our one high-priest is about
bringing all things to completion and fulfilment in God, it must
continually look in the direction of the 'last things'. It is sometimes claimed that the 'last things' were preached too much in
some Christian ages past and that they are not preached enough
today. The truth is that whenever the Christian message is proclaimed in all its 'breadth and length and height and depth' (Eph
3:18), all of the 'last things' are preached. The last things are also
the first things. Every effective proclaiming of the good news
touches, not just touches on, the last things, each of which has a
familiar name in our tradition, and all of which are about the perfecting and completing of all God's plan. It focuses our attention
on what God promised, what he fulfilled in the new covenant
sealed in his Son's blood, and what he is continually bringing to

completion. Because we have no lasting city here (Heb 13:14), the hearers of the word well preached are alerted to the meaning of the many tensions in the Christian life. They are taught to live at the same time in the present age and in the future age. They are alerted to recognise the action of the Spirit of Christ transforming our bodies into the likeness of Christ's glorified body (Phil 3:21), since our future has already begun and the 'last things' are taking place in our lives now, as we journey to the only city that will last. Each of the last things comes to be seen in the light of the relationships that are at the heart of the day to day Christian life.

Relationships, decisions and judgments

In a sense, the last things are about decisions and their consequences – God's decision to create and re-create, our daily decisions in response to his invitations, the meeting points of God's decisions and our decisions. In some gospel parables, there are close links between the words expressing 'crisis', decision, judgment and separation, and there are close links between human decisions and God's deciding judgment on us. This judgment comes in three stages:

* Now, because the Son of God has come. The moment of the death and resurrection of Jesus was the great moment of judgment of the universe (cf Jn 12:31-32). Every decision we make now about the person and mission of Jesus has the makings of a rising to life or of a rising to judgment (cf Jn 5:29). The word spoken by Jesus is continually sifting what is good from what is bad in our daily decisions (cf Jn 12:48). Our own regular examen of conscience and of consciousness is not a morbid exercise in guilt but rather an invitation to Jesus Christ to let his word go deep into our attitudes and decisions.

* In the 'particular judgment' which for some centuries now has been the way of expressing the state of our relationships at death, with God, with other people, with the rest of creation.

* In the 'general judgment' which will be the final collective manifestation of all human decisions in the light of God's decisions. The practical criterion of this judgment is one's attitudes to Jesus Christ, explicitly or implicitly, the extent to which each of us has recognised the presence of Jesus Christ in human beings made in the likeness of God (cf Mt 15:31-46). In this sense, Jesus himself is the judge and he is God's judgment. The general judgment is the

final disclosing of the implications of all our daily decisions, our daily undergoing of judgment, our daily living of the relationships to which we are called, in Christ.

Relationships changed

As Christians we believe that, in death, life is changed, not taken away; relationships are changed, not taken away. We hope that we will 'die in the Lord' (Rev 14:13) whose death gives meaning to every living and every dying. We know that 'if we live, we live for the Lord; and if we die, we die for the Lord, so that, alive or dead, we belong to the Lord' (Rom 14:7-8). What gives ultimate meaning to the mystery of death which, by any reckoning, has many connections with the chaos and disorder of human sinfulness, is the extent to which we can say, in Christ, 'every day I die' (1 Cor 15:31), until the time when we shall all 'be changed' (1 Cor 15:51).

In recent times, death is sometimes presented as an action we do rather than as something that will happen to us; a kind of decision, a conscious and free act, a moment of final choice, rather than as an event outside our control. This way of thinking looks further than the merely biological facts of death. It has value insofar as it is an incentive to take continual ownership of the direction of our lives, of our decisions, and of their final concentration at death.

Our ways of imaging the body-soul relationship in life and in death have varied over the centuries. The most familiar way of talking about death has been in terms of separation of soul and body. Some recent writing, with varying degrees of success, is groping for language to suggest a re-constituting of the whole person at death, a kind of partial resurrection. This approach, so far, has many defects and limitations. The discussion which it has engendered should help us to focus more clearly on the death-resurrection of Christ as the centre of the saving design of the saving God. It should also alert us to the fact that the plan of God is still awaiting completion and that the completion can only be brought about by the second coming of the risen and glorified Christ.

Imaging the change

Religious men and women have always been groping for images and symbols to capture something of the nature of life after death. These images and symbols have been drawn largely from the most basic areas of human experience. The Paschal Mystery has given them new riches of meaning and perspective. Examples are:

* The various shades of meaning of the words 'life' and 'death';
* Light and darkness at various levels;
* The full activating and concentration of our faculties of knowing, loving and sensing;
* Seed ripening into harvest;
* Labour and journeying leading to rest.

When images like these are seen in right relationship to the whole mystery of Christ in his whole body, we have the foundations for a theology of heaven; when they express the possibility of separation from Christ, we have a setting for the meaning of hell; when they express the need of restoration and repair, there is a basis for an understanding of purgatory.

Relationships fulfilled

From the experience of life in its various levels, we get some glimpse of heaven as the eternal life which consists in knowing the Father and Christ whom he has sent (cf Jn 17:3), not in isolated glory but integrated into a renewed people, in a perfect communion of saints, in a new creation, in a setting where knowing is loving and loving is knowing.

From the experience of various levels of enlightenment, we can think of heaven in terms of eternal light. The beatific vision, the full seeing of the face of God that alone can make us fully blessed, is made possible by the full light of God's own glory.

The Christian vocation includes an invitation to a daily sowing of the good seed (cf 2 Cor 9:11). Even on earth, the Spirit produces a harvest in people who respond to his gifts. Heaven is the full ripening of the good seeds that are sown by our daily actions and decisions under the influence of God's grace.

We can get some glimpse of eternal 'rest' if we reflect on the place of true rest in human living. One aspect of rest is the opportunity to appreciate what is good and what is true and what is beautiful. For a people who are pilgrims, Christian hope points to the rest in the land which God has promised (Heb passim). The rest which is heaven is the uninterrupted contemplation of God whom the just will see 'face to face' (1 Cor 13:12). The heavenly rest is not an inactive rest; rather it is the full concentration of the whole person on the truth and beauty of God the Father, Son and Holy Spirit 'as he is' (1 Jn 3:2), integrated into the glorified body of the whole Christ, in a new creation.

Relationships destroyed

From the gospels and from other pages of the New Testament, Christians have inherited images which indicate that it is possible to reject the continual saving offer of God in a way that has eternal consequences. The images have been drawn on and elaborated on in Christian teaching and preaching throughout the ages. In popular representation, the images have often been embellished and sometimes distorted. The Christian understanding of hell must stress both the limitless goodness of God and our freedom to reject it. It is possible to die devoid of all love. Instead of dying in the Lord, it is possible to die in a state of obstinate rejection of the eternal life offered by the Lord. It is possible to die in a state of blight rather than in a state of ripe harvest. It is possible to die in a state of unrest that will last. It is possible to die out of joint with God, with the whole of humanity, with the whole of creation.

All these possibilities must be continually re-pondered in the light of both the limitless goodness of God and the depths of the mystery of human freedom and responsibility. One is right in wondering how any human being could be so utterly perverse as to die devoid of any form of love. One is right in trusting and hoping that every human brain will finally let go of its hold on hell. One is right in believing and emphasising that God did not make hell, but that it is human beings who decide to make hell for themselves. One is right in insisting that the God who judges is identical with the loving and faithful God of the covenant who wills all to be saved (cf 1 Tim 2:4). The thought of hell should be an incentive to conversion rather than a cause for barren fear or for vain searching as to who or how many might be lost. The thought of the possibility of final loss should lead to hope in the God who saves, rather than dread of a God who punishes; to a right relationship with the God whose will is that everything he made should come to perfection and fulfilment in his Son; to a deeper realisation that God has shown us, in his Son, that he is always on our side. It is an invitation to banish out of the brain whatever is of hell.

Relationships purified

Since the Middle Ages, purgatory has been the name for the state of purification which some of the saved will have to undergo before enjoying the vision of God. The action of God's 'consuming fire' (Heb 12:29) on those who are not yet ready to see his face is a purifying and refining action. This purifying action takes place throughout all our life, in the events of history as they affect us, in the act of dying, and in what follows death. At all stages of living, the follower of Christ is invited to both active and passive purification of mind, will and senses. The state of a person experiencing purgatory after death is like that of a person needing therapy or rehabilitation or detoxification on the way to a full growth and final maturation in relationships. The Church's teaching voice assures us that those undergoing purgatory can be helped by the good works and prayers of the faithful on this earth and especially by the continuing sacrifice of the altar in which we are in living touch with the intercession of Christ himself.

Fringe relationships

The word limbo (L. *limbus*, fringe) has come to be used of the special situation vis-a-vis salvation of infants who die without the sacrament of baptism. Church thinking has developed and sometimes changed on a number of aspects of this topic. Discussion on it has focused more and more attention on the universal salvific will of God, the power of prayer and the desire of believing parents and of the whole Church, as well as our obligation to do what is humanly possible to carry out the wish of Christ about being born again (Jn 3:5). Whatever about limbo as a possible state after death, the word has become a powerful symbol of the ambiguities, the uncertainties, and the fringe situations that can be part of so much of our human relationships in our journey to completion and that make us realise our continual need of the Lord who saves.

Eternal relationships

Our days on this earth are limited (cf Ps 90). But God does not grow old, nor did he have a beginning. With the help of philosophy and of wisdom drawn from various cultures, we can get some glimpse of the eternity of God who has specially revealed himself through the Judaeo-Christian history. God has given human beings a share in his own eternity. Eternity is not an indefinite prolongation of time. Perhaps the most successful attempt at defining it is in terms of the perfect and all-at-once possession of interminable life (*Boethius*).

Relationships in a universe renewed

We look forward in hope to the promised new heaven and new earth (2 Pet 3:13). There is a close and inseparable link between the destiny of human beings and the destiny of the universe of which we form part and which we have helped to fashion. This arises from the nature of human beings who have been so much fashioned out of the elements of the earth and who, in turn, have fashioned the universe. There is a very true sense in which the present universe will come to an end and that its resources are already running out. The scriptures, especially in the more apocalyptic parts, contain many images of this ending and this running out of resources. But there is also a very real sense in which the present universe will be renewed and transformed by a new action of the creative energy of God. We cannot claim to know the exact nature of either the end or the transformation of the universe (*GS* 39) but we know that the second coming of Christ, who is the alpha and the omega of God's plan (*GS* 45), will be, above all, a saving event for the whole of God's creation (cf *LG* 48). This event will bring about a renewed set of relationships of all the members of the human family with each other, with a renewed universe, with the communion of holy persons and holy things, with Father, Son and Holy Spirit.

Here, indeed, we are dealing with ultimate questions, in the light of Christ our priest and 'fore-runner' (Heb 6:20). Here is the fullest context for every word spoken and proclaimed in his name. Here is a continual perspective for what we should put first and what we should put last in our decisions. Here is a continual priestly programme for enabling every human being to hold and hold on to God's high heaven.

Constitution on the Church, chap.7
Some Current Questions in Eschatology, (ITC, 1991).

PART VI

Looking to the Future

CHAPTER 32

A time of searching

It seems to be a characteristic of all human movements and institutions that they have to go through stages of foundation, expansion and decline. The Church of Christ is unique in having the assurance of its founder that 'the gates of Hades will not overcome it' (Mt 16:19), and that he is with his disciples 'always, to the very end of the age' (Mt 28:20). But we have no guarantee as to what precise forms the continued survival and growth of the Church will take. The assurance given to Peter, and implicitly to those who would continue to exercise the office of Peter, was a clear promise of God's strength at work in human weakness. It is the mission of the Church to be the sign of the grace of God at work in every culture and in every phase of human history. Every period of growth, of change, and of decay, in human culture, has its repercussions in the life of the Church. This is particularly true of priestly ministry and of religious life. In all of the Western world, which at one time almost identified itself with the Christian Church, there seems to be, at present, a situation of crisis, indeed of decline, in Church life. This is particularly noticeable in priestly ministry and in religious life. In many places, there has been a dramatic decline in numbers active in ordained ministry. The human weaknesses and limitations of the existing personnel have been highlighted. There would appear to be more losses than gains. Attempts at restructuring the forms of priestly and religious living do not seem to be producing impressive results.

Re-founding

All of this is an urgent call to the conversion and renewal which is at the heart of the gospel. But we can also take hope from the fact that the Church as a community of human beings is subject to the normal rhythms of growth and decline that human societies go through, and that every cultural change has its repercussions in Church life. More important still, it would seem to be true that, though the Church has been 'founded' once for all, it must be continually 're-founded' on the same foundations, on the same rock.

In the present rather critical period in Church ministry, Christian faith, hope and love are calling us to a 're-founding'. There would seem to be a call to re-structure Church ministry in a way that is faithful to both the wishes of the Church's one founder and to the living tradition which he set in motion. Those already in ministry, together with all believers, must set out on this project aware that the God who created the universe out of nothingness can still choose the foolish things of the world to shame the wise, and choose the weak things of the world to shame the strong (1 Cor 1:27). They must be aware that the gospel overturns all human understandings of what constitutes poverty and riches. They must work in humble collaboration with a loving and faithful God whose omnipotence does not keep him from somehow sharing in our human limitation and our human pain. They must work with a God whose gifts are both always free and always costly for those who are willing to receive them and to use them.

Two parables

In these questioning times, there are two gospel parables that can be of special help to us. They are of particular help for those who search not just for what is good but for what is best (Phil 1:10). Indeed they seem to provide a key to the basic structure of many of the gospel parables and a vision for all those who are 'seeking first the reign of God' (cf Matt 6:33). They are the short but ever-rich parables of the Treasure and of the Pearl (Mt 13:44-45). One could start with the man, presumably a poor man, who unexpectedly found the hidden treasure. He found, he rejoiced, he sold, he bought. After his story comes the story of the wealthy merchant. He searched, he found, he sold, he bought. We can put the two parables together and get the profile of the gospel searcher. He searches, he finds, he rejoices, he sells, he buys.

Treasure is a favoured word in St Matthew's gospel. The Magi 'opened' their treasures and 'offered' them (Mt 2:11). The Lord taught that your heart is where your treasure is (6:21). He told us how we can have treasure 'in heaven', with God (19:21). He warned that moth and rust can destroy the treasure that is stored up on earth (Mt 6:19). He talked of the good man who draws out of his good treasure and a bad man who draws out of his evil treasure (12:35). He spoke of the owner of a house who brings out of his store room new treasures as well as old (Mt 13:52). In our Lord's time, the treasure image was both an invitation to the things of heaven and a reminder to be 'down to earth'. At times of political trouble, or of disturbance between neighbours, the rich often buried their treasures in fields. Recent discoveries of precious chalices have shown that the practice was not confined to ancient Palestine. On a more modest scale, the peasant who hid coins and clothing in the ground took the risk of the threat of the moth and the rust. For rich person and poor person alike, the hidden treasure was precious. No wonder that the word 'treasure' later became a term of affection, as when a lover sings 'Il Mio Tesoro'.

As with the treasure, so with the pearl. It would appear that, in the ancient world, the pearl was regarded as the most precious of substances, even more precious than gold. In later vernaculars, the word became an expression of affection, of appreciation, of beauty. The language of love knew what it was to say 'my love, my pearl'. No wonder that the Latin word for a pearl, *Margarita*, and its variants, became a popular Christian name.

Both the treasure and the pearl were symbols for wisdom which in turn was seen to be 'an infinite treasure to men' (Wis 7:14). Those who like to allegorise draw attention to the strange origins of pearls. The pearl starts as grit coming in from the seaboard. The oyster struggles with it and tries to get rid of it. In time, in many years in fact, the oyster manages to transform it. And the greater the irritation, the greater and the more beautiful the pearl that results.

The merchant in the parable began by searching for fine pearls. His search ended when he found just one, one of great value. His experience might help us to interpret the experience of the Church in recent decades. These have been a time of great searching. There have been many helpful documents on the role of the laity, on church ministry, on religious life. All these are closely related with each other, with the total mystery of the Church, and with our understanding of the person of Jesus Christ, the only head of the Church. But we know that documents are only a stage in a process. Deep in our hearts, we all know that we will not get very far with our restructuring of lay involvement in the Church, of priestly ministry, of religious life, unless we re-discover him who is our real treasure, the real pearl. Perhaps we can be helped by the five stages of the journey of the gospel searcher:

He searched: Searching is an elementary human activity. We search for causes. We search for meaning. We search for happiness. We search for what is lost. We search for opportunities, for new beginnings. It is no wonder that the topic of searching has always played a prominent place in world literature. Nor is it surprising that the topic was often taken up by Jesus in his preaching and that he invites us to 'seek and find' (Mt 7:7).

Much of the searching and seeking which has been taking place in the Church concerns the most suitable ways of re-structuring of ministry and the recruiting of suitable candidates for the ministry of the future. It would seem that the most fruitful setting for such recruitment is among groups of young people who themselves are in a searching frame of mind. One hopes that the two-directional search will, for all concerned, result in a new fascination with the face and the person of the one who helps people to find the hidden treasure and the one precious pearl.

He found: Losing and finding go together in many of the gospel parables. For many baptised people today, being a disciple of Jesus Christ means finding in a personal way a faith which was sown in baptism and somehow got lost as the seed came to be choked by 'life's worries, riches and pleasures' (Lk 8:14). A major priority in pastoral care today must be helping each of the baptised to find the faith-treasure in a personalised way, and to combine contemplation and action in a way that will ensure the continual re-finding of the treasure.

He rejoiced: The man who found the treasure discovered, perhaps for the first time, what it was to rejoice. It is not altogether uncommon today to find a joyless local Church, a joyless presbyterate, a joyless religious community. Perhaps the source of the joylessness is the losses, the departures, the emptyings we have been experiencing on various levels in the Church. These, in turn, have generated their share of sadness and sorrow. But the life of the Church must go on. A result is that we have not yet found healthy outlets for normal grieving and bereavement. As we search for these, there is need for a renewed prayer for that fruit of the Spirit which is joy – a fruit which is assured us even in times of testing.

He sold: This is the most difficult of the five stages. One recalls that the sacrament of the unity of Christian disciples is, at the same time, banquet, memorial and sacrifice. It is consoling to find that modern studies on sacrifice emphasise that its basic connotation is not negative, not painful. And yet, it is clear that, though faith in Jesus Christ is a free gift of God, it is a gift that 'costs not less than everything' for anybody who wants to be a true disciple. The topic of sacrifice keeps raising questions about costing. The 'cost of discipleship' means that anyone who wishes to keep following the 'one teacher', must keep selling, keep sacrificing, keep giving away, in order to keep focusing, and concentrating on the 'one thing necessary' (Lk 10:42).

He bought: He bought in order to own. In one sense, we can never speak of 'owning' what is the gift of God. God's gifts are handed to us as talents to be developed, as property of God that is to be husbanded. When we have done everything we were told to do, we should say 'we are unworthy servants; we have only done our duty' (Lk 17:10). And still, there is a very real sense in which we are called to own, or rather to co-own, the riches of the kingdom. God has 'raised us up in union with Christ Jesus and enthroned us with him in the heavenly realms' (Eph 2:6). The Christian life is about 'communion' in every sense and on every level. That communion enables us to 'take ownership' of the faith that has been given us, and, in the fullest sense, to 'own up' to it at all times.

The right questions
The five stages of the journey of the gospel searcher, the person who is seeking first the reign of God, must always be lived in the context of authentic gospel wisdom, authentic gospel questions. Human wisdom tends to ask 'how many?' and 'when?'. Gospel wisdom asks 'what kind?' and 'how?'

Jesus did not answer questions about 'how many?' To the question 'how many will be saved?' his answer was an invitation to 'enter through the narrow gate' (Mt 7:13). His preferred kind of numbers were the symbolic twelve of apostolic foundations and the symbolic multiples of seven as a call to limitless forgiveness (Mt 18:22). Neither did he answer questions about 'when?', as he showed when asked about the time of the end and the timing of the restoration of the kingdom to Israel (Acts 1:6). To the question 'when did we see you …?' (Mt 25:37), his reply will be 'as long as you did it …' (v 40). The only important 'when' in gospel language is 'now'.

The great gospel questions, ones which Jesus answered, are 'what kind?' and 'how?' Mary wondered what kind of greeting she had received from the angel (Lk 1:29). The neighbours of Elizabeth and Zechariah wondered what kind of person John would turn out to be (v 66). The beatitudes are a clear indication of what kind of people will enter the kingdom. The continual gospel call to change is a foreshadowing of what kind of people we will be when we are so changed that we are 'like him' and see him 'as he is' (1 Jn 3:2). 'What kind?' leads to 'how?' Mary asked 'how can this be?' The answer was in terms of the Holy Spirit and the power of the Most High (Lk 1:34-35). To those who asked the wrong questions about the resurrection, Jesus replied that they did not know the scriptures or the power of God (Mt 22:29). In these two are concentrated God's how – the word of God and the power of God.

The continual asking of the gospel questions helps us to gain a wholesome perspective on the kind of questions that keep agitating the Church, and to keep devising a new and wholesome agenda for renewal. It also helps us to keep making the right requests to God, in our prayers of the faithful and elsewhere. Otherwise we risk being told 'you do not know what you are asking' (Mt 20:22). At each of the five stages in the journey of the one who seeks God's reign first, gospel questions and gospel requests will lead to a new appreciation of the treasure and the pearl that each of us must find anew every day. In this daily finding, we discover the meaning of the great Christian virtue of hope.

John P. Meier, *Matthew*, (Veritas Publications, 1980).
Gerald A. Arbuckle, SM, *Out of Chaos: Refounding Religious Congregations*, (Geoffrey Chapman, 1988).

CHAPTER 33

After the French School

The bishops who took part in the Synod on Priestly Formation (1990) came from two very differing backgrounds. The majority had been formed in the tradition of the French School of Spirituality. Their criteria for an understanding of ministerial priesthood came very much from that tradition. The starting point of the other participants was more focused on the realities of Church life here and now, and they were prepared to work inductively from there towards an understanding of priesthood and a programme of formation for it. However one assesses the relative merits of these two approaches, there can be no denying the enormous influence of the French School, in the past and in the present. In its beginnings, it comprised such different people as Cardinal de Berulle, founder of the French Oratorians; Fr Jean Jacques Olier, who founded the Sulpicians; Fr Charles de Condren, who was Berulle's successor in the Oratory; St John Eudes, founder of two communities so much associated with priesthood and with the heart of Christ. At the centre of the 'School', with its distinctive theology and spirituality of priesthood, was Pierre de Berulle.

The man at the centre
Berulle was, by family background and by disposition, a man of devotion. Early in his priestly life, through the influence of some holy men and women, and through his own mystical experiences, all his energies came to be focused on the mystery of the Word of God Incarnate. This mystery was to be the continual source of his teaching on the renewal of priesthood which came to occupy the central place in his life's ministry. For him, the Christian life consisted first and last of adoring Jesus Christ in each of his states, each of his mysteries, adhering to him in his inner dispositions, in each of these states and mysteries, with the consequent denials of self that this continually demands. He saw the ordained priest as one called to a state of perfection within the various 'orders' of priesthood. In his understanding of these orders, he was strongly

influenced by the schematic gradation of all things in heaven and on earth, as envisaged in the writings of the sixth century Dionysius. He saw the man in holy orders as the leader set apart and consecrated for the continual exercise of the virtue of religion and of adoring, in the name of the whole Church. Berulle was pre-occupied with regenerating the priesthood and, through the priesthood, the whole Church, by bringing about this basic atti-tude of adoration, and entering into all the mysteries of the Word incarnate. He was prepared to accept a time lag before this ideal would flower into programmes of preaching, catechising and pastoral care. What by any standards he could scarcely have fore-seen was the wonderful burgeoning of social and political action in the world of devotion which he helped set in motion and en-riched so much. The remarkable seventeenth century 'dévotes' were a moving expression of the fact that what has its source in the heart's devotion can produce fruits not only in the private world of piety but on all levels of human society.

Berulle was a busy man. Before and after becoming a cardinal in 1627, he was involved in Church politics and state politics, in con-troversies with Protestants and in diplomatic missions. And still he found ample time to interact with practitioners in spirituality and spiritual direction. He was himself spiritual director to many men and women. Through it all, he found time to bring the re-formed Spanish Carmelites to Paris, and introduce and spread the Oratory, modelled on, but not just copying, that of St Philip Neri. On many levels, he was a great disciple and a great maker of disci-ples.

Re-appraisal

The work of the French School has been the subject of much criti-cal re-appraisal in recent years. The somewhat straight-jacketed framework of 'states' and 'orders' in which Berulle situated or-dained priesthood, and the lack of what we would call ordinary pastoral action in his own life and in that of many he was forming, is one topic for questioning. His emphasis on 'slavery to Christ' has generated more opposition and misunderstanding than it deserves. It has a good scriptural pedigree, and it can provide a good corrective to an over-emphasis on mystical powers and states so much associated with the French School. The main criticism of the School concerns its teaching that Jesus Christ was a priest on the basis of his divine and not his human nature. Recent emphasis on the sacramentality of Christ's human nature has redressed this imbalance. Besides, there is no doubting the fact that, in Berulle's teaching, it is always the incarnate Word who is the priest. Recent questioning has at least had the good effect of focusing our attention on the one person of the Word of God made flesh, for us and for our salvation. In any Christian theology, the role of Jesus as mediator is sourced in the one person in whom the divine and the human are inseparably and continually united. Out of that inseparable union flows any sharing of any of the baptised in the priesthood of Christ. Berulle was in no way trying to downgrade the humanity of Christ. He was, in the fullest sense, the apostle of the Word incarnate. But his great desire was to make all Christians, not priests only, into worshippers of God, adorers; and to adore perfectly is to be in a state of complete 'self-annihilation' and total adherence to God. In this context, even the humanity of Christ is called to be completely subjected to God. This is what enables it to be such an active, living 'instrument' of God, perfectly united to the divinity.

Divinity and humanity

The emphasis by the French School on the divinity of Christ in his priestly activity had implications for its understanding of the secular and the sacred, of what is of this world and what is other-worldly. The ordained person was very much seen as a man of the sacred, a promoter of the other-worldly. The high theology of ordained priesthood associated with the School drew heavily on the imagery deriving from the Levitical priesthood and from Fathers of the Church like St John Chrysostom, St Gregory Nazianzen, and St Gregory the Great, who were strongly influenced by that kind of sacral and cultic imagery. In this perspective, the priest was very much seen as a man apart, a man separate. A result was that some words that describe the baptismal vocation came to be applied only to the ordained. The priest was separate in his theological formation, in his whole priestly life-style and prayer-style. Even in his pastoral ministry of forming the image of Christ in the hearts of the Christian people, he was separate: by the way he prayed, the way he preached, the way he gave and received spiritual direction. In all of this, the School has left us a very rich legacy of appreciation of the things of heaven. One hopes that this legacy can be wedded to the best of the contemporary emphasis on the signs of the times, on the re-assessment of the relationship between the secular and the sacred, on the importance of true human development. All of this would be in the real interest of the mystery of the incarnate Word, that mystery which the French School set out to keep exploring.

A bridging saint

A saint who provides some bridges between the concerns of the French School and some of the Church's contemporary concerns is St Vincent de Paul (1581-1660). Many would argue that he was not really a member of the French School, but that he was strongly influenced by it cannot be denied. When he came to Paris in 1610, he was searching – searching not so much for a spirituality as for a way of combining the requirements of priesthood with the securing for himself of a Church living that would bring advantage to him and to his family. The example and inspiration of Berulle and his circle had a profound influence in setting him in the direction of heroic holiness. The values and attitudes he experienced in that circle made him question many of his own priorities. Berulle became his spiritual director. In the same setting, he came under the influence of Fr André Duval, a wise and learned priest whom he came to admire greatly and who was later to direct him. He learned much about the topics of Divine Providence, the Will of God and Self-Denial from the writing of the English Capuchin, Benet of Canfield (1562-1610) who had strongly impressed Berulle and many of those associated with him. On all of these topics, Vincent was to put his own distinctive stamp.

A second and powerful influence in the shaping of his spiritual vision was the way he learned to deal with the false accusation of theft. An early biographer tells us that it was in the very enduring of this great hurt that God inspired him with a plan to lead a truly ecclesiastical life. True priesthood is about representing Christ the priest; but Vincent, in the strange ways of providence, learned to represent Christ by being himself mis-represented. It could have embittered and broken him. Instead, it helped to sweeten and re-make him.

The third great influence was the sacrifice by which he somehow took on himself the temptations against the faith of a learned theologian. The exact nature and duration of Vincent's faith trials are a matter of some debate, but there is no doubt that, again in God's providence, the temptation actuated in Vincent himself what he perceived to be virtually dead in the theologian and what mirrored for him the priestly qualities for which he himself would become famous – a zeal to catechise, to preach, to motivate other priests and likely young candidates for priesthood.

Out of the continual fermenting of these three experiences came three directly pastoral experiences which convinced him that his life must take a totally new course: the first was the vision of spiritual poverty opened up to him by his call to hear the confession of a dying man and that led him to preach his first mission sermon; the second was the vision of material poverty in the parish of Chatillon and of possibilities there of work with the local clergy; the third was the encouragement of an admiring Huguenot who was challenged by his mission work. This motivated him further to preach and to catechise.

Out of all of these very personal experiences came the shaping of Vincent's great ideal of priesthood. That ideal drew continual life from the mystery of the Word incarnate of which he had learned so much in the Berulle circle. In the same circle, he had come to appreciate the precious name of Jesus. That name was later to mean so much to him that he said to the Confraternity of Charity, simply but profoundly: 'Let us make Jesus our patron.' In this decision about choice of patron, mission and charity had met. But, ironically, while remaining always indebted to Berulle, Vincent was to break with him. It would be simplistic to say that it was a clash of personalities, or a break between the peasant and the aristocrat. It would also be over-simplifying to say that it was the praxis-oriented man breaking with the theory man. Maybe Vincent, though far from being a man who would rush providence, became impatient with Berulle's 'Dionysian' orders and ranks and pressed on with his own more 'Augustinian' view of priesthood as the kind of service by which the bread of salvation, bread for body and bread for spirit, needed urgently and daily to be broken for 'little ones'. Whatever the explanation, the focus of the two men became very distanced from each other. Both men were focused on the Word incarnate but for Vincent it was to be the Word incarnate evangelising the poor. Berulle's vocation kept taking shape in the call to pray, to study, to contemplate, to write. But it would be wrong to say that Vincent was merely a practice-oriented man. He knew exactly where his theory lay, as is abundantly clear from the rules he composed, the conferences he animated, the letters he wrote, the sharings of prayer which he led.

Disciple-learner

Much of Vincent's genius lay in his being a superb disciple-learner. He knew how to draw selectively and judiciously on every source of wisdom and experience in the Church. He learned from great men and women like Francis de Sales, Berulle, Jane de Chantal, Louise de Marillac. He learned from theologians of his time and was often heard to say 'a learned theologian told me...' He learned from his own mistakes and those of others in the planning of seminary formation, as when he eventually decided to separate the younger seminarians from the older ones in the Bons-Enfants. He kept probing the views of the 'learned theologians' as he tried to make up his mind about the orthodoxy of the leader of the Jansenists, whose services he was happy to enlist for writing the Latin text of the Rule for his priests and brothers. The last thought in his head would have been to make the Daughters of Charity into contemplatives, but he knew exactly what he was saying when he told them that they could all become St Teresas. His teaching about the interiority that blends contemplation and action and that finds God's will in all situations is well expressed in what he had to say about 'leaving God for God'.

Vincent reacted strongly against florid and rhetorical sermons and the kind of complicated catechesis that did not really break the bread of salvation. When he said no to Fr du Coudray, one of his missioners who wanted to work on the Syriac Bible in Rome, he was not despising biblical scholarship; he was recalling a preacher to his missionary vocation, a preacher whom he saw as 'co-redeemer' of the poor. When he wrote in his Rule that lay brothers should not learn reading and writing, it was for the promoting of a mission rather than for the holding back of education. Vincent was happy to leave the emphasis on academic excellence to Fr Olier who anticipated so much of the Church's present understanding of mystery and sacrament, and to Olier's Sulpician colleagues who have so profoundly affected the seminary tradition. His own emphasis, in seminary formation, was on the practical knowledge and skills that could best serve the spiritual and bodily needs of the poor and those who were to serve them, preach to them, catechise them. The extent to which he, his colleagues, and their successors, achieved and achieve excellence in attaining this ideal, and the extent of their ability to discern changing needs in changing times, is an open question.

St Vincent was the founder of the Congregation of the Mission, for the evangelisation of the poor and the renewal of the priesthood. Perhaps the loveliest line in his Rule for them is his invitation to 'live together as dear friends'. The century that produced *The Cost of Discipleship* needs no reminders that 'dear' means both 'loving' and 'at a cost'. With Louise de Marillac, Vincent was co-founder of the Daughters of Charity. They both continually invited the sisters to a life of the heart, a life of 'cordiality'. But Vincent's community-making was not confined to the missioners and to the sisters. In many ways he spent his time bridging the worlds of rich-poor, man-woman, people from greatly differing backgrounds. These bridgings provided new glimpses of the kind of gospel groupings that resulted from Peter's first preaching recorded in Acts and that are the models for all further community making. In the original groupings that were the 'charities', set up to organise and distribute relief for the poor, Vincent provided equal scope for women and men. In 1620 he set up an all-male 'charity'. In 1621 he attempted to make men and women work together in a 'charity'. He told the men that 'Our Lord is as much glorified in the ministry of women as in that of men'. When the mixed charities didn't work out, he had his own ideas about what happens when male strengths and weaknesses interact with female strengths and weaknesses. But he continued to see the gospel as the energy that produces ever new forms of communion and community. In his willingness to learn from so many sources, he continually drew on that energy.

Perhaps St. Vincent's real genius lay in not belonging to any school of spirituality. His only school was what he called the school of the cross in which we acquire the learning of the saints. As a teacher in that school, he has much to tell us about how women and men can work together in a Church that must always seek first the reign of God and that must keep daily breaking the bread of salvation.

Raymond Deville, *L'Ecole Française de Spiritualité*, (Desclee, 1987).

Elizabeth Rapley, *The Dévotes: Women and Church in Seventeenth Century France*, (McGill-Queen's University Press, 1990).

CHAPTER 34

Secular and Religious

Two expressions of priestly ministry

In the renewal of religious life since the Second Vatican Council, the charism of each religious community has had a central place. The charism of a community is a gift of the Holy Spirit. It is the particular way in which both founder and community have experienced the gospel, interpreted the gospel, lived the gospel, helped others to live the gospel. The charisms of communities are seen as gifts, divine blessings for the good not primarily of the individual but of the whole community, the whole Church and, through the Church, the whole world. Seen this way, the religious life itself is a charism. We speak of the founder's charism, the founding charism, the charisms of individuals that nurture, and are nurtured by, their congregation's charism.

Charism and lifestyle

Though the charism of a religious community is partially embodied in the lifestyle of the community, it is becoming more and more difficult to distinguish the lifestyle of the religious priest from that now envisaged for the diocesan priest. In the profile of the diocesan priest, in the decree on the *Ministry and Life of Priests*, there is a stress on the living of celibacy, poverty and obedience. Some form of common life is envisaged. The same profile is strengthened further in *I Will Give You Shepherds*, with its even stronger emphasis on ascetical practices and austerity of life. The profile is a kind of double of the traditional description of religious life. It would appear that the 'counsels' are now seen not so much as options but as the expression, for all priests and 'religious', of the radical call to all who wish to be disciples of Jesus. They are the priestly and 'religious' way of living the chastity, poverty and obedience without which no human life could be called Christian.

It cannot be that the religious priest lives the ideal of the counsels more perfectly than does his diocesan neighbour. He is not automatically more celibate, more poor, more obedient. Each of the evangelical counsels is undivided and it is inseparable from the other counsels. The diocesan priest must live his celibacy in a way that learns from the recent turbulent history of that way of life. He is entitled to all the support systems, social, psychological and spiritual, that encourage the growth of that gift of God. The religious lives the same celibacy within a somewhat different support system. The poverty of the diocesan priest will have modalities different from those of the itinerant preacher who follows the practical directives of particular constitutions. The obedience of the diocesan priest is lived out in the context of the common vision of presbyters united in mind and heart with their bishop. The obedience of the religious is set in the vision of a charism commonly owned and the call to ministry that goes beyond the confines of the local Church. In *Evangelical Witness* (par 7), Pope Paul VI said that living the evangelical counsels frees the religious from whatever might draw him from the fervour of charity and the perfection of divine worship. This freeing, perfect charity, and consecration which one normally associates with religious life, are, in fact, as much a programme for the lifestyle of the diocesan priest as they are for the religious. Common life, simple lifestyle, asceticism and austerity, must keep finding their meaning in the working out of the programme of each. In this way, diocesan priesthood and religious priesthood become partners, not competitors. Each enriches the other.

Three ways of enriching
The thrust of the Exhortation *I Will Give You Shepherds* is towards the ministry of those in diocesan priesthood. There is no special section on what diocesan priests can contribute towards the renewal of religious life. And yet, everything in the Exhortation could be read as part of such a programme of renewal. Pope John Paul devotes a short space (in par 74) to some meeting points between the charisms of religious priests and the daily life in the diocese. He sees religious clergy as forming one presbyterate with the priests of the diocese where they work. He describes their presence and their charism as enriching, challenging, and encouraging, with special reference to the ongoing formation of priests and the promoting of a suitable spirituality. He sees them as promoting communion between the various particular churches and broadening people's horizons in the giving of Christian witness.

Though it looks disarmingly simple, this is all a very demanding programme. There is a danger that it could remain a lovely ideal, with little relation to reality. How can we ensure that the enriching, challenging and encouraging will really take place? However one answers this question, there can be no denying that, drawing on their charisms and the history of their charisms, religious priests have much to give in enriching the Church in three of today's most urgent and crucial needs: 1) the promoting of the word of God; 2) the providing of special ministries; 3) the building of community.

1. Enriching with the word of God

The development of a good theology of the word of God is one of the most urgent needs of the Church today. Christians are agreed that all the baptised are called to hear the word, to pray the word, and to live by the word. But who is authorised to speak the word, to teach the word and proclaim the word? We know that the ordained are responsible for the way in which the word is spoken, taught, proclaimed. But is there a call for new ways of sharing this responsibility?

The history of the Church reflects a variety of forms of emphasis in the answering of these questions. In the assemblies of some of the early Christian communities, it would appear that all the baptised had the opportunity to 'speak in church'. There was question of the real sharing of the word. Already in the Pastoral Epistles, the special responsibility for the word was an important element in the understanding of pastoral office (cf 2 Tim 4:2). At the time of St Dominic, the episcopal office was so identified with the preaching of the word that some people wondered whether Dominic wished to found an order of bishops. At the same time, in another part of Europe, Francis, the layman, had no problem about preaching and motivating his brethren to preach. The preaching of the word, to believer and unbeliever, was an important ingredient, indeed a priority, in the mission of the new apostolic orders and congregations that began to come into existence in the early sixteenth century.

The close links between the word and the office of priest and bishop is a partial reason for the virtual monopoly of the proclamation of the word which, up to recently, was so characteristic of Catholic

Church life. One example was that the homily was seen as the preserve of the ordained only. Any other speaking allowed in
Church was called by another name. But our experience of the
richness of the ministry of the word has, of late, been bringing
about some change. The instituting and developing of the ministry
of lector, the scope given to catechists and teachers in children's
Masses, the post-synodal papal exhortations on evangelisation,
on catechesis, and on the lay vocation, a growing appreciation of
the prophetic vocation of all the baptised, have all contributed to a
desire for a wider and richer sharing of the word, by all the baptised, within the Church assembly and outside it. While the duty
and responsibility of bishop and priest to proclaim and guard the
word remains unimpaired, it would appear that it is time to look
in a new and creative way at the lesson of the Church assemblies
in Corinth, of Dominic, of Francis, of the apostolic preaching orders. There is no doubt that the new forms of sharing the ministry
of the word, in the Christian assembly and outside of it, will have
profound implications for all Church life and all Church ministry.
The wide and varied experience of religious orders and of societies of apostolic life throughout the centuries, in a prophetic
proclamation of the word, has very much to contribute to this new
growth. Maybe it is in this setting that religious priests will make
their best and most realistic contribution to the promoting of a
suitable spirituality.

2. Enriching with special ministries

There is very good evidence that nearly all the orders and congregations of men founded since the thirteenth century were founded
for some special ministry or ministries. The realisation of this
should be a crucial ingredient of their renewal. All their consecration, all their desire for perfect charity, should be refracted
through the prism of ministry. Priests in every order and society,
no matter what the time of their foundation, must be very exact
today in naming or re-naming their ministry. This principle applies, of course, to those in monastic communities, to those in
apostolic societies, and to those in communities that are delicate
blendings of the two.

As priests in societies of apostolic life try to re-discover today
what are their special ministries, there is a real concern that their

services might be more and more absorbed into regular parish ministry. This issue becomes more acute in the growing number of areas where there is a shortage of diocesan clergy. It is not the only issue affecting identity. With the deepening of appreciation of the prophetic and other aspects of the baptismal vocation, many priests in religious communities are wondering whether there is a future for large groupings of priests involved together in ministries which, no matter how good, do not require priestly ordination. This question extends to those involved in the area of seminary formation and of formation for other kinds of Church ministry. Is there a good case for saying that priests who are involved in such formation should be required to have a continual experience of pastoral ministry that goes wider than the community of those they are helping to form? Is it a matter of urgency that religious priests be re-directed from some of their present good ministries to ministries more in accord with the foundation charisms of their communities? Some of these questions affect diocesan priests as well as religious priests. Answers to them should be dictated less by the reality of diminishing numbers than by a clearer vision of what constitutes baptismal priesthood and ordained priesthood. The questions give rise to other questions. In what sense, for example, are religious and diocesan priests to form one presbyterate in the local church? The diocesan priest belongs to the diocesan presbyterate. With a growing involvement of the laity, he could also be described as the maker of new groups of 'elders' in the parish, a new kind of 'presbyterate'. The religious priest, as well as somehow belonging to the diocesan presbyterate, belongs to the presbyterates of his local religious community, of his province, of his society worldwide. This belonging to many presbyterates can be very enriching. It can also be impoverishing, encouraging a kind of dissipation of spiritual energy and a blurring of ministerial accountability. In the end, the best way of ensuring that the charism of religious priests is really enriching the local Church is the effective performance of the ministries that both correspond to the charism of their order or congregation and are clearly and obviously seen to be of benefit to the Church, universal and local.

Apostolic religious societies were founded to meet specific needs. The discerning of these needs was usually done by men and women who had no prominent Church office. In the renewal of the same societies today, the discerning of needs is done largely by the local bishops or by the full college of bishops. This is what has been happening in the synods of recent years. The list of topics of these synods, and of the key words in each topic, can be a mirror in which religious see reflected the particular ministries to which their charisms call them today: atheism, ministerial priesthood, justice, evangelisation, catechesis, family, reconciliation, lay vocation, priestly formation. For each of these topics, there is a corresponding urgent need in every diocese or group of dioceses. Each of these needs is today's mirroring of a need that called a religious community into existence in the past. In the effective and visible responding to the needs that are discerned today, charisms from the past speak to priests and people in the present, and the community of apostolic life does not need to justify its existence to either priests or people. The fact that ministries which in the past were associated exclusively with religious are done effectively today by some diocesan priests is a good development. But it can also be a salutary reminder to religious communities to find again the ministries which are the real expression of their founding charism. Maybe it is in this context, too, that the fear of some religious of becoming too caught up in parish ministry will find its level. In a diocese fully alive, there is room for a rich variety of ministries, a wide variety of kinds of parish.

At many points, this second way of enriching coalesces with the first. It is good to keep remembering that all clerical societies of apostolic life were founded for providing some form of special ministry of the word.

3. Enriching with community
Every priest is a builder of community. To build community you must first experience community. The diocesan priest, after his time of formation in the seminary community, belongs to the community of the bishop's presbyters and to the community of pastoral leaders who shape the parish community. Every aspect of the spirituality and ministry of the religious priest is coloured by the life and traditions of the community to which he belongs. The reality is that many priests, diocesan and religious, live their lives in a less than healthy isolation. Of the areas in which there is

a gap between ideal and reality, there is none more alarming than this; there is none with a greater bearing on priestly life-style and celibacy-related issues. For a priest caught in this isolation gap, there can be nothing more effective than the stumbling on a real experience of community. It can mean the re-discovery of the joy of his vocation.

The priest's need for community cannot be separated from recent developments in the topic of community. A phenomenon of our time is the emergence of new forms of Christian community. These include communities of lay people who welcome the liturgical and pastoral services of priests. They also include communities comprising a cross-section of laity, religious and priests, with a common programme of prayer and work. In reflecting on their experience of such communities, many priests are finding the beginnings of a vision for the future. In the attempts to help build new Christian communities in imaginative ways, the diocesan and religious experiences of community should not pass each other by. They should enrich each other. Many religious priests belong to communities founded to comprise 'priests and lay-brothers'. Perhaps the same communities will one day be described rather as comprising 'lay people and priests', the priests being the 'co-adjutor brothers' helping the lay people to re-alise the hitherto undreamt of riches of their common baptismal vocation; at the same time, the lay people will help the priests to re-discover the fulness of their own vocation.

Conclusion
The details of the future forms of community are unknown to us. In helping to shape them, religious have much to give out of their community experience and tradition. In this service to diocesan priesthood and to the whole community of the baptised, they themselves can discover again their own service to the word of God. They can discover the ministries to which they are now called. They can discover again the community to which they were once called, as well as the communities to which they are now being called.

T. P. Rausch, *Priesthood Today: An Appraisal*, (Paulist Press, 1992).
Lawrence Cada, SM, et al, *Shaping The Coming Age of Religious Life*, (Affirmation Books, 1985).

CHAPTER 35

Holy and glorious wounds

On Holy Saturday night we are at the nerve-centre of the whole liturgical year. Indeed we are at the nerve centre of the workings of the universe, the celebration of the rising from death of the one who by dying gave meaning to every living and every dying. As a result, the liturgy of the vigil is so loaded with meaning that one could easily miss some of its most precious ingredients. But, fortunately, some of the contents of the vigil are celebrated more fully at other stages of the liturgical year. An example is what takes place early on in the service of light. The Easter candle is lit from the new fire. If the candle is to be blessed, the cross is brought to the celebrant who cuts a cross in the wax. He traces the letter 'alpha' above the cross, the letter 'omega' below, and the numerals of the current year between the arms of the cross. He says: 'Christ yesterday and today, the beginning and the end, alpha and omega; all time belongs to him, and all the ages; to him be glory and power, through every age and forever, Amen.' When the cross and other marks have been made, the priest may insert five grains of incense in the candle. He does this in the form of a cross, praying 'by his holy and glorious wounds, may Christ our Lord guard us and keep us. Amen.' He lights the candle from the new fire, saying 'may the light of Christ, rising in glory, dispel the darkness of our hearts and minds.'

The Sunday liturgy a week later provides a kind of celebration of this series of actions at the Easter Vigil. The gospel for the Second Sunday of Easter (Jn 20:19-31) highlights the endless reserves of the 'holy and glorious wounds' of the Lord. The man at the centre of that gospel reading has come to be known as 'doubting Thomas'. It would, perhaps, be more correct to call him 'believing Thomas'. His experience provides us with a rich programme for coming to believe. He was not with the rest of the twelve when Jesus came. To the disciples' assurance that they had seen the Lord, he replied 'unless I see the holes that the nails made in his hands and can put my finger into the holes they made, and unless

I can put my hand into his side, I refuse to believe'. Eight days later, Jesus stood among the disciples. He gave them a message of peace. Turning to Thomas, he said 'Put your finger here; look, here are my hands. Give me your hand; put it into my side. Doubt no longer but believe.' The contact of Thomas with the transformed and transforming wounds of Christ elicited his great act of faith: 'My Lord and my God.' This, in turn, drew the blessing of Jesus on those who have not seen and yet believe.

The 'holy and glorious' wounds of Christ put us in touch with the holiness and glory of God, a process which is the purpose of all worship, all priesthood, all ministry. The holiness of God is God's unique trinitarian way of knowing and loving. The glory of God is the shining forth of that holiness. The wounds of Christ are the wounds out of which came the Lord's life-blood, the blood of the new covenant of which he is mediator (Heb 9:15). Without the shedding of that blood, there is no remission of sins (Heb 9:22). The life-giving blood coming from the Lord's wounds in the sorrowful mysteries spills into the joyful mysteries and the glorious mysteries. At the Easter Vigil the symbols of the five wounds are inserted into the paschal candle in the form of incense, a prayer and an act of worship rising up to the Father from the whole body of Christ. The transformed wounds of Jesus, like their bearer, are a continual act of intercession for us (Heb 7:25), a continual sacrifice, and a continual source of new faith and life.

The wounds of the body of Christ are reflected in the whole Church at every stage of her history. Preachers and teachers have always alerted the Church to the forms which the five wounds of Christ seemed to be taking in various events in Church and world. The saints have at all times been willing to identify with these wounds and to carry the marks of Jesus Christ on their bodies (cf Gal 6:17). The virgins and martyrs especially saw their call to witness in these terms. The wounds of Christ in the whole Church have been reflected, in turn, in the state of priesthood and Church ministry. One could also say that the wounds in priesthood and other ministries are always reflected in the whole Church. There is no doubt that our generation has its own share in the weakness and wounds of Christ. It could be said that Christ's Church was never as much seen to be vulnerable as it is today. It could also be said that never was it harder to convince Christians generally that the way to discipleship must be the way of the cross. In the meantime, devout believers continue to look for consolation in the 'five most precious wounds'. The wounds are being experienced by those exercising baptismal priesthood and those exercising ministerial priesthood. There are wounds today in our attempts to exercise faith, hope, love and in the two qualities which are our sharing in the covenant qualities of God. In the perspectives of faith, all these are our entering into the five 'holy and glorious' wounds by which Christ our Lord mysteriously 'guards and keeps' us.

Head-wounds

Over the centuries, the most popular way of naming the five wounds was in terms of the head, each of the hands, the feet nailed together, the side. The wounded head of Christ should have a special appeal today for those in ordained ministry. Ordination to priesthood is a call to a share in the headship of Christ. As wounded healers, the ordained are coming more and more to realise their need of a power greater than themselves. This power resides in the head and face of the Church's Head.

Hand-wounds

Two of the five wounds of Jesus Christ were on his hands. These were the hands which had continually blessed. One recalls that little children were brought to him, so that he would place his hands on them and bless them. But the disciples rebuked those who brought them. Jesus said 'Let the little children come to me, and do not hinder them, for the kingdom of heaven belongs to such as these.' Then he placed his hands on them (Mt 19:13-14) and blessed them (Mk 10:16). With the same hands, in the context of another kind of blessing, he was later to take the bread and the cup which would inaugurate the new covenant (Lk 22:19-20). The final recorded blessing that came from the hands of Jesus is in St Luke's account of his ascension: 'He lifted up his hands and blessed them.' The effect was that they worshipped him and they returned to Jerusalem in a spirit of joy and praise (Luke 24:50-53). The hands that blessed were also the hands that healed and that restored life. One day a ruler came and knelt before him and said, 'My daughter has just died. But come and put your hand on her and she will live '(Mt 9:18). When Jesus eventually reached the ruler's house he assured the noisy crowd that the girl was not dead but asleep. Their laughter was changed to amazement when he 'went in and took the girl by the hand and she got up' (v 25). The same touch of his hand brought sight to a blind man whom people brought to Jesus in the hope that he would touch him. He took the man by the hand, spat on his eyes, and again put his hands on him. After some questioning, Jesus put his hands on his eyes. 'His eyes were opened, his sight was restored and he saw everything clearly' (Mk 8:22-25).

Others who benefited from the helping touch of the hands of Jesus were the man with the shrivelled hand whom he healed on the Sabbath Day (Mt 12:13), and Peter's mother-in-law whose hand he touched so successfully that she was able to get up and to wait on him (Mt 8:14-15). Sometimes the touch of the hand of Jesus was allowed to be distorted into a judgment, as when his betrayer turned out to be the man who 'has dipped his hand into the bowl with me' (Mt 26:23). Shortly after this event, Pilate was to protest his own innocence by taking water and washing his hands in front of the crowd (Mt 27:24). When the moment came for him to die in consequence of these symbolic actions of men's hands, Jesus was to commend his spirit into his Father's hands (Lk 23:46). In the beginnings of his resurrection glory he showed his disciples his hands and his feet (Lk 24:39-40). St Mark's gospel closes with the assurance that among the signs that would accompany those who believe would be 'they will pick up snakes with their hands...They will place their hands on sick people, and they will get well' (Mk 16:18). Having sent the disciples on their mission, 'he was taken up into heaven and he sat at the right hand of God' (v 19).

The hands of Jesus were hands that blessed, hands that healed with a whole range of blessing and healing. The disciple who was the author of 1 John was happy that his own hands had touched 'that which was from the beginning, which we have heard, which we have seen with our eyes, which we have looked at'. This is what he wished to 'proclaim concerning the word of Life' (1 Jn 1:1). From the beginning, that experience of the touch of Christ must have been an ingredient in the understanding of the imposition of hands whenever the grace of special ministry was passed on (2 Tim 1:6). Following the whole range of movements of the hands of Jesus is a programme for all discipleship and all ministry. Entering into the power of their wounds is a requirement for every disciple, for every minister, in every generation.

Feet wounds

The wounds of the hands of Christ are closely linked with the wounds in his feet. In his risen appearance, he showed both hands and feet to his disciples (Lk 24:39-40). His short public ministry had been a time of many journeys, many walkings. He knew what it was to have tired feet, as when he was 'tired from the journey' (Jn 4:6). His walking led him into situations in which he condoned some actions which were against the law, as when the disciples began to pick ears of corn as they walked along on the Sabbath (Mk 2:23). In his walkings he had his agonising moments, as when 'he no longer walked publicly among the Jews' (Jn 11:54), and his glorious moments, as when he came to Peter walking on the water (Mt 14:25). His whole message was an invitation to walk not in darkness but in light (Jn 8:12). The walking image was later taken up by Paul, notably in his consoling assurance that we walk by faith, not sight (2 Cor 5:7), and Peter when he invites us to 'walk in his steps' (1 Pet 2:21).

The missionary walkings of Jesus, as he preached the good news, reached a great high point in the action which the fourth gospel regards as important as the taking and blessing of the bread and the cup at the Last Supper: 'After the journey to the supper room, he began to wash his disciples' feet and to wipe them with a towel' (Jn 13:5). The action elicited from an astonished Peter a desire for a more complete washing (v 9). This, in turn, elicited from Jesus a programme or rather an outline for a style for all ministry (vv 12-17). The message must have got a new poignancy when the feet of Jesus himself were nailed to a cross, after a trying journey on foot.

Wound in the side

The fifth wound of Jesus is the wound on his side (Jn 19:34). The account of the opening of his side evokes the whole mystery of the blood of the new covenant, the water of baptism, the water coming forth from the side of the new temple which was already in process of being raised up again (Jn 2:19), the mysterious union between man and woman issuing from the side of the new Adam (cf Gen 2:22).

A programme for disciples

The head, the hands, feet and side of Jesus are a kind of shorthand for his whole mission and ministry. Their wounds are a short-hand for the rejection which he had to endure from a 'world' which hated him because he testified against what was evil in it (Jn 1:7). His disciples who minister in his name today are to expect the same rejection (Jn 15:18). They must make sure, of course, that the rejection results from their living of the gospel rather than a failure to live it. It is in the 'holy and glorious wounds' that the Church today, as always, must seek its real strength. The five wounds of the Church today are wounds in faith, in hope, in love, in mercy, in fidelity

We are experiencing wounds in faith. From outside the Church we are being persistently challenged by the implications of world views other than the accepted Christian one. From within the Church is coming a search for re-statements of the faith which will take account of the many developments in scholarship and the Church's lived experience. The laudable efforts to re-state the Church's beliefs, and to find the real 'hierarchy of truths' in a changing world, is having some shattering repercussions in the faith of many. This, in turn, can present the man who proclaims the word at its 'highest level of sacramental intensity' with challenges and wounds for which he is not always prepared.

We are experiencing wounds in hope. Changing world views have been challenging our understanding of and approach to all the 'last things', and indeed the 'first things'. Growing numbers are wondering how to make religious sense of the 'immortality of the soul' and the 'resurrection of the body', Christ's and ours, in a society strongly coloured by the assumptions of new scientific world-views. With so many shakings of so many foundations, many teachers and preachers of the gospel are experiencing much challenge and not a little confusion.

We are experiencing wounds in loving. Nobody can deny that the great Christian virtue is the agapé form of love but many

Christians today, married and celibate, are questioning accepted attitudes towards loving. The emphasis is on the goodness of every part of creation and especially on every aspect of the human body. This has happily led to the disappearance of many taboos and cautions. But it has generated new problems about human loving. Those in celibate Church ministry are finding that the emphasis has changed from loving as an activity of the will to include loving as an expression of the affective side of our human-ness. Many celibates were not ready for the change. This has gen-erated its own share of wounds. Even with all the helps of contem-porary holistic approaches, it will take a while till we all learn all the implications of what it is to love God with all the heart, all the soul, all the mind and to love both ourselves and our neighbour in a way that flows from that love (Mt 22:37-39).

We are experiencing wounds in tender mercy. The two great qualities of the God of the covenant were tender mercy and fidelity. These two qualities are praised in several pages of the Hebrew Bible, notably in Ps 89 and the very short Ps 117. Jesus was the human face, the sacrament, of the Father's tender mercy and fidelity, and his Church is called to be the sacrament of these same qualities. A challenge for the Church today is to live that ideal and at the same time to distinguish between sin and sinner, and al-ways provide laws and a discipline which will help enable this to happen. The effort to combine the two provides its own wounds and heartaches.

We are experiencing wounds in fidelity. The move from a static world view to a dynamic one has been affecting every area of Church life. Many believers do not feel bound now by a commit-ment, which they made earlier in life, in very different circum-stances. The attitude has had many repercussions in Church ministry. One would hope that the confusion and pain which often ensue will lead to a new appreciation of the fidelity of the God of the covenant, made visible and tangible in the costly fidelity of Jesus Christ.

The Church, the body of Christ, will never be without its wounds. It will have to bear the marks of Jesus branded on its body (Gal 6:17). Every age of the Church's life brings its own wounds. For the believer, this should be a source not of sadness but of boasting (Gal 6:14). Wounds borne in faith, hope, love, and in a spirit of continual conversion, keep us in living touch with those wounds that were inflicted as an act of rejection on the earthly body of Christ and were themselves changed into something holy, glorious, and life-giving.

CHAPTER 36

Houses and householders

As we search for an understanding of the mission of the Church in the world today, there is a question that can help put both Church and world in suitable focus. What have the following five words in common?: economy (of salvation); ecology; ecumenism; parochial; diocesan. It is easy to recognise something in common between the first three, but the connections with the other two are not so obvious. All five, in fact, come from the Greek word for a house: *oikos, oikia*. The economy of salvation is God's saving plan for the whole house and household of the universe. Ecology expresses a concern for the condition of the house in which the one human family lives. Ecumenism is the move to unite, in accordance with God's design in his Son, the hearts and minds of all human beings in the whole inhabited house of the universe. Parochial concern began, literally, with Christians seeing themselves as resident aliens, provisionally housed (Eph 2:19). The diocese is, literally, the network of the many house-churches. Much of the renewal called for by the Second Vatican Council could be seen as an invitation to widen and deepen our understanding of each of these house-words. It is also a continual invitation to see how the five are in many ways connected.

Economy and the household
The economy of salvation began, not with the call of Abraham, not even with the creation of the universe, but with the plan of the Creator before time began, 'before the foundation of the world' (Eph 1:4). Until creation, the great mystery of the plan had been hidden in the mind and heart of the Creator (cf Eph 3:9). The working out of the plan was the disclosure of God's decree, for our glory (cf 1 Cor 2:7-8). The great houseplan reached a decisive stage in the various big movements of creation, in the billions of years before the emergence of the first human beings, in the many thousands of years that passed before the call of Abraham, in all the saving events between the call of Abraham and the coming of the word of God in human flesh. The special manifestation of

God's saving economy was the incarnation, life, death and resurrection of his Son. In the whole mystery of his Son (cf Eph 1:10) the limitless riches of the house-plan made by God are contained and revealed. The plan is revealed as one of communion, on many levels – a communion of all human beings with each other, with the rest of creation, and with Father, Son and Spirit. Since that communion had been ruptured and damaged in many ways, as far back as human memory could go, the work of repairing, redeeming and re-creating emerged as being of the essence of God's houseplan, in Christ.

Reflecting on God's economy of salvation helps us to enter into the 'economic' aspects of the mystery of the triune God. We are invited to keep wondering what is going on 'immanently' in the intimate life of the Father, Son and Spirit, as we ponder on what each of them has been doing as the story and destiny of the human family has unfolded. Since all human beings are made in the 'image' of God (Gen 1:27), by studying the image we come to know something of the triune God who shaped the image. As we try to take in the full message of the person who, by the will of the Father and the working of the Holy Spirit, so identified with our human condition that he 'in every respect has been tested as we are, yet without sin' (Heb 4:15), we discover something of the inner life of the divine persons themselves. Every time we experience love, understanding, communion, we sense and glimpse something of what is eternally happening between Father, Son and Spirit. The creation of the universe and the unfolding of God's economy, God's houseplan, come to be seen as a kind of overflow of divine love, energy, relatedness. Human living comes to be experienced as a being drawn into the community life of the divine persons. We find a new meaning in the invitation of Jesus to love him. The result will be that the Father will love us and they will come to us and make their home with us (Jn 14:23). The economy becomes an invitation to open the house of our hearts to the divine persons. Our house becomes their home.

Ecology and the house
Our generation has experienced the first ever earth-summit. It is a forceful reminder that the state of the house of the universe is no

longer a concern just for the few. Ecology raises the question of how we relate with and treat the rest of the universe. It alerts us to the fact that we could become destroyers of the universe rather than its stewards. We are finding a new urgency in words like holistic and interrelatedness. We are learning what it is to come from the earth and to return to it; to be part of the earth and to let the earth be part of us; to cultivate and care for the earth with which we are in many ways one. We are seeing new meanings in the fact that the world has been called the cosmos, the thing of beauty loved into existence by God. We recognise that in the making and shaping of the world we are God's partners, fellow-workers, collaborators. We are re-discovering the riches of words like pro-creation, co-creation. We are tuning in better to the words of Jesus 'We must work the works of him who sent me while it is day; night is coming when no one can work' (Jn 9:4), and we are seeing more meaning in his call for 'labourers' (Mt 9:38). In this context, it would be good to read the Genesis accounts of creation in the present tense and to see the commission to till and keep the garden (Gen 2:15) as an invitation to be sharers now in the work of creation. The priestly account of creation envisages human beings as being at the head of creation. Here perhaps we are most in touch with the great question which once dominated the schools of theology – how to harmonise the supremacy of the Creator and the autonomy of the human will, how to image the ways that God and humans work together. All human beings were made in God's image (Gen 1:26). Every generation has nuanced this teaching in its own way. In the light of this continual nuancing we can now say that the vocation to be human is one to full intimacy with God, Father, Son, and Spirit; to represent God, to be in partnership with God. It is a call to be sharers in his dominion, in his power.

The fact that God created human beings, male and female, leaves scope for a limitless variety of images of co-creation, nurturing, fostering, inventing. The advances in science and technology can be abused by a search for the wrong kind of domination, the wrong kind of power, but, in the design of the Creator, these are so many invitations to let the earth preserve its own autonomy and still produce the fruits that nurture and support the whole human family. This demands a gentle dominion rather than a ruthless domination. It calls for the kind of management and stewardship of creation that is alert to every threat of pollution and destruction. William Wordsworth spoke of the youth who remains 'nature's priest'. The full human vocation also comprises being nature's prophet and king. In our task of freeing creation from the futility to which it has been subjected (Rom 8:19-21), there is a continual call for collaboration between priest, prophet and king, between the science that deals with God and the science that deals with the earth. It is a call to beautify further the one cosmos; to make the best use of all the earth's resources; to provide for the one human family in the one house of earth.

The ecumenical house

For centuries, Christians have been professing in the Creed that they 'believe in the Catholic Church'. Implicit in this profession is belief in the ecumenical vocation of the Church, since to be 'catholic' is to have concern for the whole inhabited world. 'Catholic' concern is concern for what is in every sense, universal, whole. But the word has different connotations for different Christians. Over the centuries it came to have both exclusive and inclusive meanings. It came to connote doctrinal orthodoxy and integral gospel truth. It came to suggest both that which is universal and worldwide and what leaves place for diversity and variety.

Up to the Second Vatican Council, the Catholic Church in communion with the See of Rome was at ease in applying to herself, sometimes in an inclusive way and sometimes in an exclusive way, all the meanings that the word catholic suggests. Her members felt secure in their unity and catholicity, in doctrine and in basic discipline. The Council decided not to identify absolutely the Catholic Church and the one true Church of Christ. Instead, the one true Church of Christ was described as 'subsisting' in the Catholic Church (*LG* 8). There is some diversity in the interpretations of this word, but all are agreed in saying that it recognises authentic expressions of the Church of Christ outside the visible confines of the Catholic Church. Catholics are described as 'fully incorporated' into the Church (*LG* 14). Catechumens are 'embraced by the Catholic Church as her own' (ibid). Other Christians, principally as a result of baptism, are seen as possessing various levels and degrees of communion with the Catholic

Church (par 15). Those 'who have not yet received the gospel' are described as being 'in various ways related to the people of God, the Church, that is, of Christ' (par 16). Five classes of people who have not yet received the gospel are named: the Jewish people, Moslems, those who 'in shadow and images seek the unknown God', those 'who sincerely seek God', those 'who without blame on their part, have not yet arrived at an explicit knowledge of God'.

It would be hard to draw lines of demarcation between some of these groups, notably the last three. But the great vision behind the whole teaching is that of a God who wills all to be saved, who has revealed himself in a totally unique and definitive way in his Son Jesus Christ whose saving grace, flowing from the events of his life, death, resurrection, and exaltation is offered to every human being. It is because the Church as body of Christ on earth is, through the Spirit, the 'universal sacrament of salvation' (LG 48) that all those who are saved must be in some way related to the Church. We cannot name all the possible ways. We are dealing here with sacrament in its richest connotation of sign, instrument, mystery. What a vision is opened up here for a programme of ecumenism, inter-faith dialogue, and dialogue with non-believers, not merely for the foreseeable future, but until the end of time! What a vision of the God who built the house of the universe, for all his family, in preparation for the eternal transformed dwelling-place to house a family saved!

House of the parish; house of the diocese

It would appear that the original Christian parish (cf 1 Pet 2:11; cf 1:17) was an effort to meet the needs of those who were 'strangers and aliens' (Eph 2:19), and that the word 'diocese' connotes the communion of those who are in various ways 'housed'. In our days, we have experienced much searching for what constitutes the ideal local Church, the ideal parish, the ideal diocese. On paper, the ideal is clear enough. The diocese is a section of God's people entrusted to a bishop assisted by his clergy; to be formed into one community through gospel and eucharist; constituting one particular Church in which the one, holy, catholic and apostolic Church is present and active (SC 11). In the communion of churches which is the Church universal, the diocese embodies and makes manifest the mystery of the universal Church. The liturgical life of the diocese is centred round the bishop, especially in his cathedral church. God's people, presided over by the bishop, surrounded by priests and ministers, give the principal manifestation of the Church in one eucharist, one prayer, one altar (SC 41). All this, in turn, is reflected in the parish. In the parish, the word is preached; all the sacraments are at various stages celebrated; pastoral care is exercised. The ideal is that there is a continual and harmonious interaction between diocesan pastor and parish pastor, in the celebration of word and sacrament, and in the exercise of pastoral care. A phenomenon of our time has been the emergence of parishes that transcend territorial boundaries, and are more oriented towards persons and groups sharing a particular culture and lifestyle. There is also the occasional phenomenon of the non-territorial diocese. Could this be a symbol of the Church's desire to develop a more personal pastoral style, one that makes contact with people's hearts and minds in the grouping in which they are most 'at home'?

A serious concern of our day is about the growing number of homeless people. It would also seem that a growing number of people are no longer 'at home' in traditional forms of Church life. As parishes and dioceses seek renewal and even re-structuring, it may be good to keep remembering that both 'parish' and 'diocese' were originally house-words and that the earliest Christian churches were house churches. Parish and diocese must continue to be communities of households who keep searching for new ways of being home-makers and at-home makers for the growing numbers of the homeless and the alienated.

Building the one house
The author of 1 Timothy wrote of the importance of knowing how we ought 'to behave in the household of God, which is the Church of the living God' (1 Tim 3:15). Our one teacher in the household of the faith, the house-builder's son (cf Mt 13:55), was himself trained in a good school of building, though he himself freely decided to become homeless (Mt 8:20). No wonder he returned so often to images about house, household and building. No wonder that the house-church became the basic unit for the early groupings of his disciples. According to the Letter to the Hebrews, Jesus

was faithful over God's house as a son (3:1ff). As son in his Father's house, Jesus is the builder of a new community. In 1 Peter, Christ and Christians are seen as living stones in the new house, the new temple (2:4ff). This, in turn, provides a setting for what constitutes Christian priesthood, and Christian sacrifice (1 Pet 2:5-9). Ultimately, it is God himself who is the 'master of the household', as is clear from many of the parables of Jesus (e.g. Mt 10:25; Lk 13:25; Mk 14:14). His care extends to everybody and everything in the house.

The purpose of all apostleship and all Church ministry is to build up, to edify (2 Cor 10:8; 13:10). Sometimes one apostle lays the foundation, and another builds on the foundation (1 Cor 3:10ff). Believers are to build each other up (1 Thess 5:11). The gifts of the Spirit are to be used for the upbuilding, encouraging and consoling of the whole community (1 Cor 14:3). In the building, Jesus is the cornerstone who can be maltreated and turned into a stone of stumbling by those who reject him (1 Pet 2:5). The apostles and prophets who are the foundation, are united in one construction with the cornerstone (Eph 2:19-22). In this setting, apostolic ministry is one of stewardship (cf Lk 12:43; Mt 24:45ff). Paul saw himself as a steward called to trustworthiness since he was entrusted with the treasures of the gospel (2 Cor 4:7). According to Titus 1:7, the bishop is God's steward. According to 1 Peter 4:10, every Christian is to be a steward of the gift he has received. All stewardship, whether in the discharge of one's office (Lk 16:1ff) or in carrying out the divine plan of salvation (Eph 3:9), implies accountability to the giver of the office, the one who is the ultimate maker of the plan for the whole household. There is a unified programme here for all ordained and non-ordained ministry, for all economy, all ecology, all ecumenism, every parish, every diocese.

Francis A. Sullivan, SJ, *The Church We Believe In*, (Gill and Macmillan, 1988).

John R. Sachs, SJ, *The Christian Vision of Humanity*, (Liturgical Press, 1991).

CHAPTER 37

Men and women in ministry

The covenant at Mount Sinai came to occupy the central place in the understanding of the relationship between God and his chosen people. A covenant involves a lived agreement between persons or between peoples. Since the time of Abraham, God had been speaking to his people in various forms of covenant language. At Sinai, he assured them that they would be his 'treasured possession out of all the peoples ... a priestly kingdom and a holy nation' (Ex 13:5-6). The covenant bonds into which he entered with his people were expressed not in legal language but in words of deep personal intimacy. The most intimate expressions of these bonds were in terms of the husband-wife relationship and the father(mother)-child relationship, those two elementary human relationships that are the foundation of all other relationships.

The formula expressing the covenant relationship was modeled on the marriage formula: 'I will be your God, and you shall be my people' (Lev 26:12). Like marriage, the covenant relationship was to be worked out in terms of loving-kindness and fidelity. These special qualities of the God of the covenant were to persist in spite of all human infidelity. The Book of Deuteronomy was written specially to underline the relationship of love and fidelity that was at the heart of the covenant. The covenant of God with the Davidic dynasty added a new dimension to the Sinai covenant but it indicated no change in the loving and faithful God. The prophets picked up the covenant theme and they played especially on the marriage symbolism. The idolatry which had at various times characterised God's people was seen by prophets such as Isaiah, Hosea, Jeremiah and Ezekiel as a form of adultery. But God would not abandon his spouse. He had allowed her to be taken into exile so that she would be purified and led to return to him with all her heart (Hos 2:16-22; Is 54:6-8). Through Isaiah, God reminded his people that 'Your maker is your husband' (54:5-8). Through Jeremiah, the same husband tells his wife 'I remember the devotion of your youth, how as a bride you loved me'

(2:2). Hosea's understanding of the covenant was coloured by his own brittle relationship with his wife (2:4-23).

The father(mother)-child relationship flows obviously from the husband-wife relationship. It is expressed in such images as Israel being the first-born (Ex 4:22), God's love for the child Israel (Hos 11:1-11), the impossibility of a mother forgetting the baby at her breast (Is 49:15), God's plaintive disappointment that his people did not call him 'Father' (Jer 3:19).

The ministry of Jesus
Both the husband-wife imagery and the parent-child imagery are seen in even richer light in the ministry of Jesus. Jesus came as the bridegroom who 'has the bride' (Jn 3:29). As bridegroom, he at the same time calls for joy and celebration because he has come (Mt 9:15) and vigilance and readiness because he will return (25:1-13). His final meal with his disciples was a covenant meal. It indicated the coming into existence of the new covenant promised by the prophets. It was established by the 'giving' of his body and the 'pouring out' of his blood (Lk 22:19-20).

The spousal overtones of this language were picked up in the letter to the Ephesians, in the prescription that husbands should love their wives 'just as Christ loved the Church and gave himself up for her' (5:25), and in the various marital images of the Church in her relationship with Christ (1 Cor 6:17; 2 Cor 11:2). The same imagery is taken up in the Book of Revelation. The marriage of the Lamb is a time for rejoicing, exulting, and giving glory (19:7-9). The New Jerusalem is portrayed as the bride (21:2). The book ends with both Spirit and bride saying 'come' (22:17), after God's own assurance that 'they will be his peoples, and God himself will be with them' (21:3).

All this nuptial imagery is closely related to the parent-child imagery so central to the teaching of Jesus. Becoming like little children is not an optional extra but rather a requirement for those who would enter the kingdom of heaven (Mt 18:3). The pattern of all prayer is the Our Father (Mt 6:9-15). The Father reveals himself only to 'little ones' (Mt 11:25-27). Jesus gave the right to become children of God to all who received him (Jn 1:12). The high point of intimacy in one's relationship with God is the ability to say 'Abba

Father' (Mk 14:36; Rom 8:14-17; Gal 4:6). This revelation of God as Abba Father is the basis for the revolution in all familial language introduced by Jesus (Mk 3:31-35).

A new covenant

Over the centuries, the Church has continually drawn new energy out of her reflection on her origins in the new covenant in which she was both bride and mother (cf Gal 4:26-27). At the Second Vatican Council, the bishops often returned to the cluster of images that came from that setting. Christian married couples 'signify and share the mystery of the unity and faithful love between Christ and the Church' (LG 11). The bonds of religious life 'show forth the unbreakable bond of union between Christ and his bride, the Church' (LG 44). By means of celibacy, priests are dedicated to 'espousing the faithful to one husband': they recall that mystical marriage 'by which the Church holds Christ as her only spouse' (PO 16).

Sacraments of the covenant

The covenant relationship with God was the key to the whole story of God's people before the coming of Jesus Christ. The new covenant in the blood of Jesus has always remained the key to the mystery of the Church which he called into existence. In the Catholic Christian tradition, and to some extent in other Christian traditions, there is one word that particularly helps to link together all the experiences of the covenant. That word is sacrament. Since its origins in the Greek world of mystery and its development in many Latin settings, it has captured and absorbed all the richest implications of signs and symbols. It expresses both that which is a sign and that which contains and makes present the very reality which it signifies. No wonder that, for several years now, the Church has been continually finding new possibilities in this very evocative word. We speak of Christ, in his humanity, as sacrament of God's saving activity. On account of her unique relationship with Christ, his Church is the universal sacrament of salvation; the whole Church is sacrament of all the saving activity of Christ; in one sense, she already is that sacrament; in another sense, she is always becoming that sacrament. All her efforts at renewal, in ministry and otherwise, must be efforts to keep entering more deeply into the movements of his once-for-all sacrifice.

After much searching for ways of expressing the relationship of the eucharist to that once-for-all sacrifice, it is interesting that the authors of the Lima ecumenical statement (1982) found a key to consensus by the use of the word 'sacrament': 'The eucharist is the sacrament of the unique sacrifice of Christ' (par 4). In the ecumenical agreements on ministerial priesthood, the notion of sacrament has also been found to be invaluable: 'The action of the presiding minister ... is seen to stand in a sacramental relation to what Christ himself did' (ARCIC 1, par 13); 'in this sacramental act, the gift of God is bestowed upon the ministers' (par 15); 'the ordained ministry is called priestly principally because it has a particular sacramental relationship with Christ as High Priest' (*Elucidations*, No 12).

A context for ministry
The covenant; husband-wife symbolism; parent-child symbolism; the meaning of sacraments. It all seems like a very long preamble to the topic of man and woman in ministry. Yet it is in the ambit of these words, and of the many links that unite them, that the Catholic Church over the past few decades has been expressing her teaching on the relationships between man and woman in ministry. It is only in the context of the covenant, of basic familial imagery, and of sacrament, that this teaching can be properly understood. The teaching has found its strongest expression in the *Declaration on the Admission of Women to the Ministerial Priesthood* (1976). The Declaration was issued not by the Pope but by the Congregation for the Doctrine of the Faith. It is subject to the same historical conditioning that affects all Church statements. It is not an infallible statement, but it expresses official Catholic teaching and it calls for its own level of assent. Its contents require careful and prayerful study and reflection.

At the heart of the Declaration is the statement that 'the Church, in fidelity to the example of the Lord, does not consider herself authorised to admit women to priestly ordination' (Introduction). The reason given is the unbroken Christian tradition of ordaining only males. The arguments supporting this reason are presented in the rich language of sign, symbol, and sacrament, and leading to the conclusion that 'in actions which demand the character of ordination and in which Christ himself, the author of the

Covenant, the Bridegroom and Head of the Church, is represented, exercising the ministry of salvation – which is in the highest degree the case of the eucharist – his role ... must be taken by a man' (par 5). This teaching was taken up again and developed in Pope John Paul II's *The Dignity of Women* (1988). The letter reflects much of the Pope's teaching on the 'nuptial meaning of the body', a topic to which he is well known to devote much attention. In his concern to highlight the radical equality of woman and man before God, he spells out the nuptial implications of Eph 5 and related texts. In these texts, he distinguishes the 'old' elements inherited from Judaism and the 'new' elements introduced by Christ. With the help of this distinction, he concludes that 'whereas in the relationship between Christ and the Church the subjection is only on the part of the Church, in the relationship between husband and wife the 'subjection' is not one-sided but mutual' (par 24).

The teaching of Pope John Paul II on the equality between man and woman in the marriage partnership is only one expression of the search for ways of expressing the riches of the Judaeo-Christian nuptial symbolism. The search has continual implications for our understanding of the man-woman partnership in Church ministry, and especially in ordained ministry. In the ways it is being applied in this area, it has tossed up many questions, some old, some new. Some of these will wait a long time for fully adequate and satisfying answers; some are already touching on many of the Church's nerve-centres:

How tied are we today to the various layers of the covenant and spousal imagery in expressing the relationships of God with his people, of Christ with his Church, of the ordained priest with the Christian community? The imagery is attractive in itself but is there a possibility that we might use it in a way that enslaves rather than liberates? Are we giving too central a position to metaphors that are fascinating but obsolete? In the variety of possible approaches to questions like these, it is good to remember that God, who is beyond gender, could have revealed God's self in a variety of ways. Among questions now asked are: could revelation have taken place in a matriarchial society? could God have become incarnate in a woman? could the Church have had a very different history? Allowing for these questions, the Church today must do her best to keep reflecting for believers what God has actually done in the one history which has taken place, not what God might have done in other possible economies of salvation. The Church must continually sacramentalise the abiding message of what God has done in the only salvation history that we know.

How sure is the Church that she is being faithful to the practice of Christ and to tradition? To deal with the implications of this question, it is good to bear in mind that tradition is somehow the memory of the Church.

* The Church keeps remembering her God who made both man and woman in God's own image and likeness (Gen 1:27) and who shows a mother-love as well as a father-love (Is 49:14-15; 66-13).

* As she remembers her founder she tries both to recapture what he did in history and to know what he wishes for his Church now. She knows that her access to the mind of the historical Christ is principally through the pages of the gospels. These represent him as choosing twelve men to be the symbolic foundation people for the new Israel. They also represent him as calling women to discipleship and friendship in ways that broke through many of the conventions of his time.

* She remembers St Paul who involved women as 'ministers', 'fellow workers', 'apostles' (Rom 16) and who, though he had no problem about the fact of women prophesying in church, was very much influenced by some contemporary conventions about how both men and women should behave. In this remembering, she tries to distinguish, in his teaching, between what is permanent and what is so culturally conditioned that it is for its own time only. The distinction is not always easy to draw.

* She remembers the authors of the Pastoral Epistles who gave strong directives against some forms of Church leadership by women.

* She remembers the theologians and mystics who, over the centuries, helped to disclose the feminine aspects of God's love.

* In spite of some recent questioning, she remembers her own unbroken practice of not ordaining women as priests or bishops.

* Drawing on all this memory, she endeavours to shape a ministry faithful to the past, suited to the present, and looking to the future.

How do we reconcile the contemporary Church emphasis on the equality of women and men with the various expressions of the subjection, subordination, and exclusion that undoubtedly characterised some Church attitudes to women in the past and have left their residue of hurt and anger? A partial answer to this complex question is the recognition that the covenant values have been transmitted to us through patriarchal societies and in a patriarchal Church. One hopes that the emphasis today on such topics as justice and human rights, and a growing sensitivity to feminist concerns, will contribute to a process of real forgiveness, real healing and real growth.

Is the use of the bridegroom-bride imagery helping to perpetuate the mentality that associates woman with sin and infidelity and man with fidelity and integrity? Is this question further compounded by reserving the description 'in the person of Christ' for the priest, who must be a man? Any imbalance in the answering of these questions should be offset by the fact that the priest also acts 'in the person of the Church'. He represents the faith, devotion, and communion of the holy Church. But he also represents the unholy and sinful bride which is the whole Church and with whom he must fully and repentantly identify. This remains true though he first represents Christ himself, who is the head and shepherd of the Church. He is the sacramental sign of the presence and saving activity of the bridegroom; but he is not the bridegroom.

In the theology of ministerial priesthood, has too much been made of the maleness of Christ rather than of his humanness? Is ministerial priesthood not about being a sacrament of his humanness rather than of his maleness? Certainly, the eucharist is not an exercise in drama; though the word persona does come from the world of theatre, priestly ministry is not about people acting parts – the priest represents Christ; he is a sacramental representation, not a stage representation, of Christ. But we are living in the world of the incarnation, the world of sacraments. God became human in the personality of Jesus of Nazareth. Though we worship 'in spirit and truth' (Jn 4:23), we worship in a way that does full justice to the body. As we worship our one mediator 'the man Christ Jesus' (1 Tim 2:5) we are helped by the ministry of a man who focuses us in a bodily way on him who gathered together in his own earthly body all the loving and faithful qualities of the God of the covenant. The president of the eucharistic assembly and minister of the sacrament of reconciliation, which is so closely connected with the eucharist, is called to be an 'icon' of Christ, both in the moral sense of expressing the bridegroom's love and fidelity and the more easily recognisable sense of providing a visible, audible, tangible communication with the bridegroom who is sacramentally meeting his bride. The priest's sacramental headship is continually linked with his pastoral headship. Both are for the sake of the whole body, which comprises all the baptised. This is why the spousal image stands beside the images of head and shepherd in the description of ordained ministry in *I Will Give You Shepherds* (par 16).

A continual search

In the Church today, many women are becoming more aware of their distinctive ways of experiencing God and human relationships, and of their need to articulate and embody their experience. In the story and memory of the Church over the centuries, they are re-discovering many forgotten expressions of that feminine experience. At the same time, all baptised men and women are being called to a vast range of ministries in the building up of the one body of Christ. As our vision of the mission of the Church becomes clearer our vision of ministry becomes clearer. In the working out of who does what in the whole range of ministries that promote our common vision, it would be easy to label some human characteristics as feminine and some as masculine. One could be led by a contemporary anthropology rather than by a continual searching into the Christian memory. One can get lost in doubtful thickets of gender symbolism and gender differentiation. Only in the humble, prayerful, and collaborative ministry of women and men in the spirit of him who said 'with you this must not happen' (Lk 22:26), will the whole Church be able to shape the new forms and styles of leadership suited to a Church that keeps bringing out of her treasure what is new and what is old (Mt 13:52). Only in that setting can we learn the riches of the complementarity of woman and man. Only in that setting will every eucharist reveal both the father-face and the mother-face of God.

Only in that setting can we learn how God would define a woman and how God would define a man.

Sara Butler, 'The Priest as Sacrament of Christ the Bridegroom' in *Worship*, 66 (1992), pp 498-517.

Hervé Legrand, *'Traditio Perpetuo Servata*? The Non-Ordination of Women: Tradition or Simply an Historical Fact?' in *Worship*, 65 (1991), pp 482-508.

CHAPTER 38

Young elders and old

The Church has only one mission. She must proclaim the good news of the reign of God; she must live by that good news; she must help others to live that good news. To further her mission, she has a great variety of ministries, a great variety of forms of serving. In a sense, there are as many Christian ministries as there are baptised people. To each of the baptised is given 'the manifestation of the Spirit for the common good' (1 Cor 12:7). This common good is the wellbeing and building up of the whole body of Christ, the enabling of the whole body to grow to maturity 'in him who is the head, into Christ' (Eph 4:15). Out of this growth, this maturing, the whole human family, indeed the whole universe, is enriched.

From the earliest stages of her existence, the Church was able to name a large number of the gifts of ministry which had come from the activity of the Holy Spirit working in all her members. For the fostering of all the ministries to the body, in the spirit of the commissioning which Jesus gave to his first disciples and apostles, three titles in particular came to be associated with Church leadership. These were bishop (lit. *overseer*), presbyter (lit. *elder*), deacon (lit. *servant* – or *agent*?). In the literal sense of these words, the whole Church must always remain episcopalian, presbyterian, diaconal. It must always have people who exercise good oversight; it must always have leaders who are elders by age or by maturity; it must always be a serving Church, a community of agents of Jesus Christ who came 'not to be served but to serve' (Mt 20:28). In time, the connotation of each of these words came to be more clearly delineated. Already in the beginning of the third century, there were signs that this threefold form of leadership was to become the norm for the whole Church. The threefold ministerial leadership of bishop, priests and deacons, developed over the centuries. It has been the subject of much study in recent ecumenical dialogue, notably in the *Lima Report* of the World Council of Churches (1982). It is clear that, for various historical and theological reasons, the Catholic Church upholds and will continue to uphold the threefold ministry. In the teaching of the Second Vatican Council on the one sacrament of holy orders, all three offices are seen as a special sharing in the priestly, prophetic, and pastoral mission of Christ the head of the Church, for the well-being of the whole Church.

Recent history

The time since the Second Vatican Council has been characterised by much searching into the meaning and structuring of the sacrament of holy orders. It has been equally characterised by the emergence of many new ministries in the Church, and the re-emergence of ministries that had somehow gone into abeyance. Three significant contributions to these developments were Pope Paul VI's Apostolic Constitution *Certain Ministries* (1972), his exhortation *Evangelisation Today* (1975), and Pope John Paul II's exhortation *The Lay Faithful* (1988). In these, as in other official teachings, the call to ministry is seen as emanating both from the sacraments of baptism and confirmation and from the present needs of the Church. Ideally, both ordained ministry and the great variety of other forms of ministry should flourish in the Church at the same time. The reality is that, in a growing number of areas of the world, and sometimes to an extent that could be described in terms of crisis, Christian communities are so lacking in ordained ministers that they are unable to celebrate the eucharist, the very sacrament that 'makes' the Church. In this situation, believers are making many valiant and creative attempts to celebrate together in ways that derive from their common baptismal faith. There have also been attempts that, while well motivated, are unlikely to bear any long term fruits. One is the encouraging of a greater mobility of priests, enabling them to celebrate several Masses at several centres. Another is the combining of the liturgy of the word and the receiving of holy communion from hosts consecrated at another time, in ways that can blur the real meaning of both word and sacrament.

Many questions

The anguish generated by this contemporary reality has made many searching questions to surface:

Can human regulations about requirements for ordained ministry be allowed to deprive the Church anywhere of the eucharist to which the baptised have a basic right? A reflection on the history of the presidency of the eucharist would seem to make this question even more pointed. In the early Church, it would appear that the local Church leaders, many or most of whom were heads of families, were seen to be the obvious presidents of the eucharist. This situation would eventually change and there emerged in the course of time a clear teaching on such topics as the essential difference between ordained priesthood and the priesthood of the baptised, the character conferred in the sacrament of orders, and the ontological change effected by the conferring of the sacrament of orders. The presidency of the eucharist came to be reserved to bishops and priests. It is sometimes suggested now that, in a way that is both faithful to existing teaching and a genuine response to contemporary realities, the Church should reconsider her requirements for presidency of the eucharist and for other forms of sacramental empowering.

In assessing these and related topics, it is good to remember that the Church is a learning Church. As Christians grew in appreciation of the eucharist as the communion in the once-for-all sacrifice of Christ and as the great sacrament of unity, they came more and more to realise the crucial importance of providing for its presidency. Long before the end of the first Christian century, St Paul had to complain that when the Christians at Corinth came together it was 'not for the better but for the worse' (1 Cor 11:17). When they came together it was 'not really to eat the Lord's Supper' (v 20). Experiences such as this contributed eventually to the ensuring that only the bishop or the presbyter could preside at the eucharist. This was seen not as a restrictive, disciplinary measure but as something called for by the very nature of the sacrament of the unity of Christians.

Essential difference

Out of the same conviction there came to be articulated the teaching on the essential difference between the two expressions of Christ's priesthood, the fact that in the words of the ARCIC Statement on *Ministry and Ordination* (par 13), ordained ministry 'is not an extension of the common Christian priesthood but belongs to another realm of the gifts of the Spirit'. The gift of the

Spirit given at priestly ordination establishes so unique and indivisible a relationship to word and sacrament, especially in the sacrament of the unity of the body of Christ and in the ministry of reconciliation, that it cannot be equiperated to or replaced by any other ministry or set of ministries. It is in this context that one can best understand Church language about ontological change and about function. Ontological language deals with who a person is. Functional language deals with what a person does. Ordination effects an ontological change. It establishes the ordained person in a new and enduring set of relationships with the rest of the baptised and with Christ their head. Ordination does, of course, set a man aside for the performing of various functions in the Church. But these functions derive from what the ordained person is. Out of what he is derives all that he is called to do. Both what he is and what he does are expressions of the qualities of the God of the covenant, the God who continues to show his tender compassion, and to call the ordained to be, like him, faithful forever.

Does the insistence on priestly celibacy restrict the number of candidates who might freely present themselves for ordination to priesthood, thus placing a Church discipline that can be changed above the far more important right of the people of God to the eucharist? In our attempts at evaluating this question, it is important to see the place of celibacy not as one discipline among others but as part of a whole way of life. In official Church teaching, celibacy is more and more coming to be seen as one facet of the radical living of the whole message of the very radical gospel. It could, of course, be argued that this form of radical discipleship should be encouraged as just one way of living the call to priestly ordination. It could also be argued that this way of radical discipleship might be very suited for missionaries whose task it is to set up new Christian communities, but not for the Church leaders in fixed and stable Christian communities. But, in a rapidly changing society and a rapidly changing Church, one might wonder where are the fixed and stable Christian communities, where is the Church that is not missionary. Jesus presented his own celibacy 'for the sake of the kingdom of heaven' (Mt 19:12) in words that were enigmatic, provocative and shocking. It may well be that the special demand on all the priestly leaders of today is to be more in tune with this very radical way of presenting and living the Good News.

Dealing with the pain

While the Church lives with the pain of a growing number of Christian communities deprived of the eucharist, and seeks for ways of dealing with it, we can recognise providential opportunities for the promotion of two great teachings of the Second Vatican Council. The first is the teaching on the many ways in which Christ is really present in his Church. In many places, both where there is an abundance of priests and where there is a shortage of priests, Catholics have only begun to explore the riches of the assurance that Christ is 'always present in his Church ...'(*SC* 7). In God's providence, perhaps the priestless communities are the very places where those who are baptised and confirmed can learn to recognise and celebrate non-sacramental forms of the real presence of the risen Christ in the members of his body who are in various forms of human need. Perhaps this form of glorifying and carrying God in their body (1 Cor 6:20) will be the greatest achievement of many of today's 'basic Christian communities'. Related to this re-discovery of the many ways in which Jesus Christ is really present to his people is the re-discovery of the importance of the place of the word of God. In the eucharist, the word of God is proclaimed at its highest level of sacramental intensity. The once-for-all sacrifice of Christ is made present sacramentally. One hopes that, especially in places where the eucharist cannot be regularly celebrated, the Church will learn new and powerful ways of proclaiming and celebrating the word of God at non-eucharistic levels. This effective proclaiming and celebrating can take many forms in the baptised community. It is significant that at the very time in which he suppressed the minor orders, Pope Paul VI established two ministries, one for the service of the word of God and one for the service of the eucharist. The effective proclaiming of and promoting of the word of God may provide the very setting in which more people will be called to the presidency of the eucharist. If the word of God is well proclaimed, the eucharist will again be well celebrated.

New colleges of elders

It would appear that in the early Church the most common pattern of Church leadership was a collegiate one exercised by a group of presbyter-elders. With the development and stabilisation of the role of head of the presbyteral college, and with the growing sacramental role of presbyters, the monarchic episcopate became normative in the Church. This settled down into the pattern of bishops, priests and deacons, a pattern with which we are now so familiar. In communion with the bishop, and collaborating closely with him, is the *presbyterium*, the college of priests. Collaborating with both bishop and priests are the deacons.

It would appear that in the unit of the diocese which we now call a parish, whether territorial or based on more personal groupings, the pattern of leadership emerging today is once again in terms of what one might call a 'college of elders'. In the Church of the future, with the development of various forms of baptismal ministry, it is unlikely, indeed undesirable, that ordained priests and deacons will be the only 'elders'. The ordained priest will be one of a body of elders, in close collaboration with the other members of the new kind of 'college' of elders. One would hope that, with due regard for the health of his body and mind as well as of his spirit, he will be more freed to do that for which he was ordained, to be the man defined by the word of God, the word which he keeps internalising and externalising, especially in the Church's sacramental life and in his exercise of overall pastoral leadership. His fellow 'elders' will be involved, each according to his or her competence, in the full range of services for the building up of the local community. These will include various services of management, administration, parish development, catechesis, spiritual direction, as well as various services to inter-faith and inter-church dialogue and to word and sacrament. The exact shape that the college of elders might take will vary from particular church to particular church. In a Church which more and more sees itself as a community of disciples, parish will learn from parish; diocese from diocese; episcopal conference from episcopal conference. All will learn from, and will in various ways contribute to, those areas of the Church where there is a shortage or lack of people in ordained ministry. In his role of headship in the name and person of the Head, the priest will provide a ministry that has its source in his special relationship to the word of God. This headship will always provide him with at least a symbolic leadership in the Christian community. But he must never let this symbolic leadership take the place of the leadership that is a real competence in proclaiming the word of God. In his interaction with his fellow 'elders', clearer answers will keep emerging to questions like the following: to what extent are lay men and women authorised to preach in the liturgical assembly?; what acts of blessing are reserved to those in ordained ministry?; what acts of worship require the presidency of an ordained person?; to what extent should the ordained person be involved in the social and political activities of the local community?

As the forms of leadership of the future take shape, the Church can keep drawing on the accumulated wisdom of the ages:

It will keep drawing inspiration from the many forms of ministry which arose in the early Church both by the action of the Spirit and in response to the needs of the day (cf 1 Cor 12:4-12, 26-30; Eph 4:11-13; Rom 12:4-9). Some of these forms of ministry arose from the needs of a Church at the time of its founding; some were more related to the building up of an existing Church. Some had their setting in administrative needs; some in the inspirational and prophetic word that built up the faith of the baptised.

In *Evangelisation Today* (No 73) Pope Paul VI set new Church ministries in the perspective of both the experiences of the early and growing Church and the emerging needs of today's Church. He listed specific ministries which both capture much of what was good in the past and point a direction for the future. He emphasised the importance of careful preparation for all those involved in the field of evangelisation, and especially for those who devote themselves to the ministry of the word. In *The Lay Faithful* (pars 18-20, 25-26) Pope John Paul II places the exercise of various ministries in a rich context of communion and community.

The experience of pastoral councils and synods at various levels of the Church over the past few decades has helped to indicate where some of the Church leaders of the future might come from. It has also suggested new ways of designating, approving, commissioning, and installing leaders and pastoral assistants, in a temporary or permanent capacity, according as the needs of the

Church suggest. It has pointed to ways of seeing the relationship between the unique pastoral leadership which derives from ordination and the many forms of leadership that derive from baptism.

The implementation of the *Rite of Christian Initiation of Adults* has already been disclosing many possibilities for the future of church leadership and church ministry.

Institutes of consecrated life and societies of apostolic life are part of both the local Church and the wider Church. The living of the charisms appropriate to each institute and society should enrich the leadership of the Church on both levels.

There is scope for creative and innovative ways of exercising a permanent diaconate that truly bridges liturgical action and social action.

The Lord keeps calling
All calling to Church ministry comes ultimately from the Lord of the harvest. He is as active as ever in calling labourers into his harvest, in calling to new ministries and old, in the calling of elders young and old. At a time when we are experiencing a new structuring of Church ministry and seeking new models for constituting 'elders' in our Christian communities, there is an urgent need for prayer, to discern the ways in which the Lord's calling is being mediated, and for courage to follow where that call is leading us.

Michael Casey, *What are we at?*, (Columba Press, 1992).

Pro Mundi Vita Studies, No. 12, Nov. 1989, Leuven.

CHAPTER 39

One, good, true – and beautiful

In the days before the Second Vatican Council, candidates for priesthood were introduced early on to the one, the good, and the true, the transcendental properties of being. They were also introduced to an understanding of the human person in terms of a body-soul unity. Regard for the unity, the goodness and the truth of every human being and indeed of every created being, were somehow the a, b, c of the seminary course in philosophy. Whatever its limitations, it was a noble preparation for the study of theology, and indeed for a whole life's ministry.

The one: In the study of theology, unity was seen as the first 'note' of the one, true Church. We spoke of the Church as being one, in a kind of exclusive, triumphalistic way. Other Christian groups – we didn't call them churches and ecclesial communities then – just did not have that oneness. The great shift since the Council is that we use the word 'one' in a more inclusive way. We are encouraged to see the world as one great house, housing the one human family, with the Church as the one great sacrament of salvation, having living links with all the members of the family, to all of whom it has a mission of unifying. Our understanding of priesthood concentrates more and more on a service of transparency to the one priesthood of our one priest who has offered his one sacrifice, once-for-all. The ordained priest is seen as a sign of one-ness, a kind of sacrament of the 'one Lord, one faith, one baptism' (Eph 4:5); as a person who gives expression to the unity of priesthood, prophecy and kingship in Jesus Christ and in his body which is the Church.

The good: The good had a prominent place in our moral theology, in the efforts, for example, to express what constitutes a good deed and an evil deed. Admittedly, this search was not always related to the conviction that every being is good. Since the Council, we have made great strides in seeing the goodness of all creation, of human sexuality, of marriage. Gnosticism, manichaeism, dualism, dichotomies of all sorts, have taken a trouncing. But was the trouncing really effective? On second thoughts, it looks as if the questions raised by the Manichaeans never really went away and will never go away. In the past, many of the great religious movements have had to grapple with questions about the nature of good and evil. St Dominic had only moderate success against the Albigensians. Why? Because they had an over-simplified and attractive, but ultimately unsatisfying, approach to the complexities of good and evil. Martin Luther battled with many variations on the questions 'how good are we? how corrupt are we?' He didn't resolve them. Our generation has banished the devil from respectable discourse, but satanism, in its many forms, is alive and well. Since Auschwitz, the most nagging objection many people find against belief in a good God is a variation on St Augustine's 'if God cannot prevent evil, he is not all-powerful; if he will not, he is not all good'.

This good-evil question, what has been called the 'biggest question on earth', is as much with us as ever. The shelves of bookstores at airports and railway stations do not show a bias in favour of religion. But there are two books with a religious theme that continue to feature on all the racks. Both concern the 'biggest question'. The first is actually called *When bad things happen to good people*. In the context of the sadness of his own family situation, the author, a Jewish rabbi, searched the whole of his religious tradition for an answer. His treatment of the Christian answer is brief but illuminating. In essence, it is that the experience of the bad can help us to discover a lot of unrecognised good. This is the answer that is worked out more elaborately by the author of the second book, *Blessings*, again in the context of a family sadness that turned into a multiple blessing. The answer provided by Karl Rahner in his essay 'Why does God allow us to suffer?' is just a more learned variation on the same theme. 'There is no blessed light to illumine the dark abyss of suffering,' he writes, 'other than God himself.' The goodness of God can draw reserves of good and growth out of every being and every experience. Recently, the stories of hostages and of people in concentration camps have given us glimpses of this great truth. But the mystery remains. A continual task of Christian ministry is to recognise the good in the most unlikely places and to help others recognise it.

The true: Before the Council, theology put a lot of emphasis on the true religion and the true Church. Very often, the opposite of 'true' was 'wrong'! An achievement of the Council was to re-situate much of our theology in the context of the covenant. In that context, the opposite of true is unfaithful, inauthentic. The God of the covenant is the God who is true. His truth is his telling us both who he is and who we are. His truth is his faithfulness, his trustworthiness, his loyalty. In dealing with the covenant qualities of God, we are dealing with the very basics of all personal communication, in an atmosphere of trust. We are dealing with the loving heart of God that is 'ever kind and true'. Much recent theological writing has been trying to reclaim this covenant language. Priestly ministry is being helped by the search. Recent writing on the character of the sacrament of ordination keeps emphasising the covenant qualities of God, especially his 'truth' and fidelity. The God who, by ordination, calls us, has hands laid on us, has us anointed, will never treat us as disposable containers and used up dispensers of his grace. He will remain 'true' to what he has done. He calls for the same 'truth' in us. The faith of the people, the needs of the people, and their continual right to suitable ministers is grounded in the same truth of God. The character of ordination exists in order to sustain that faith, those needs, that right. It is a life's programme modeled on the covenant qualities of God.

Enter the beautiful: So much for unity, goodness and truth. Then there was the 'poor relation', beauty. In the older courses in philosophy, we bowed to it as the splendour of the true, 'that which, when seen, pleases'. We didn't go much farther than that. In theology, too, beauty was peripheral, almost non-existent, if the truth were told. This was not a problem for the seminaries only. Philosophers throughout history never quite agreed as to how beauty related to the good and the true. In recent centuries, many of them had closed an eye to the beautiful. The Greeks certainly had got it right with their *kalokagathia,* that vision of how the beautiful fuses with the good, the good with the beautiful. For Plato, the beautiful and the good are inseparable; beauty suggests proportion, measure. For Aristotle, things are beautiful if they are in the condition in which they ought to be. Plotinus stressed radiance, light, the luminous. Some of the Greek vision was carried

over into Christian thinking. Augustine saw the source of all
beauty in the beauty 'so ancient and so new'. For Bonaventure,
beauty was a transcendental in its own right and in its relationship to the four causes. Because order is a sign of beauty, he saw
holy orders as an on-going expression of the beauty of God and of
the Church. Albert located beauty in the measuring up to each
other of the good and the true. For Aquinas, who took beauty seriously, and may have regarded it as a transcendental in its own
right, the key word is proportion. For him, truth is a kind of goodness, goodness a kind of truth; the due proportion coming from
both truth and goodness delights even the senses, especially the
sight, when it recognises the 'colourful'; beauty implies integrity,
right proportion and radiance. Aquinas, like Bonaventure, situated
holy orders in the context of divine order; God established order
in the Church so that his own beauty might not be lacking in it.

Beauty and glory

The beautiful may have been the poor relation. But she has come
of age. It is time for her to get adult status in the family. As we
wonder about what is the most urgent need of the Church, there is
a good case for saying that it has to do with the re-discovery of the
beautiful, at the very time when there is much confusion and even
scepticism about what actually constitutes the beautiful. Earlier
this century, G.K. Chesterton wrote that there are two gates into
the Church, the gate of truth and the gate of beauty. Most, he said,
entered by the gate of beauty. As examples of the draw of the
Church's beauty he gave the magic of the medieval cathedral and
the continuing attraction of the Church's classic way of worshipping. These were examples from a past culture, but he also in-
stanced contemporary examples of the truth continually dawn-
ing in the beautiful eyes and face of the Church.

As we search for the biblical equivalents of the beautiful, we
would do well to ponder on the glory of God, a topic of which the
bible is full. The glory of God manifests the beauty of God. Both
his glory and his beauty are disclosed when we glimpse his
majesty, his power, his holiness, his lofty deeds, the great theophanies. They are disclosed in what his hands have made and in
the best of what human hands have made. They are fully disclosed in the man Christ Jesus: 'We saw his glory' (Jn 1:14), 'full of

grace and truth'; 'what we have heard, what we have seen, what our hands have touched' (1 Jn 1:1). It is the Christian conviction that the same glory is intended to be revealed fully in our own bodies, and in a restored and renewed creation. This message was picked up accurately by St Irenaeus when he told us that the glory of God is a human being fully alive, and that to be fully alive is to see God, and by Ignatius of Loyola, who so much furthered the ideal of a life lived for the greater, indeed the greatest, glory of God.

An urgent need

But how can one speak of the re-discovery of the beautiful in terms of being the most urgent need of the Church? In recent times, the splendour of the face of the Church has become somewhat overcast, if not eclipsed. It would appear that some of the major issues for which Christians, and especially Catholic Christians, are known to stand have detached themselves from the one, the good, the true, the beautiful. Who, for example, would ever think that some of our laudable and valiant efforts to promote human life are sourced in the wish of the one who came that we 'may have life and have it more abundantly'? (Jn 10:10). Our best intentioned efforts in the cause of human life sometimes come across more like an exercise in the peripheral and the eccentric than a revealing of the glory of God. Who would guess that the Catholic Church has such a beautiful ideal of celibacy as a 'stimulus to and expression of pastoral charity'? Even our laudable efforts towards justice and peace, human liberation, and the preferential option for the poor, have to be continually and urgently re-sourced in the one, the good, the true – and the beautiful. The examples could be multiplied.

Theology and beauty

The re-discovery of the beautiful had a central place in the life work of the late Hans Urs von Balthasar. His avowed aim in all his writing was to articulate the full Christian message 'in its unsurpassable greatness' – to lead people to contemplate the beauty and the splendour of the Christian faith, in all its uniqueness and originality. He became totally absorbed by the realisation that being as a whole possesses the transcendental properties of unity, goodness, truth, beauty. The basis of his theological vision became the one, the good, the true, the beautiful – all interpenetrating. This vision is unified by his perception of the beautiful. In Christ, the beauty of the divine plan is uniquely made visible, and not least in Christ's self-emptying, disfigurement, and dying. In these especially we have to learn to perceive God's glory. The glory of God is manifested in the incarnate Word, radiated to the world by the Church, and celebrated in the eucharist by Christians.

Von Balthasar was convinced that the aesthetic perspective, properly presented, will always 'attract our gaze, stimulate our imagination, and invite contemplation', and even call us to conversion. Jesus, for him, was the definitive, historical expression of God, knowing the true, loving the good, enjoying the beautiful. Here we have what really pleases, what is really radiant. We are invited to share in this knowing, loving and enjoying as we enter into the total paschal mystery of the beloved Son of God, the beautiful one. And von Balthasar pointed out that joy differs from pleasure; animals can have pleasure, but joy includes the appreciation of values.

A daily programme
How can we express the beauty, the glory, of the Church, in today's society? A few pointers may be in order:

The various historical approaches to beauty can be an outline of a programme of continual renewal: proportion; good measure; the condition in which things ought to be; radiance; light; the luminous; the shining forth of the one, the good, the true; what is both ancient and new; engaging mind and senses; in proportion; pleasing when seen; in a word, a continual reflection of what is happening between Father, Son and Spirit, and a promotion of what is inspirational and imaginative.

The beauty of the Church must be seen in things and in buildings, in the work of artists, craftsmen, and musicians, on whom we often pray an outpouring of the Spirit; above all, it must be seen in people. The current expression 'a beautiful person' contains a lot of theology and wisdom. It is significant that the biography of our most successful ambassador of the Christian faith today was entitled *Something Beautiful for God* – shades of the times when beauty was associated with moral excellence, and holiness with the gifts and fruits of the Holy Spirit that beautify a human life.

The 'souled-body' of our psychology days comes into its own in the living body of the one who said, on coming into the world, 'You do not want sacrifice and offering of animals, but you have prepared a body for me' (Heb 10:5). Out of the earthly body of Christ there rose up a daily perfect and beautiful sacrifice to the Father. No wonder St Paul saw his own priestly ministry as one of enabling the gentiles to do the same with their bodies and to make 'an offering acceptable to God, sanctified by the Holy Spirit' (Rom 15:16).

One hopes that the first fruit of the new emphasis on evangelisation will be that preachers and teachers of the gospel will themselves discover anew the beauty of the word of God. One hopes that they will keep discovering the beauty of the souled-body and the many ways in which it can become a continual sacrifice giving glory to God.

The beauty of the body of Christ in human bodies must be revealed most characteristically in the celebration of the eucharist. Some church designers claim that the only colour in the space where the eucharist is celebrated should be provided by the people. This is open to debate, but it touches on a profound truth. Maybe St Thomas' 'bright colour' which he saw as an important aspect of beauty, could be a good starting point for describing Christians at worship. Christians are called to be, in many senses, a 'colourful' people. In the same context, maybe the statement that every eucharist should be a 'new appearance of the Risen Lord' is more than a nice figure of speech. And is there a more lovely description of ministerial priesthood than the 'ministry of transparency' that theologians have talked about and that the recent synod on priestly formation made its own?

Vocation and vocations must be seen as a call to a life that is beautiful. For the Greeks, the beautiful was *to kalon*, a word which comes from *kaleo*, to call, to beckon. Pursuing the Christian vocation in any of its forms means fascination with the good and the beautiful as they call and beckon to us. The only authentic 'vocation programmes' are the ones that engender a fascination with our one, good, true, and only teacher, who keeps disclosing the glory and the beauty of the Father.

The glory will not depart

When the wife of Phinehas gave birth to a son, she named him Ichabod, because the glory had departed (1 Sam 4:21). Ichabod can never be a satisfactory name for a Christian. The Lord of glory is with us always to the close of the age (Mt 28:20). Christians are people anointed into Christ, the anointed one. In biblical times, one of the purposes of anointing was to beautify. We have been anointed into the glory and beauty of Christ. When he returns, he will change our lowly bodies to be like his own glorious body, his beautiful body (cf Phil 3:21). In the meantime, much anointing remains to be done.

Hans Urs von Balthasar, *The Glory of the Lord*, Volume 1 (T & T Clark, Edinburgh, 1989).

Patrick Sherry, *Spirit and Beauty*, (Clarendon Press, Oxford, 1992).

CHAPTER 40

Living and transparent images
The Message of *Pastores Dabo Vobis*, 1992

The topic of the Roman Synod in 1990 was the formation of priests. The publication of the Apostolic Exhortation, *I Will Give You Shepherds*, in March 1992, was the fruit of the Synod deliberations. It includes much material from the Synod propositions; it draws heavily on the teaching of the Second Vatican Council; it is unified by Pope John Paul's characteristic approaches to priesthood. The whole document is a loving invitation to discern the best ways of exercising ministerial priesthood in a society which is at the same time indifferent to God and hungering for God (chap. 1).

It is a call to 'contemplation' (par 11), to a new focusing on the name and person of Jesus Christ the priest. It is an invitation to be deeply and fully immersed in the mystery of Christ (par 18). In that sense, it is an invitation to priests to become 'mystics', men steeped in mystery. The call to contemplation is, in turn, the basis of a call to the fascination by which the young will be drawn to follow Christ, and by which those who are already following him will find new heart on their journey.

It is a call to be like the group in the synagogue whose eyes were all fixed on Jesus (par 11; cf Lk 4:20). This fixing of one's eyes on Jesus is seen as a lifelong programme. It is in the spirit of the letter to the Hebrews which, after its portrayal of Christ the priest offering in his body the once-for-all sacrifice, invites us to 'fix our eyes on Jesus, the author and perfecter of our faith' (12:2).

It is a call to make the Church into the kind of community where young people can be invited to 'come and see' (Jn 1:39). This is presented as providing a dynamism for sowing the seeds of vocation, and of developing them by 'seeking Christ, finding him and staying with him' (par 34).

It is a call for a life-long search and discovery, the kind of discovery of the Lord that drives one to invite others to leave all and follow him (pars 38, 46).

It is a call to keep bringing together 'the permanent truth of the priestly ministry and the characteristic requirements of the present day' (par 5).

According as we learn to fix our eyes on the Lord, we become more perfect images of him. In a sense, the 'image' idea is itself the core image in the document: 'The priest is a living and transparent image of Christ the priest' (par 12). The call to be an image is a call to be like Jesus Christ who is the image, the icon, of God (Col 1:15; 2 Cor 4:4). An image, an icon, must be seen in relation to the original. The Bible had said severe things about graven images. The reason was the continual danger of worshipping false gods. The only acceptable image of God was the human image that God himself had made (Gen 1:26-27). St Paul rejoiced to see that image of God restored by the union of humans with Christ, the perfect image; the Christian programme is one of being transformed into that image 'from one degree of glory to another' (2 Cor 3:18; Col 3:10; Rom 8:29).

Ministers of the Head
A 'figure' has a meaning similar to that of an image. Every Christian is called to be an image of Christ and to be con-figured to Christ (cf Phil 3:21). The ordained, 'by virtue of the consecration they received in the sacrament of orders' are 'configured in a special way' to Christ as 'Head and Shepherd of his people' (par 12); they are 'ministers of the Head' (par 20). Headship connotes leadership and authority. For St Paul, who drew on the medical insights of his time, the head also suggested the communication of life to all the members of the body. Contemporary exploring into the workings of the human brain would indicate that these insights are not outdated. The ordained is configured to Christ the Head, Christ the Shepherd, and Christ the Spouse (par 16). The 'pastoral charity' that should characterise a good shepherd flows from this triple relationship. It is one of the most recurring themes of the document. It suggests a life-long programme of good headship and good shepherding by one wedded to the Church.

Shepherd, priest, prophet
The inter-connectedness of shepherding, priesthood and prophecy, in Christ, in the call and mission of all the baptised, in ordained

ministry, in the formation of future priests, provides the warp and woof of the whole Exhortation. Christ, anointed as shepherd-king, priest and prophet, is the one on whom our eyes are to be continually fixed. Some recent writing on ordained ministry has placed the emphasis on the proclaiming of the word of God as the first, and in a sense, the primary duty of the priest. This approach highlights the prophetic aspect of the ministry. The emphasis on dealing with sacred things, especially in the presidency of the eucharist, focuses on the 'priestly' aspect. The emphasis on leadership and on service to the people of God derives from the 'pastoral' approach. It would be hard, even wrong, to say that the document favours any one of these three approaches. All three are seen as crucial to the ministry of the ordained. The priest is seen as one who continually studies, reflects on, prays, preaches, and celebrates, in the sacraments and in the liturgy of the hours, the word in which he himself is the first 'believer' (par 26). This concern for the living and proclaiming of the word is not seen as conflicting with the other aspects of priestly ministry. Priests are described as existing and acting in order to proclaim the gospel to the world and to build up the Church in the name and person of Christ the Head and Shepherd (par 15). From an intimate union with the Head and Shepherd comes the pastoral charity which should characterise all priestly activity. Pastoral charity, in turn, finds its 'full expression and supreme nourishment' in the eucharistic sacrifice (par 23). The Pope makes a very personalised appeal to ensure that good foundations for priestly ministry are laid as seminarians become convinced that the eucharistic celebration is the essential moment of each day (par 48). Almost equally pressing is his appeal, in the same context, to rediscover, in spiritual formation, the beauty and joy of the sacrament of reconciliation.

Word, sacrament, pastoral charity

One could say that, in the perspective of the document, word, sacrament and pastoral charity are inseparably interwoven. It is the living and proclaiming of the word that nurtures the priest's relationship with the Word made flesh and with his body, the Church. The heart of one in that relationship must be a heart of love and service. By its very nature, the ministry of the word is for others, towards others. The heart of the preacher must be the heart of a good shepherd. The man of pastoral charity keeps breaking the bread of the word in every situation in which human beings need to be fed, by the preached word, by the sacraments which are special highpoints of the word, and by every form of pastoral care and service. The heart of the good shepherd should be of the kind hoped for by God's prophet, 'after God's own heart' (Jer 3:15). The heart is the meeting point of his ministry of word, sacrament, and pastoral care. In the daily life of the man of pastoral charity, the word of God keeps going out to people wherever they are, and gathering them for sacramental worship. That going out and that gathering authenticate each other.

Representing
The Exhortation gives prominence to the representative role of the ordained persons. They are a 'sacramental representation of Jesus Christ, the Head and Shepherd' (par 15). This is closely related to their vocation to act 'in the name and person of Christ' (par 15) and the hope that all pastoral ministry will be 'as incarnate as possible' (par 32). To 're-present' is very closely related to the mystery of Christ's being present in many ways in the life of the Church. The ordained person represents to all the members of Christ's body their living Head who is always present to his Church; and, in the liturgy especially, he represents the members before their Head. Being 'in the person of Christ' involves acting with his authority, making present his sacrifice, being in his presence, standing before his face, speaking with his voice.

Transparent
'Transparent' is a word that has had some prominence in recent writing on priesthood. Pope John Paul highlights its value by describing the priestly ideal as to be 'a living and transparent image of Christ the priest' (par 12). The expression speaks for itself. One recalls St Paul's assurance that 'we see the Lord's glory as in a mirror' (2 Cor 3:18), and the inadequacy of all reflections of God, since the mirror reflection is obscured by the fact that our God-talk has something of the riddle about it (1 Cor 13:12). The appeal to transparency is closely linked to the ideal, presented by some recent writers, that every eucharistic celebration should be like a new appearance of the Risen Lord. This way of speaking is in line with the First Letter of John which speaks of the many ways in which

Christ has appeared and 'appears' (1:2; 3:2,5,8,10; 4:9) to those whose minds are anointed to receive him. In this perspective, every eucharist should be a manifestation, an appearance, of the Lord's glorified humanity. Those participating should get some vision of his hands, his eyes, his heart, his transformed wounds. In this spirit, the document calls for 'an evangelisation which never tires of pointing to the true face of God' (par 37) and the kind of liturgical celebration that reveals the same true face (par 38).

Participation

'Participation in', 'sharing in', 'being instruments of' the priesthood of Christ are expressions that recur in the document. The whole priestly people which is the Church is said to receive from Christ a 'real ontological share in his one eternal priesthood' (par 14). The ordained is described as 'a living instrument of Christ the eternal priest' (par 20). The priest finds his identity in being 'a specific participation in and continuation of Christ himself' (par 12). All of these expressions touch on the great mystery of how human beings can in any sense be co-workers with God. They touch on all the classic questions on how good works are related to faith. Certainly, no human being can add to the work of God, to the all-sufficient mediation of Christ our one priest, to the sheer gratuitousness of God's grace. But the mystery of our being made in the image of God and re-made in the image of Christ reveals the generosity of God in which the work of our salvation is all divine and all human, all his and all ours.

Radical discipleship

More than once, the document calls for a radical following of Christ (par 27), 'embodying his way of life and making him visible' (par 15). A major expression of radical discipleship, for both seminarian and priest, is seen to be the living of the 'evangelical counsels', obedience, celibacy, poverty.

Obedience is set in the context of facilitating the full mission of the Church, expressing 'a marked spirit of asceticism' and 'responsible freedom' (par 28).

Celibacy is presented in terms of the love of Christ towards his bride the Church, and our living out of the nuptial meaning of the human body (par 22-23), now and at the resurrection.

Poverty is linked to being configured to Christ the head (par 26) and the call to a simple and austere life-style (par 30). There is also a call for a search for suitable forms of common life (par 80) and a recognising of the importance of the liturgy of the hours (par 28, 72).

With all of this, one may well ask whether the line of demarcation between 'diocesan' priesthood and 'religious' priesthood has now become more difficult to draw. It seems a long, long way now from the days when the presbyteral ideal was of mature 'elders' who could be good heads of family households, while the monastic ideal took a course of its own. The Synod vision is clearly in favour of concentrating on the formation for priesthood of 'boys, adolescents, young men' (par 38), while not excluding the older vocation (par 64). This is the Synod's way and the Pope's way of calling all the Church to an enrichment of priestly ministry by continually giving of her first fruits. For younger vocation and for older vocation, the radical gospel life-style envisaged is essentially the same. It would appear that, as the centuries have progressed and as the presbyterate has come more and more to be seen in terms of priesthood, sacrifice and sacrament, the emphasis has come to be on radical gospel living, for diocesan priest as well as for religious priest. Radicality is about roots. In the understanding of priesthood, obedience, celibacy and poverty are, more and more, coming to be seen as root areas. This vision of radicality has reached a high point in the Synod document. All priests, diocesan and religious, are seen to be called to 'radical' discipleship, fully transparent with the radical style of the gospel. Radical discipleship is seen to be one and undivided. Its ingredients are inseparable.

An on-going programme

Gospel radicalism is nurtured by the faith, hope and love that flow from and lead to the eucharistic sacrament-sacrifice which is 'the centre and root of the whole priestly life' (par 23). The radical response of the man receiving the radical gospel call must be 'conscious, free and responsible' (par 25). From the beginning, his formation must be holistic, involving every aspect of being human, with special attention to the 'essentially religious dimension of the human person' (par 45). His formation on all levels must be ongoing and lifelong (pars 70-81), in response to the God who continues to call (par 70). His world vision and spirituality must be kept alive by intimate communion with the Father who keeps calling us to hallow his name, with the Son who calls us to follow him, with the Holy Spirit who makes us holy and enriches the Church with charisms (pars 19, 31). This communion overflows into our communion with the whole Church at every level: with one's fellow priests and with one's bishop (par 28), with the laity whom one encourages and directs in every aspect of their vocations and ministries (par 59). It is in this setting of communion that candidates for priesthood are to be 'accompanied' along their whole journey (par 42), from the earliest years, through minor and major seminary and through various forms of prior preparation (par 62), and of being part of the local Church. Formation for priesthood should, in various ways, be the work of the whole people of God (par 66). Though he belongs to a particular Church, the priest, having been formed by the whole people of God, should be open to the mission of the whole Church (par 31, 32).

A spirituality of relationships

This life of full communion provides a continual enrichment for all the relationships that comprise ministerial priesthood: relationships with Jesus Christ, with all the members of his body, with all those with whom we collaborate in ministry, and through them with all the human family. The priest's spirituality flows from this communion and from all these relationships. In the spirit of the document, the whole of the priest's life is seen as being suffused with a spirit of constant prayer and the constant exercise of pastoral charity. All this is implied, in the 'multiple and rich interconnection of relationships which arise from the Blessed Trinity and are prolonged in the communion of the Church' (par 12).

It was fitting that Pope John Paul II should end the Apostolic Exhortation with a long and moving prayer to the woman who at the Second Vatican Council was seen as the 'type' of the whole Church, and who at the end of the Council was declared Mother of the Church. We can have every confidence that the mother of the mothering Church will be sure to keep providing living and transparent images of her Son.

First fruits always

Good priestly ministry ensures a Church in tune. The whole Church is called to be in tune with Jesus Christ, the shepherd-king, prophet and priest who continues to exercise his priesthood, in the form of intercession, at his Father's right hand. From there, he sends his Spirit into the hearts of believers, inviting and enabling us to participate in his own pastoral, prophetic, and priestly mission. This triple mission is one mission. From heaven, Jesus keeps inviting and enabling us to enter into the flow of eternal life that unites Father, Son and Holy Spirit since each of us was made in the trinitarian image of God. The trinitarian life comprises limitless knowing, limitless loving, in a way that produces fruit without limit. The inviting and enabling of Jesus is the source of the whole network of relationships that constitute the Christian life. On account of the reality of sin, these relationships suffer continual damage and even breakdown. As we experience this damaging and this breaking, we need re-entry into the community life of Father, Son and Spirit. Only Jesus Christ can provide us with this re-entry. His whole priestly work consists of inviting and enabling us to enter and re-enter into the flow of eternal life. Our graced life means our continual entry and re-entry into God's own way of knowing and loving. This graced life enables us to see God, not only in the final beatific vision but in every human experience. In our daily seeing of God, as St Irenaeus put it, the glory of God is expressed in human beings alive.

Our entry and re-entry into the life that unites the divine persons has been made possible because 'the Word became flesh and lived among us' (Jn 1:14). In the pastoral, prophetic and priestly work of the Church, the word continues to become flesh, to be embodied. All the members of the Church are called to be instruments of the word, fully in tune with the word. The ordained person is authorised and empowered to proclaim the word at its highest level of sacramental intensity. He is ordained to be a servant of the word and a servant-leader of all the rest of the baptised in their relationships with the word. This is why his sharing in the priesthood of Christ is called ministerial. In his work of service, he must have the qualities of two very significant gospel figures, the shepherd and the fisherman; he is called to a life of pastoral charity and to exercise the diligent and confident care which makes him continue to 'put out into the deep water' (Lk 5:4) and to 'fish for people' (Mt 4:19). In this he must daily live out the triple call to be human, to be a baptised person, to be minister of word, sacrament, and pastoral care. This triple call has its own variety of rhythms and seasons, from spring through to the harvest-time that is followed by winter, the winter that makes its own contribution to each of the other seasons. In this rhythm of the seasons, the exact pattern of which is not always predictable, the ordained person, and indeed every baptised person, is called to be patiently in tune with the great interceder (cf Heb 7:25) whose continuing priesthood knows no seasons.

The pages of the bible have much to say about the topic of first fruits. This image has a lot to tell us about priesthood, about sacrifice, about Christian living, about order in human life, about holy orders. From ancient times, the first fruits of the earth were presented to God in a spirit of sacrificial offering. They thus became the guarantee of a good harvest. In the Christian perspective, God keeps giving us the Spirit himself as a first-fruits (Rom 8:23). Christ has been raised from the dead and he is 'the first-fruits of those who have died' (1 Cor 15:20). His rising is the source of all order in the Church. Since he is the first fruits, he keeps giving first fruits, in the form of life and growth to all his members, 'each in his own order' (v 23). From early Christian times, the emergence of good leadership has been seen as a sure sign that the Church is continuing to bear fruit in abundance. In living out the full rhythm of the seasons of the Paschal Mystery, the whole Church today is called to 'sing to the Lord a new song' (Ps 149:1). The song must be sung to the tune of the one who is himself the first-fruits and in whom the whole harvest is assured. It must express the Church's desire to keep offering her first and best fruits, in providing for good priestly ministry and in other ways. It must be the song of an ever-new faith, an ever-new hope, an ever-new love. The life of every one of us is part of the new song.

Bernier, Paul, *Ministry in the Church: A Historical and Pastoral Approach* (Mystic, CT: Twenty-Third Publications, 1992).

Brown, Raymond E. SS, *Priest and Bishop: Biblical Reflections* (London: Geoffrey Chapman, 1971).

Brown, R.E., Joseph A. Fitzmyer SJ, Roland E. Murphy, O.Carm. (eds) *The New Jerome Biblical Commentary* (London: Geoffrey Chapman, 1990).

Cooke, Bernard, *Ministry to Word and Sacraments: History and Theology* (Philadelphia: Fortress Press, 1976).

Donovan, Daniel, *What Are They Saying About the Ministerial Priesthood?* (New York/Mahwah: Paulist Press, 1992).

Dunn, Patrick J., *Priesthood: A Re-Examination of the Roman Catholic Theology of the Presbyterate* (New York: Alba House, 1990).

Evans, Michael, *Why Priests?* (London: Catholic Truth Society, 1989).

Fink, Peter E., SJ, (ed) *The New Dictionary of Sacramental Worship*, (Dublin: Gill and Macmillan, 1990).

Flannery, Austin, (ed) *Vatican Council II: The Conciliar and Post Conciliar Documents* (Dublin: Dominican Publications, 1975).

Flannery, Austin, (ed) *Vatican Council II: More Postconciliar Documents* (Dublin: Dominican Publications, 1982).

Freedman, David Noel, (editor-in-chief), *The Anchor Bible Dictionary*, Six volumes. (New York: Doubleday, 1992).

Galot, Jean, SJ, *Theology of the Priesthood* (San Francisco: Ignatius Press, 1985).

Greshake, Gisbert, *The Meaning of Christian Priesthood* (Dublin: Four Courts Press, 1988).

Komonchak, Joseph A., Mary Collins, and Dermot A. Lane, (eds),

The New Dictionary of Theology (Dublin: Gill and Macmillan, 1987).

Lawler, Michael G., *A Theology of Ministry* (Kansas City: Sheed and Ward, 1990).

Lecuyer, Joseph, CSSp, *Le sacrement de l'ordre: Recherche historique et théologique*, Collection 'Theologie historique', (Paris: Beauchesne, 1983).

Leon-Dufour, Xavier, *Dictionary of Biblical Theology*, Second Revised and Enlarged Edition. (London: Geoffrey Chapman, 1973).

Marliangeas, Bernard-D, *Clés pour une theologie du ministère. In persona Christi. In persona Ecclesiae*, Collection 'Theologie historique' (Paris: Beauchesne, 1978).

Mitchell, Nathan, OSB, *Mission and Ministry: History and Theology in the Sacrament of Orders*, Message of the Sacraments, 6 (Wilmington, DE: Michael Glazier, 1982).

Murphy, James H., CM, (ed), *New Beginnings in Ministry* (Dublin: The Columba Press, 1992).

Neuner, Josef, SJ, and Dupuis, Jacques, SJ, (eds) *The Christian Faith in the Doctrinal Documents of the Catholic Church*, Revised and Enlarged Edition. (London: Harper Collins Religious, 1992).

Nichols, Aidan, OP, *Holy Orders: The Apostolic Ministry from the New Testament to the Second Vatican Council*, The Oscott Series, 5 (Dublin: Veritas, 1990).

O'Meara, Thomas F., OP, *Theology of Ministry* (New York, Ramsey: Paulist Press, 1983).

Osborne, Kenan, B., OFM, *Priesthood: A History of Ordained Ministry in the Roman Catholic Church* (New York/Mahwah: Paulist Press, 1988).

Power, David, N., OMI, *Ministers of Christ and His Church. The Theology of the Priesthood* (London: Geoffrey Chapman, 1969).

Power, D.N., *Gifts That Differ: Lay Ministries Established and Unestablished* (New York: Pueblo, 1980).

Shaefer, Mary M., and J. Frank Henderson, *The Catholic Priesthood. A Liturgically Based Theology of the Presbyteral Office*, Canadian Studies in Liturgy, 4 (Ottawa: CCCB Publications Service, 1990).

Schillebeeckx, Edward, *The Church with a Human Face: A New and Expanded Theology of Ministry* (London: SCM, 1985).

Schwartz, Robert M., *Servant Leaders of the People of God: An Ecclesial Spirituality for American Priests* (New York: Paulist Press, 1989).

Tavard, George H., *A Theology for Ministry*, Theology and Life Series, 6 (Dublin: Dominican Publications, 1983).

Vanhoye, Albert, SJ, *Our Priest is Christ: The Doctrine of the Epistle to the Hebrews* (Rome: Pontificio Istituto Biblico, 1977).

Wister, Robert J.,(ed), *Priests: Identity and Ministry*, (Wilmington, DE: Michael Glazier, 1990).

Abbreviations

AA *Apostolicam Actuositatem* (Decree on the Apostolate of the Laity, 1965)

AG *Ad Gentes* (Decree on the Church's Missionary Activity, 1965)

CD *Christus Dominus* (Decree on the Pastoral Office of Bishops in the Church, 1965)

GS *Gaudium et Spes* (Pastoral Constitution on the Church in the Modern World, 1965)

LG *Lumen Gentium* (Dogmatic Constitution on the Church, 1964)

PO *Presbyterorum Ordinis* (Decree on the Life and Ministry of Priests, 1965)

SC *Sacrosanctum Concilium* (Constitution on the Sacred Liturgy, 1963)

Biblical texts are from *The New Revised Standard Version* (OUP, 1989) and from *The Revised English Bible* (OUP/CUP, 1989).

Index